JANE AUSTEN AND MARRIAGE

Jane Austen's Hampshire

Jane Austen and Marriage

Hazel Jones

continuum

Continuum UK, The Tower Building, 11 York Road, London SE1 7NX
Continuum US, 80 Maiden Lane, Suite 704, New York, NY 10038

www.continuumbooks.com

First published 2009

British Library Cataloguing-in-Publication Data
A catalogue record for this book is available from the British Library.

ISBN 978 1 84725 218 0

Typeset by Pindar NZ, Auckland, New Zealand
Printed and bound by MPG Books Ltd, Cornwall, Great Britain

Contents

Acknowledgements

I am grateful for the help and advice given by many institutions and individuals in the course of my research. These include Helen Scott, Sarah Parry, Jacqui Grainger and Corrine Saint at Chawton House Library; the staff at the British Library, Hampshire Record Office, Bath Fashion Museum and Bath Record Office; the Revd Michael Kenning, Rector of Steventon Church; Jessamy Sykes at Lambeth Palace Library; Camilla Seymour at Bonhams; Christopher MacDonald at Asprey Jewellers, London; Miss Helen Lefroy; Mr Tom Carpenter and Louise West of the Jane Austen Memorial Trust and Dr T. K. Brandreth for the use of his extensive library.

I also thank my critical readers Charlotte Reilly, Lorna Blewitt and Dr Pat Ensum for their constructive comments and all of my Jane Austen students for their tireless encouragement, over the past year in particular. Lorna Blewitt also created the map of Jane Austen's Hampshire featured on the frontispiece.

Ben Hayes, Eva Osborne, Sarah Patel, Pen Whitson and Alice Eddowes at Hambledon Continuum, Jane Gadd, Kim Pillay and Dina Cloete at Pindar NZ deserve thanks for guiding me through the publication process.

For permission to quote from various publications and annual reports, I am grateful to The Jane Austen Society and to Dr Katherine Beaumont for permitting the use of material from the Austen Papers. In addition, the British Library, Hampshire Record Office and Chawton House Library have allowed me to use references from a number of eighteenth- and nineteenth-century texts and archives. The idiosyncratic spelling, grammar and punctuation found in extracts from primary sources have been retained for the sake of contemporary colour and flavour, with errors indicated only where the sense is compromised.

I owe a special debt of gratitude to Deirdre Le Faye, for answering my queries with promptitude and kindness and providing accurate transcripts of the Austen Papers. Without her definitive biography, *Jane Austen, A Family Record*, the invaluable *A Chronology of Jane Austen* and her collection of *Jane Austen's Letters*, I could not have written this book.

Finally, I am indebted to my dear husband David, for his practical help and considerable technical skill, for driving me to Hampshire, London and Bath on demand and for the hours he has spent delving into his collection of the *Gentleman's Magazine*.

Every effort has been made to contact all holders of copyright. The publisher will be happy to rectify in future editions any errors or omissions brought to its attention.

Introduction

Any book about marriage in Jane Austen's time is sure to feature contradictions and complexities and this one is no exception. These were years of great change and great resistance to change, creating a state of flux in that trickiest of personal relationships, marriage. While the final pages of every Austen novel celebrate the very best kind of union, based on compatibility, affection and respect, alliances contracted as the result of other inducements provide significant counterpoints. The level of society with which the author was most familiar, comprising large landowners, the armed services, the professions and the lower gentry, increasingly viewed the companionate marriage as the ideal and conjugal happiness as a legitimate aim, yet marriages of convenience were common. At the top of the social scale, some aristocratic families still arranged marriages for money and political power, yet love matches were not unknown. Not all titled or wealthy parents manoeuvred their children into mercenary alliances; not all gentry families allowed their sons and daughters to marry where they chose. The differences in attitude to marriage between these discrete ranks became blurred as one certainty emerged: that marriages based on love and esteem were more likely to endure the test of time than those contracted for material gain. Foreign visitors who recorded their impressions of English society at this time were unanimous in their verdict, that young men and women were granted more freedom than their continental counterparts to choose marriage partners and that friendship within marriage, first cultivated over a long period of courtship, was lasting rather than fleeting. This was not the whole story. Eldest sons who inherited family acres and fortunes were more often than not subject to parental sanction in their choice of wife, and fathers of General Tilney's persuasion expected to command an influence over the selection of all their children's marriage partners. Parental veto remained a powerful weapon where money and land were at stake. Daughters in all ranks of society were in a particularly vulnerable position and the pressures on them to marry were of a different order, because their present and future economic security lay in male hands – fathers', brothers', husbands'. Sir Thomas Bertram's liberal-minded expectation that both of his sons would find compatible wives is counterbalanced by his lack of sympathy for the women under his care: his endorsement of Maria's contemptible match; his anger and incomprehension when Fanny refuses to accept a rich man whom she does not love. The problems facing single women, with money or without it, are clearly delineated in Jane Austen's novels, while her letters and the correspondence of other women recognize the mental and physical dangers encountered by married women in real life.

Conduct literature proliferated in Jane Austen's lifetime, in response to the anxieties and uncertainties created by the problem of finding the right mate. Sons and daughters allowed to exercise a degree of choice over whom they married needed advice on how to assess character, how to behave in the assembly rooms springing up in every notable town in England, how to attract the opposite sex, how to make or refuse a proposal, and – finally – how to fulfil their roles as husbands and, more especially, wives. From fox-hunting parsons to aristocratic ladies, every conduct writer had opinions on manners and morals, etiquette and dress, accomplishments and education, and they promoted them unstintingly. The Reverends Gregory, Blair, Fordyce and Gisborne, to mention only a few among the many Church of England clergymen who advised men and women on their duties to God, their spouses and themselves, tended to adopt a conservative approach, unequivocal enough to be delivered from the pulpit and popular enough to run to many editions. The main thrust of their argument was that God had made men stronger than women, both intellectually and physically and that this superiority gave them a divine right of authority which women must not seek to challenge. Equality, they cautioned, was neither possible nor desirable; female interests were best served by the cultivation of refined helplessness, guaranteed to stimulate the male protective urge and soften the male heart. Women were put on this earth to please men, after all, and happiness in marriage could only come through an unquestioning acceptance of male dominance.

Attitudes towards wives, however, were changing fast as a direct result of affective marriages, occasioning widespread concern about the balance of power within the household. As late as the 1730s, a man's right to apply 'reasonable correction' to his wife was still upheld by the courts; in 1782, when a prominent judge voiced his support for wife-beating, provided the stick used was no thicker than a man's thumb, there was a general outcry. Yet wives promised to obey their husbands in the marriage service and relinquished their limited autonomy, as well as their legal identities and any money they might possess, on achieving the elevated status of married women. Two radical writers, Mary Wollstonecraft and Mary Hays, attacked the system as it stood and those who supported it, arguing for female rationality rather than physical and mental frailty; for vocational female education in place of superficial accomplishments acquired merely to please future husbands; for conjugal companionship rather than wifely subservience. Inevitably, they attracted a barrage of criticism from the traditionalists, targeting their unconventional lives as well as their ideas. Catherine Macaulay, a staunch promoter of female education, adopted a less combative tone, holding that husbands had the right to expect obedience from their wives, but that they should in their turn treat those wives as their best friends. Reactionary pronouncements on women's marital roles did not emanate exclusively from the male camp; Hannah More and a number of other female conduct writers supported the belief that women should defer to men in all things and accept male protection with gratitude. Some recognized the double standards operating within marriage, but counselled acceptance of the status quo as the safest option. Those who focused on the less controversial area of dress and deportment gave advice geared specifically to catching husbands, and admitted as much.

Men and women were exposed to the same contradictory messages, but that does not mean that they took any notice of them. That conduct books were so prolific points to the fact that existing behaviour was already causing concern and if Jane Austen's characters and plots reflected real people and real situations, as contemporary critics seemed to think they did, then conduct literature was taken for the most part with a pinch of salt. The *British Critic* review of *Persuasion*, published in 1818, attacked the questionable moral of the story, which appeared to be that where marriage was concerned, the young could avoid certain and prolonged misery by listening to their own hearts rather than to those older and wiser than themselves. The satirical final sentence of *Northanger Abbey* emphasises the author's ambivalent response to the dubious wisdom peddled by the exponents of both traditional and liberal moral values. It is left to the reader to decide whether parental tyranny or filial disobedience is to be applauded, since everyone gets what they wished for in the end. Jane Austen herself read conduct manuals and the ways in which she used their precepts in her fiction reveal her opinion of them. She hated Hannah More's overt didactic moralising and altered an early composition, *Catharine, or The Bower*, so that the heroine's narrow-minded aunt can limit her niece's reading matter to Hugh Blair's Sermons and More's *Coelebs In Search of A Wife*, an account of a fastidious bachelor's successful quest to find an unrealistically virtuous mate. Mr Collins spouts Fordyce, Mary Bennet has a quotable moral maxim for every eventuality. Her heroines possess no more than an allowable number of virtues and although Fanny Price is less flawed than most, it is not moral rectitude that saves her from Henry Crawford, but her love for Edmund. Jane Austen presents us with fallible women, who learn from their mistakes, because this is how experience is gained. They are individuals and respond to whatever happens to them with intelligence and common sense. Elizabeth Bennet's method of dealing with the vagaries of life and love is not Fanny Price's, or Anne Elliot's, or indeed any of the other heroines' ways. Their marriages will certainly not turn them into exemplary spouses either – it is difficult to imagine Lizzie or Emma as silently submissive wives, Darcy and Mr Knightley marry them for entirely different qualities – what is more important is that they possess an acute self-knowledge and appreciate the moral and intellectual qualities of their partners. Jane Austen allows her heroines a year at least to make keen character assessments and shows that matches based on physical attraction alone are doomed to failure, yet she questions the assumption that alliances formed after only a short acquaintance were similarly disadvantaged. The Crofts achieve lasting happiness in marriage after only weeks in each other's company. Austen novels highlight the exceptions and reflect the contradictions in late eighteenth- and early nineteenth-century approaches to marriage. Conduct writers could not expect one size to fit all.

From the 1790s to the end of her life in 1817, Jane Austen became an increasingly critical observer of the marriages which came to her notice. She recognized that affection, friendship and respect were fundamental elements of any workable relationship, but discovered for herself that a man who combined the ability to inspire the necessary degree of love and esteem with the essential qualification of a good income was not easily come by. Financial inducements alone were not enough to tempt her into matrimony – she turned down one wealthy suitor in the full knowledge that, at the age of twenty-six and with eligible men in scarce supply, she might never receive another proposal of marriage. Although she would probably not have gone as far as Mary Wollstonecraft in claiming that the marital state was little more than legal prostitution for those women who traded their bodies for economic security, she did indicate in her novels and letters that such sacrifices were made. No Jane Austen heroine marries for money: affection is always part of the equation – yet the recognition that romance alone would neither keep body and soul together nor sustain marital accord is a crucial element underpinning all of her writing.

In real life and in the novels, the psychological preparedness of those entering the marriage state interested Jane Austen far more than the external show of the wedding itself. She left it to others to detail the satin and lace, the feathers and pearls, the cakes and carriages and a selection of their accounts are included in this study, together with contemporary experiences of courtship and marriage, childbearing and birth control, adultery and elopement, the trials and comforts of the single life. The marital histories of Jane Austen's brothers and sisters-in-law, her neighbours, friends and acquaintances and those unfortunates whose scandalous alliances came to her notice through the newspapers, provide the background against which her minor and major characters make their assesments and choices and, consequently, the beds they have to lie in.

1

The Advantage of Choice

A single man in possession of a good fortune was not in want of a wife, unless he chose to be. Inviting a woman to dance or proposing marriage, was, as Henry Tilney points out to Catherine Morland in *Northanger Abbey*, the man's privilege, but in his choice of a wife he had to think beyond his initial inclinations and the superficial obligations of the dance floor. Few men could act completely independently, unless they were very rich, very foolish, or had no family to consider. Money, character and connections were crucial concerns for both parties, as Jane Austen and other writers stressed in novels, letters, journals and the conduct literature of the day. Popular sentimental fiction may have glamorized love matches, with or without parental sanction, but not many men or women could afford to ignore the absolute necessity of an adequate income. 'Love in a cottage?' asks one unconvinced realist. 'Give me indifference and a coach and six.'[1] If it was morally indefensible to marry solely for money, it made little sense to marry without it and in reality, many choices were made with an eye to monetary gain *and* emotional happiness. Affection was desirable, but if a good income made the heart beat a little faster, well, that was understandable.

The scarcity value of men in Jane Austen's lifetime, together with women's dependence on husbands for status and financial security, gave eligible bachelors the power to behave like connoisseurs. Men with the means to marry occupied an enviable position and a Fitzwilliam Darcy, with a sizeable yearly income and a large estate, could thwart the expectations of young ladies and their mothers in assembly rooms up and down the country, by refusing to make himself available as a dancing or a marriage partner. Men with independent fortunes or lucrative professions, naval captains back on land with prize money in their pockets, clergymen with comfortable livings, gentlemen with private incomes, all possessed the wherewithal to raise or to dash female hopes. The younger sons of peers and gentlemen with small estates and expensive habits might consider themselves restricted in their exercise of choice, but it was a self-imposed constraint, based on procuring the income necessary to maintain an accustomed lifestyle, to keep a stable of hunters or finance the glittering social round in London and Bath. In the early nineteenth century, one out of every four younger sons remained a lifelong bachelor. If they married at all, they tended to do so in their early to mid-thirties, after they had worked their way far enough up their professional ladders and perhaps attracted a woman with money. An eldest son, with his property and income guaranteed, usually married between the ages of twenty-seven and twenty-nine. Clergymen might have to wait for ten to twenty years for a good living to become vacant, so marriage for them was postponed until their thirties and forties. Professional men in the law and medicine were slightly better off; in 1800, they were marrying at twenty-eight, on average.

Unscrupulous men who decided that their incomes were not sufficient to achieve their aspirations had no consideration beyond marrying for money and used the advantage of choice to the full. There were enough of them in evidence for conduct book writers to issue warnings to unsuspecting women:

> When they chance to think of MARRIAGE, it is with feelings of the most perfect indifference; for as in this step a mercenary view is the great incentive, should one Lady refuse their Proposal, they cooly turn round, and seek for another who may be weak enough to accept it . . . an inquiry into her pecuniary circumstances is made, as an indispensible preliminary to an union, which if they find below their expectations, they quickly banish all thoughts of making her A WIFE; . . .[2]

How to identify a man intent on gaining money through an expedient alliance, with scant concern for the woman in the case, is a question debated at length by Elizabeth Bennet and her Aunt Gardiner. When George Wickham turns on his charm for Miss King with £10,000, Elizabeth claims to consider it natural that he should attempt to gain a degree of independence by acquiring a wife with money, especially when he possessed so little of it himself. Mrs Gardiner, with less reason to excuse his sudden interest in a girl with little to recommend her other than her recent fortune, views his actions as mercenary; but how could a woman determine the difference between self-interest and prudence? Where did sound judgement end and cupidity begin, particularly when money was at the root of both? Miss King and Miss Darcy are both saved from Wickham's gold-digging ambitions by their families, but some women in the real world were not so fortunate. A former neighbour of the Austens, the desperately plain but moneyed Mary Russell, fell prey to George Mitford, a charming fortune-hunter, who pretty soon frittered away his wife's assets.[3]

Beleaguered heiresses of a later date might have benefited from the advice offered in a popular lovers' handbook for both sexes, published in 1809. One exemplar letter, purporting to be 'From a Gentleman to a young Lady of Superior Fortune', attempts to alert the vulnerable to the duplicity of the disingenuous: '. . . were our circumstances reversed,' he claims, 'I should hardly take to myself the credit of doing a generous action in overlooking the consideration of wealth, and making you an unreserved tender of my hand and fortune.' The lady's reply is encouraging – she appears to swallow his assertion of disinterestedness – but at the same time circumspect: 'I must refer myself entirely to the direction of my father.'[4] According to some moral advisers, however, inequality of wealth in itself should create no hindrance to marriage:

> . . . if one of the Parties has an Independence, and loves a person who is not in affluence, there can be no reasonable objection to the Alliance, provided the affection be mutual and the CHARACTER of the less wealthy party be unblemished.[5]

In reality, such alliances were rarely greeted with unalloyed pleasure by families with money. No matter how spotless the character of the less fortunate in terms of wealth or status, suspicions of self-interest would inevitably be aroused. When the only legitimate son of General Sir Robert Sloper chose to marry the former governess to his illegitimate brothers and sisters, the marriage appeared to please no-one other than the couple themselves.[6] Jane Austen allows Mr Weston, with money made from trade, to choose Emma's 'portionless' companion, with the blessing of his friends and son, although in this case, the distinctions of rank are not offended. In contrast, his first marriage to an heiress had caused a family rift and brought no material benefit to himself. The headstrong Miss Churchill had determined to have him, but her extravagance proved more than his small private income could stand and she never allowed him to forget her condescension in marrying beneath her. His second match, twenty years later, provides 'the pleasantest proof of its being a great deal better to choose than to be chosen, to excite gratitude than to feel it.'[7] A letter from Jane to Cassandra in 1800, reporting Miss Sawbridge's marriage to Mr Maxwell, told a similar tale, but one where the woman possessed the fortune. He was only a humble tutor, who stood to gain materially from the match, in terms of status and a good home. Jane concluded that Miss Sawbridge must be head over heels in love to contemplate such a penurious suitor.[8]

That the match was based on infatuation on her side and acquisitiveness on his is mildly implied here, although the motivation behind the alliance might have been less cynical, especially since Jane added that she had heard Mr Maxwell's character highly spoken of. Whatever the truth of the matter, Jane Austen leaves her novel readers in no doubt that single *women* with little money must be in want of husbands with ample fortunes, especially if they had no male relatives to support them. In *Sense and Sensibility*, Marianne and Elinor Dashwood openly discuss the annual income necessary for a comfortable married existence: for Elinor £1,000, for Marianne, £2,000. It is not surprising that Mrs Bennet's sole aim in life is to get her daughters married off – there are five of them, all facing a narrow existence on the interest of £5,000 a year between them when their father dies. So, when Mr Bingley with his £4,000 a year settles at Netherfield Park, she sees in him an insurance policy against future privations. Contemporary readers would have understood her motives, but deprecated her determination to marry her daughters off to *any* man with a decent income, regardless of affection or compatibility. Elizabeth has a firm enough character to oppose Mrs Bennet's manoeuvrings, but her more tractable sister Jane, with a strong sense of duty and obedience to her mother's wishes, would surely have been browbeaten into accepting the oily Mr Collins. Luckily for her, a richer suitor is already on the horizon.

With few opportunities for earning money, women ignored the necessity of marrying men with reasonable prospects at their peril. If a young woman hoped to avoid a penny-scraping existence, she must learn to value self-preservation above inclination. Conduct literature supplied ready-made arguments for fathers faced with reckless, love-sick daughters who had read one too many sentimental novels. One example from the early 1800s provides a list of questions aimed at dissuading a girl from accepting a young soldier's proposal:

> Is his pay sufficient to maintain himself? If it be, will it be sufficient for the support of a family? Consider, there will be no opportunity for you to increase his poor income, but by such means as will be very grating for you to submit to. Be cautious of pushing yourself into ruin.[9]

In a similar vein, Mrs Gardiner warns her niece against becoming attached to George Wickham and Elizabeth accepts her sensible advice without resentment, but makes the realistic point that caution often comes a poor second when affection is part of the equation – a consideration often overlooked by the conduct books, most of which reprobated mere personal liking as a sound basis for marriage. Despite her claims to the contrary, Elizabeth is wiser than many of her gender, but the only promise she makes is to do her best to take things slowly. She promises more than Jane Austen herself was willing to when she met Tom Lefroy, the twenty-year-old nephew of the Lefroys at Ashe Parsonage. In her letters to Cassandra, covering an acquaintance of three weeks in January 1796, her partiality is plain enough for her sister to issue an Aunt-Gardiner-type warning about the dangers of unguarded behaviour.[10] After the final ball at Ashe on January the 15th, his aunt and uncle had seen sufficient to unsettle them, and Tom was sent back to London. In later life, he admitted to feeling 'a boyish love'[11] for the twenty-year-old Jane, so presumably he would have chosen to marry her if circumstances had allowed, but with his way to make in the law and younger brothers and sisters to support, he could not marry without money. As matters stood, they were forced to part and the Hampshire Lefroys ensured that any future visits by their nephew occurred in Jane's absence, or were kept secret. Mrs Lefroy in particular blamed Tom for behaving thoughtlessly towards a young woman whom he knew he was in no position to marry. Single men needed a fortune in order to want a wife and this particular single man became engaged to Mary Paul, the sister of a rich Wexford friend, only a year later. 'If *his* love had continued a few more years, he *might* have sought her out again – as he was *then* making enough to marry on—' wrote Caroline Austen to her brother James-Edward. Instead, 'he married an Irish lady – who certainly *had* the convenience of *money*.'[12] In fairness to Tom Lefroy, his wife's fortune only materialised on her brother's early death, several years after the marriage, but this early experience taught Jane a lesson about love and money that she never forgot.

Women were also capable of fortune-hunting and the man's advantage of choice proved no advantage at all if he lacked a knowledge of the world. Innocence in such matters serves *Northanger Abbey*'s James Morland a painful lesson. As a woman with no fortune, Isabella Thorpe's initial fears are that James will fail to gain his father's consent to marry. Her assertion that he would be her only choice if she had '"the command of millions"' belongs in the pages of a sentimental novel. Her expectation of future wealth is apparent in her dreams of a villa in Richmond, her own carriage, a new name on her visiting cards and a dazzling display of rings on her finger. When Captain Tilney and his better financial prospects arrive on the scene, she rapidly transfers her mercenary affections to him. Edward Ferrars, too, is a victim of his own youth and inexperience – he becomes attached to Lucy Steele as a result of naïvety and lack of occupation. Lucy is determined to do better than merely economise on a small income and despite her protestation that she would be willing to suffer poverty for Edward's sake, she plans to wait however long it takes for his mother to part with a substantial sum. Elinor recognises that Lucy will give Edward up only if a better opportunity presents itself – which it does, in the shape of Edward's credulous younger brother, Robert. His vanity makes him susceptible to Lucy's flattery: 'Instead of talking of Edward, they came gradually to talk only of Robert, – a subject on which he had always more to say than on any other . . .'[13]

Any green young man might have benefited from reading *The Advice of Experience to the Young of Both Sexes*, which claimed to know all about the Isabellas and Lucys of this world:

> To you, my young Lords of the Creation, my advice is, not to marry too unadvisedly, for on your present choice depends your future happiness. If the lady you intend to pay your addresses to destroy her time in dress, frivolous entertainment, public spectacles, or unprofitable reading; if she be enamoured of her own person, coquettish, and love flattery; if she laugh much, and talk loud; if she prefer the street to her father's house, and her eyes glance eagerly at those of men; . . . be not captivated by her beauty, but turn away . . . contemplate the misery which will ensue where beauty, that perishable flower, is the only foundation on which your happiness is built.[14]

Male flirts exercised their advantage of choice in a different way, entertaining to themselves, less amusing for their victims. Mary Wollstonecraft recognised the extent of their power: 'There are quite as many male coquets as female, and they are far more pernicious pests to society, as their sphere of action is larger, and they are less exposed to the censure of the world.'[15] Henry Crawford fits this mould perfectly. He is an accomplished flirt, having gained plenty of experience in London, practising his techniques on his sister's friends. A wife, he declares, is '"Heaven's *last* best gift."'[16] In the meantime, he means to enjoy breaking hearts without putting himself at risk; the Miss Bertrams are attractive and gullible and fair game. His winning manners have a softening effect even on Fanny Price's resolve, and Jane Austen describes how successful the attack of a practised deceiver on *any* young woman is likely to be, no matter what conduct literature maintained to the contrary:

> although there doubtless are such unconquerable young ladies of eighteen . . . as are never to be persuaded into love against their judgement by all that talent, manner, attention, and flattery can do, I have no inclination to believe Fanny one of them, or to think that . . . she could have escaped heart-whole from the courtship (though the courtship only of a fortnight) of such a man as Crawford, in spite of there being some previous ill-opinion of him to be overcome, had not her affection been engaged elsewhere.[17]

Ascertaining character was vitally important for both men and women, and for the families concerned on both sides, for, as Catherine Morland puts it, '"People that marry can never part"', and if they wished to, divorce and separation were prohibitively expensive options. It is to be hoped that Jane Austen's prediction of certain unhappiness for Miss Jackson and

Mr Gunthorpe was wrong, since their marriage lasted for thirty-six years, but his character – 'He swears, drinks, is cross, jealous, selfish & Brutal' – appears unredeemable.[18] When even an intelligent Lizzie Bennet could be taken in by a handsome face and assured manner, what hope was there for those of inferior penetration? Plenty of conduct manuals attempted to provide an answer and while some offered genuinely helpful advice, others were of uncertain benefit. One female moralist advised women to make a purely rational choice of marriage partner:

> Comply not to give your heart before you have well weighed and advised what you are about to undertake. Let not love blind you, but make your choice with the eye of reason . . . Consider not of riches and a high birth so much as of virtue and agreeableness.[19]

Choice here, of course, did not imply that women could make proposals; they could only give or withhold encouragement, but the advice given, although eminently sensible, expects rather too much in the way of cool evaluation on the part of an inexperienced young woman, in love perhaps for the first time. An even less practical approach to choosing a suitable husband was adopted by another writer who stated that physical attributes reflected the inner character:

> If the man you contemplate have thick red lips, he will be simple, good-natured and easily managed . . . If he speak quick but distinct, and walk firm and erect, he will be ambitious, active, and probably a good husband . . . If he be what is termed a NICE MAN, he will not have dirty nails, dirty shoes, a cravat soiled, and hair like brush-wood: his stockings will be tight, his apparel dusted, and his gait not as if his limbs were at variance with his body.[20]

At least this writer recognized that good looks had a direct bearing on female interest. Most conduct literature attempted to deny it, but Jane Austen undermined this absurd attitude with wit and common sense in her early writing and in her later fiction. In *Frederic and Elfrida*, she has the young, lovely, but far too obliging Charlotte Drummond accept the marriage proposals of two men in a single evening, one a sallow-faced, aged gentleman, whom she cannot bear to make unhappy by a refusal, the second a young, handsome fellow in a fetching blue coat, whose appearance 'influenced Charlotte in his favour . . . she could not account for it, but so it was.'[21] The proud Charles Adams, in *Jack and Alice*, is a self-proclaimed paragon, fully aware of his dazzling effect on women: '"I look upon myself to be a perfect beauty – where would you see a finer figure or a more charming face?"'[22] Jane Austen does not ignore the seductive power of physical appeal – Emma Woodhouse is attracted by Mr Knightley's firm, upright bearing as well as his intelligence and her feistiest heroine, Lizzie Bennet, is particularly alive to it. To Jane Bennet's list of Mr Bingley's qualities, her sister adds the fact that he is handsome, as every young man should be to make his character complete. Her favourable first impression of Mr Wickham is based entirely on his tangible charm and she is not immune to Darcy's physical presence.

First impressions, however, often lead to ill-informed judgements, as Jane Austen is quick to point out. Darcy's initial attraction for Meryton society is based on his tall, good looks and his £10,000 a year, but when his disinclination to mix becomes obvious, he is pronounced proud and disagreeable, a superficial view with which Elizabeth Bennet concurs, her pride having been dented by his rejection of her as a dancing partner. Yet during her stay at Netherfield, she might have seen a better side to his character, if she had chosen to look with an impartial eye: he writes long letters to his sister and is an articulate, thinking, reading man. On his home territory, at Pemberley, Darcy's wider social responsibilities as a landowner and master are evidenced in his restrained taste and judicious exercise of power. Unlike Lady Catherine, he does not parade his wealth, nor seek to impress, and Elizabeth must reassess her prejudiced view of him. Her later claim that she began to fall in love with Darcy after seeing his beautiful house and grounds is no joke. By the time she accepts his second proposal, she fully comprehends his character and her own state of mind. Jane Austen allows each of her heroines about a year to assess their future husbands' qualities; forming an attachment too precipitately invariably carried a health warning:

> In the choice of a companion for life, no one will be hardy enough to deny that great circumspection, and a proper knowledge of the disposition of each party by the other, is absolutely necessary. Yet how often do we find this unattended to, in the most material concern of life! Hasty matches are formed; and subsequent misery is but too often the result of them.[23]

In *Love and Freindship* the idea of marriage contracted on a short acquaintance is taken to ridiculous lengths when the heroine marries a total stranger the very same night he turns up on her doorstep. Mr Collins' decision to choose Jane Bennet as his wife is made almost as fast – on the first evening of his visit to Longbourne. She is the prettiest and he is confident that he is enough of a catch to stipulate for a 'handsome' partner. The following morning, Mrs Bennet cautions him against fixing on her eldest daughter, so, while she is poking the fire, he transfers his hopes from Jane to Elizabeth. Mr Collins can now choose to marry because he has a good house and a sufficient income, but he does not consider the character of his future partner beyond the vague virtue of 'amiability'. He allows himself eleven days in which to secure his companion for life and expects to expend little energy on courtship. He will inherit the Longbourne estate; his suit, therefore, will be highly acceptable. In real life, a faster worker than Mr Collins secured a wife, fortune and all, in record time. Mrs Bland writing to Miss Heber in 1791, described the whirlwind courtship:

> Pray do you know in Northamptonshire a Mr Pinckard? He has Lately married a Mrs Lethieullier that Lives in Portman Street, a maiden Lady, near £20,000 at her own disposal. Her friends thinks she had better not have had it. She talks much of his Beauty &, when he is in the street, he is taken for the Prince of Wales. They met at Margate, & that there first acquaintance, & that in about 10 days tack'd 'em together for Life.[24]

She had fallen for his good looks, he for her £20,000. How the relationship prospered is anyone's guess, but the unequivocal assumption that an acquaintance of brief duration inevitably led to an unhappy marriage is a truth not substantiated in fiction or in life. If the couple involved were of good character, there was every chance of success. Admiral and Mrs Croft, Jane Austen's cousins Thomas and Jane Williams, reach an understanding after days rather than months in each other's company, although for the majority, any certainty of conjugal compatibility resulted from a more leisurely evaluation. A Frenchman noted with surprise in the 1780s that three English marriages out of four were based on affection, attributing this to fairly rigorous character appraisal beforehand: '. . . the Englishman makes more effort to get to know his bride before marriage;

she has a similar desire', but he was not at all sure about the English ideal of companionate marriage. Marrying at a later age was wise, he thought, if wives and husbands were to live always together, otherwise life would be a misery.[25]

Women were free to exercise judgement, but they could not be initiators. Emma Woodhouse, with all her money and influence, is not allowed to invite Mr Knightley to dance, although she can tell him quite directly that she would like him to ask. By the same token, women had to wait to be asked to marry, although they might angle for the proposal. If men were reluctant, or uncertain, or inexperienced, there were ways of bringing them to the point of no return. Isabella Thorpe shamelessly angles for James Morland from the moment of their first meeting. Her 'instant' friendship with Catherine, her compliance with James' every thought, are calculated to further her aim. Augusta Hawkins, also on the *qui vive* for a husband in Bath, as she has been for several winters, knows just how to ease Mr Elton into making a proposal. His damaged pride is delightfully responsive to the 'distinguishing notice', following hard on the heels of the first introduction; the 'accidental rencontre'; the various dinner and party invitations; the lady's 'smiles and blushes', 'consciousness and agitation' and willingness to be impressed. She signals very clearly that, if asked, she will not turn him down.[26] For the sake of a home of her own, Charlotte Lucas makes a bid for Mr Collins as early as the Netherfield Ball, when she 'goodnaturedly' relieves Elizabeth of his tedious conversation. Charlotte is sharp enough to interpret his behaviour to her friend and predict an outcome which could work to her own advantage. Following Elizabeth's refusal, Charlotte learns that Mr Collins' sole object is to find himself an acceptable wife, and realising that she can manoeuvre him into a position where he will consider her, she lures him away from Longbourne to Lucas Lodge. She listens to his pompous pronouncements for two days and is rewarded with his proposal speech early on the third.

It was considered highly improper for a woman to fall in love before the gentleman's preference was declared, but Catherine Morland, like most of Jane Austen's heroines and plenty of women in real life, does not follow conduct-book principles. Henry cannot help but notice her attraction to him when her obvious dependence on his good opinion is so plainly, if unconsciously, revealed. He is mature enough and sensitive enough to read all of the signs and Catherine, 'in finding him irresistible', becomes so herself. 'That a young lady should be in love, and the love of the young gentleman undeclared, is an heterodoxy which prudence, and even policy, must not allow', declared Samuel Richardson, and many other moralists agreed with this principle.[27] Any attempt to communicate interest in a man could be read as potential entrapment, the natural order overturned, man as hunted rather than hunter. Jane Austen jokingly cast herself in this predatory role, stating in a letter to her sister after a party in Bath that she had only been prevented from using all her wiles to snare one of the men there by the inconvenient fact of his having a wife and ten children.[28] In *Sense and Sensibility*, she has Sir John Middleton, a huntsman himself, employ the vocabulary of the chase when he accuses Marianne Dashwood of scheming to 'catch' John Willoughby, merely because she asks questions about his character. Marianne particularly objects to the expression 'setting one's cap at a man', yet she exposes her preference for Willoughby without reserve, laying herself open to ridicule, especially when he abandons her for an heiress.

Jane Austen saw both sides of the coin. In *Pride and Prejudice* she shows that concealment could also have potentially disastrous consequences. Elizabeth, reflecting on Jane's circumspect behaviour towards Bingley, is satisfied that she will not be the object of gossip, but Charlotte makes the sensible point that if Bingley himself remains blind to Jane's affection, there will be little comfort in the rest of the world being ignorant of it also. The world, it seems, took delight in deriding disappointed hopes, which provided one strong argument in favour of discretion. Charlotte is proved right in this case, as Elizabeth later admits – Bingley gives up all hope of Jane when he is persuaded, by her too guarded behaviour, that she is indifferent. When merely dancing more than once with the same partner could appear 'particular', it is little wonder that men themselves should take care to avoid raising the expectations of single women or their families. Believing that he has paid Elizabeth enough attention to give her ideas, Darcy resolves to ignore her completely on her final day at Netherfield. Bingley is less circumspect in hiding his preference for Jane – he chooses her as a dancing partner over other women, he fails to respond when people speak to him, but do these signs add up to love? When Bingley leaves the neighbourhood, ostensibly for good, neither Jane nor Elizabeth is entirely sure. Willoughby's total lack of concealment appears more unkind in comparison – even in public, he shows a marked preference for Marianne and acts like a committed lover.

Fishing for a marriage partner might be done by the family on either side. That marriage could be 'a manoeuvring business' was only too apparent, with the interference ranging from the cold calculation of the arranged marriage to more benevolent coercion. Jane Austen at almost thirty-three could joke about marrying the forty-five-year-old Rector of Chawton, 'whatever might be his reluctance or my own', in order to please Mrs Knight,[29] or speculate on the likelihood of a dead father bequeathing his four unmarried daughters to noblemen,[30] but the powerless sons and daughters of aristocratic families could only hope that they might find some reward for sacrificing themselves to fulfil their parents' dynastic aspirations. 'I had not the least guess about it till the day papa told me,' wrote Harriet Spencer of her arranged engagement to the Earl of Bessborough's son and heir in 1780:

> I wish I could have known him a little better first, but my dear papa and mama say that it will make them the happiest of creatures, and what would I not do to see them happy . . . I have a better chance of being reasonably happy with him than with most people I know.[31]

Her sister, Georgiana, appears to have possessed a more realistic view of such matches: 'Marriage now is a necessary kind of barter, and an alliance of families; – the heart is not consulted.'[32] It was common for a would-be suitor from the higher classes to bypass the woman completely and go straight to her father for permission to marry. The first she knew of any proposal was when Papa summarily brushed away all objections, insisted on compliance and packed her off to the library to give the expected answer. The ideal of the companionate marriage was far from influencing every father's dealings on the marriage market; the arranged marriage was alive and well, despite the change in attitude and century. Mamma might do her best to soothe her distraught daughter with the likelihood of love after marriage, 'and it did come' confided one fortunate victim in 1823,

'– but oh the sunshiny morning of youth.'[33] What made the situation even worse for this particular woman was that her elder sister had fallen desperately in love with the suitor on his previous visits. Sisterly affection must have been severely tested for some while. Eugenia Stanhope, an aristocrat herself, voiced her disapproval of such matches in her letters to a young female relative in the late 1790s, exposing the questionable assurance of love after marriage:

> There is no one, you well know, holds in so much contempt the general Opinion, that Persons of good Tempers will love one another after they are married, tho' they were indifferent before . . . I have differed with all our Family, and with all the Families of Prudence, as they call themselves, in the World, about those Marriages which are made by Parents, and in which those who are most concerned have no Business but Compliance.[34]

Not only aristocratic families were guilty of such stratagems, as Jane Austen illustrated. The Honourable Miss Morton with her £30,000 becomes the focus of Mrs Ferrars' machinations in *Sense and Sensibility*. When Edward refuses to comply with his mother's directive to make the heiress his wife, the younger son, Robert, is substituted, prompting Elinor to wonder wryly whether Miss Morton herself would have any say in the matter. Her brother's reply clearly expresses the mercenary principles on which he, his wife and mother-in-law expect everyone to be operating – Miss Morton is little more than a commodity on the marriage market and now that Robert is the heir to property and a fortune, he will automatically be acceptable.

The advantage to families of a good match could be considerable – '"The luck of one member of a family is luck to all."'[35] Isabella Thorpe, because she is beautiful, is expected to catch a man with money and provide greater opportunities for her younger sisters to find good husbands. Mrs Bennet relies on a match between Jane and Bingley for the same reason; her younger daughters will move in a higher social circle and mix with rich, eligible bachelors. Elizabeth's marriage to Mr Darcy introduces Kitty into more edifying company and Lydia and Wickham are benefited, too, by a steady supply of money from Elizabeth's allowance. On Darcy's side of the equation, Georgiana gains a sister who injects a sense of fun into her serious life. Charlotte Lucas' brothers can breathe a sigh of relief that their sister will not be a future burden on their finances and her sisters entertain hopes of mixing in adult society sooner than they had expected. Even Fanny Price can see one definite advantage in marrying Henry Crawford – she imagines him agreeing to her sister Susan's removal to Everingham, far from the deprivations of Portsmouth. The rest of the Price family would also benefit from Fanny's alliance – her brother William in particular, through the Admiral's influence over future promotion in the Navy. Examples of the wider implications of marriage choices abound – the richer Musgroves aid the poorer Hayters, Sir Thomas Bertram supports his wife's less fortunate sisters.

Family opposition to a match could prove powerful, or ineffectual. Henry Tilney may go against his father's orders and propose marriage to Catherine, but the Morlands will not sanction the match until the General relents. Henry's position is an uncomfortable one – his living is in the gift of the Abbey and open defiance of his father leaves him isolated. Charles Bingley's sisters are successful at the outset in detaching him from Jane Bennet, but their hopes for a match with Georgiana Darcy are not realised and their brother returns to Netherfield to marry his first choice. Anne Elliot suffers for eight years from her father's cold disdain and Lady Russell's well-meaning but rank-obsessed advice to refuse a man with uncertain prospects. Unfortunately for Lady Catherine de Bourgh, her determination to influence Darcy against Elizabeth has the opposite effect of taking him back to Hertfordshire to make a second proposal.

The proposed marriage, in 1781, between Jane Austen's cousin Eliza Hancock and a French officer stirred up a certain amount of family panic back in England. John Woodman, a trustee of the Hancock funds, wrote anxiously to Eliza's godfather, lamenting the Frenchman's lack of ready funds and Mrs Hancock's intention to 'give up to them the sum which was settled on her for life'. Mr Woodman stated that this request had been declined by himself and the second trustee, Mrs Hancock's brother George Austen. Mr Austen had other concerns – apart from giving up all their English friends and their country, he feared his sister and niece might turn Catholic. Given his opposition and Eliza's propensity for independent thought, her claim that she married 'much less from my own judgement than that of those whose councils & opinions I am the most bound to follow', is questionable. The advantages of the match are openly admitted in her letter to Philadelphia Walter: her husband 'literally adores' her; her circle of acquaintance is 'numerous & brilliant'; she is 'mistress of an easy fortune with the prospect of a very ample one', although Woodman claimed that the couple were draining Mrs Hancock of every shilling she had. She signs off with a flourish, 'Countess de Feuillide'.[36] There is no mention anywhere of affection for her husband, and Phylly herself, in a letter to her brother, revealed that although Eliza professed respect for the man, she did not love him.

The Austen parents themselves appear not to have stood in the way of their children's choice of marriage partners. One match in particular pleased Mrs Austen: her eldest son's choice of Mary Lloyd as his second wife, and she wrote to welcome her into the family in November 1796:

> Had the Election been mine, you, my dear Mary, are the person I should have chosen for *James's Wife, Anna's Mother*, and *my Daughter*; being as certain, as I can be of anything in this uncertain World, that you will greatly increase & promote the happiness of each of the three . . . I look forwards to you as a real comfort to me in my old age . . .[37]

Following his first wife's death, James Austen had danced his way into the hearts of several Hampshire ladies, until the choice had narrowed down to two clergymen's daughters, Mary Harrison and Mary Lloyd. Why he eventually settled on the smallpox-scarred Mary Lloyd is uncertain; her fortune was small, but it did clear the debts he had accrued during his first marriage. The Lloyd family were already well-known to the Austens and Mrs Austen may have had it in mind to promote Mary's interests when she invited her to Steventon for a week in September.

Familial intervention invariably finds its way into Jane Austen's fiction: a guardian locks up his wealthy ward until she agrees to marry his eldest son; a father drops heavy hints about breakfast china and shows off his opulently furnished abbey; two titled sisters plan an alliance between their babies; a baronet holds a ball, so that his niece's rich admirer can dance with her; another one deigns to be seen with his eldest daughter's choice at Tattersall's and in the lobby of the House of Commons; one mother sends a daughter three miles on horseback into certain rain, to ensure a lengthy recovery under the potential suitor's roof; a second bribes a son to marry an heiress and when he refuses, disinherits him; a third rewards a flannel-waistcoated suitor of thirty-seven with a young wife of nineteen; a sister employs trickery to promote her brother's advances. Sojourns with inhospitable relatives are extended, lovers are left alone in drawing rooms or sent off for long walks, invitations to dinner are issued, carriages made available or denied, character and accomplishments vaunted. The whole mechanism of choice proved far more complex than a straightforward decision to marry as soon as finances allowed and, while the man still made the final move, he might find himself either abetted or obstructed by whoever possessed the ultimate power of refusal.

2

The Power of Refusal

The choice made, nothing remained but to pop the question, either in person, by letter, or through an intermediary. The form of words used in face-to-face proposals was rarely recorded and although a few conduct manuals suggested various plans of campaign, there is no evidence that their efficacy was ever put to the test. Interestingly, references to men delivering proposals on bended knee, either in fictional accounts, conduct literature, or letters, are negligible;[1] surely Jane Austen would have had Mr Collins adopt this position when he makes his speech to Elizabeth, had a book on etiquette decreed that he should. It is hardly likely that he would have done so in the lane where he proposes to Charlotte Lucas. Those uncertain of their own powers of persuasion, or doubtful of a positive answer, could make an offer indirectly through a third party or by letter. The self-assured might wax lyrical on the extent of their properties and fortunes, leaving the more romantic to deliver ardent speeches, perhaps on their knees, and the less prolix to simply ask the direct question, 'Will you marry me?'

Rebecca Solly's painfully shy suitor carried out the initial courtship negotiations with her mother, who replied with a letter of encouragement dictated by her daughter. The following week the man rode over to spend a short time alone in the library with his intended, but the power of refusal or acceptance did not belong to her at this stage of the proceedings. Her mother and brothers decreed that money matters had to be decided before any definite answer could be given, despite the twenty-nine-year-old Rebecca's obvious desire to marry:

> . . . I believed myself as free when I left the library that day as when I entered it – however I will now acknowledge . . . my meditations were not very old maidish and I certainly wished that money at least might not conclude the Affair.[2]

Neither his request nor her answer are available, but we can guess at the embarrassment of such an encounter for both sides and the nail-biting uncertainty they must have suffered while the financial bargaining dragged on for another fortnight. When all was finally settled to everyone's satisfaction, the lovers were recognized as engaged and permitted to kiss for the first time.

William Chute of The Vyne, one of James Austen's hunting companions, showed a greater sense of strategic timing when he proposed to Eliza Smith in June 1793. Eliza's diary covering the period of courtship is remarkably economical on detail: after several 'Mr Chute to dinner' entries in early June, 'Sopha conversation', 'Answer' and 'Final decision' appear on the 10th, 12th and 13th; then the very next day the Smith family left London for a prolonged holiday in Weymouth and Lyme, Mr Chute joining them in the final week of July. He danced attendance throughout August and September, turning up most evenings and striding in at odd times during the day, his restlessness most likely a symptom of his impatience to get back home to his hounds and foxes at the start of the hunting season. It was probably no coincidence that he chose to secure a wife during the early summer months although, during September, he managed to squeeze in a day's shooting on the Smiths' estate in the country. The marriage settlement was signed on October the 14th and the wedding took place on the 15th, after which Mrs Chute's diary records her husband's hunting pursuits on an almost daily basis throughout the rest of the year and into the next.[3]

'Allow me to say that you are the only person in whose Society I can find Happiness and to whose example and care I could entrust the welfare of my children,' wrote Sir Edward Knatchbull in his proposal letter to Jane Austen's niece, Fanny Knight, in 1820, adding that she could be certain of his 'most unremitting and constant attention' if she became his wife. He had been a widower for six years and perhaps his decision to marry again came about through necessity – he had inherited his father's property and his seat in Parliament in 1819 and now needed someone to look after his children. Despite Fanny's professed antipathy to second alliances, 'particularly if there is any family', she accepted him. She referred to his 'excellence of character', her own 'prospect of as much comfort as this world can bestow' and her family's 'greatest satisfaction', but professed no warmer feelings. She was twenty-seven and, perhaps anxious that she would never find the perfect mate, settled for a thirty-nine-year-old widower. Aunt Jane's assessment of her niece's excellent judgement in matters of the heart may have been borne out by Fanny's behaviour in this case, maybe not. She gained a title and became Lady Knatchbull, but took on six step-children and produced nine more of her own.[4]

Successful proposal and acceptance scenes in the novels withdraw into third-person narrative, or near-silence as soon as the critical point is reached. The majority of Jane Austen's heroes exhibit a deep mistrust of fine words, but they also possess strong feelings. This is particularly applicable to Darcy and Mr Knightley, who both voice their unwillingness to make speeches – if they had felt less, they claim, they might have said more. There is no suggestion of elegant speeches rehearsed before a mirror – these proposals are spontaneous. Mr Knightley follows Emma into the garden with no idea of revealing the true state of his heart; it is described as 'the work of the moment' and the declaration that follows is the only proposal to be delivered in direct speech by the suitor himself. On this occasion, it is Emma who is temporarily tongue-tied. At the end of *Persuasion*, Captain Wentworth's feelings also flow unchecked, but this time in a letter which is, effectively, a proposal: 'I offer myself to you again with a heart even more your own, than when you broke it eight years and a half ago.'[5] All he asks of Anne by way of response is a word or a look. Edmund Bertram's proposal is hardly in evidence at all – once he has decided that Fanny will do as a wife, he is 'very steadily earnest in pursuit of the blessing.'[6] Edmund transfers his affections to Fanny in more time, granted, than Mr Collins takes in switching from Jane to Elizabeth, but his passions and inclinations are weaker than they were when Mary Crawford attracted him. He is on the rebound, and his anxiety to marry Fanny seems like an inevitable, worn-out kind of reaction. Fanny is a safe option: she is *not* Mary. Edward Ferrars' proposal is also sidestepped in a very determined fashion: 'in what manner he expressed himself, and how he was received, need not be particularly told.'[7] He is agitated enough beforehand to hack a scissors case to bits and has to take himself off for a long walk in the village before he can make his intentions intelligible to Elinor.

Henry Tilney, with greater wit and eloquence, has more to say for himself on the walk between Fullerton Rectory and Mrs Allen's and he expresses himself so well that Catherine would have given anything to hear it all over again, but the reader, as usual, is left behind on the path, just out of earshot. The heroines themselves all avoid sentimental or agitated responses, no hysterics, no swooning, just a warm but considered acceptance: 'What did she say? – Just what she ought, of course. A lady always does.'[8]

Refusals, on the other hand, present the novelist with an opportunity for combative dialogue – nothing will ever be the same afterwards. Mr Elton's proposal to Emma, like Mr Darcy's first proposal to Elizabeth, is reported for the most part indirectly, but the ensuing exchange is given in glorious detail. Armed with the courage to blurt out his 'violent love' to Emma by a surfeit of Mr Weston's wine, Mr Elton declares extravagantly that he is 'ready to die' if she refuses to reward his 'ardent attachment and unequalled love and unexampled passion.'[9] Emma is forced to disabuse him in strong terms, since he will not see reason, leaving him in no doubt as to his position as a social inferior. Mr Collins' proposal speech is so obviously rehearsed that Elizabeth is unable to interrupt him until he reaches the point where he takes her acceptance as read. Mr Collins has had little to do with women and his ideas about the opposite sex have all been gleaned from Fordyce's *Sermons* and similar texts. Like Mr Elton, he has digested everything that conduct books have to say about 'elegant females' rejecting proposals out of a sense of modesty, while all the time meaning to accept. His comments on suspense find an echo in a letter written by the Revd John Gregory to his daughters in the 1770s, the entire collection of which ran to many editions in Jane Austen's lifetime: 'a state of suspense' it claimed, is a 'very great incitement to attachment, and (is) the food of love in both sexes.'[10] He is so convinced by this argument, that an exasperated Elizabeth is forced to refuse him five times, in increasingly firm language, thus creating a powerful refutation of the view of women expressed in some conduct literature. She questions the existence of overly modest young ladies who would risk their future happiness by refusing a first proposal in the hope that a second attempt would follow. Women are rational creatures, she claims, who know their own inclinations and are capable of judging for themselves. When they say no, they mean no.

The absence of a clear negative was often interpreted as encouragement – but a woman's silence sometimes just gave her a breathing space before she did say no. Emma's initial speechlessness is taken as an auspicious sign by both of the men who propose to her, whereas she has no thought of accepting the first and every intention of saying yes to the second. Darcy certainly interprets Elizabeth's stunned response to his first proposal as an invitation to air his unconquerable, but not altogether gratifying, love for her. Convention requires him to express some anxious doubts about a favourable reply, although Elizabeth sees that he has no real qualms on that score. Her refusal is such a shock that he turns pale and has to struggle for composure. After her dismissal of Mr Collins, Elizabeth is still mistress of her own feelings, calmly determining her future plan of action, but the heated, highly charged exchange with Mr Darcy leaves her so mentally and physically exhausted that she collapses onto a chair to cry for half an hour. Her refusal has powerful consequences for both of them: Darcy is stung into a mortifying review of his ungentlemanly conduct and Elizabeth is forced to re-evaluate her unfounded prejudices. This is the beginning of a better knowledge of themselves and each other and from this point on they draw closer together.

Elizabeth Bennet is so splendid at handling refusals that Jane Austen cannot resist allowing her a third – a refusal in reverse. She refuses to promise that she will never become Darcy's wife, propelling Lady Catherine straight to London, to rehearse to her nephew all of his own previously held arguments against an alliance, together with Elizabeth's spirited resistance to her demands. Given Lady Catherine's celebrated candour, Darcy would feel the full force of Elizabeth's change of heart. Her final refusal has the most powerful consequence of all – it brings a hopeful Darcy back to Hertfordshire to make a second proposal of marriage.

Not every woman could expect Elizabeth's luck, but rejected suitors who were determined enough made multiple attempts to overcome disinclination. One particular clergyman, 'a plain Sensible man between thirty and forty years old with a pair of beautiful black Eyes to recommend a person otherwise not at All handsome', was refused seven times in one year by the woman he wished to marry, before she was prevailed upon to accept him. On the day of the marriage, by special licence in a private house, the groom exacted his revenge – he disappeared on the afternoon before the wedding and failed to turn up for tea at 8 p.m. The whole city of Dublin was searched from end to end, but he could not be found. He finally arrived late for the ceremony, claiming that he had been shopping for gloves, 'but as he was a sensible little man, every one thought it was a piece of Satyrical Revenge on his long demurring Spouse.'[11] The story ends entertainingly enough, but the woman's extreme unwillingness sounds a darker note and brings Fanny Price sharply to mind. Perhaps the reluctant bride faced the same kind of coercion, her refusal interpreted as the result of inexperience and modesty. Her father, offended that she had not seen fit to consult him before making up her own mind, applying pressure by laying before her all of the advantages to herself and her family that a marriage to an eligible man would provide, impressing upon her that she may never receive another offer; the sanguine lover encouraged to persevere and allowed frequent access to her company, her resistance finally worn down and overcome, the power of refusal no power at all.

Emotional blackmail operated successfully in some instances. If the woman could be persuaded to believe that her refusal had resulted in the would-be lover's near-death, she might repent enough to change her mind. Dorothea Herbert was having none of it. She remained completely immune to a hot-headed lover, who penned long poems of undying love and followed her everywhere, wringing his hands and shedding tears. On receiving a very passionate letter from him, threatening desperate consequences should she continue to refuse him, she decided that his sentimental foolishness had gone quite far enough and passed the letter to her parents. He beat a hasty retreat, leaving Dorothea with some residual guilt, although news of his subsequent dealings soon restored her common sense:

> I was quite Miserable at thus banishing him from his Eden – And my Conscience was never easy till I heard some Months after of his Marriage with a Miss Rolleston a Lady of large fortune – who besides got him good church Preferment being related to some Person in the Ministry – As I heard he was perfectly happy with his Choice – I thought myself quite exhonorated from all further feeling on his Account.[12]

Helen Bourne's capacity for self-preservation was less developed than

Dorothea Herbert's. She rejected Thomas Martineau's desperate suit, then later agreed to allow him to write to her, because she felt sorry for him. She had learned of his poor physical and mental state, but she was also quite aware of her own susceptibility to human suffering and the danger to herself in agreeing to a correspondence:

> I was indeed deeply grieved some weeks ago to hear of such unfavourable accounts of yr health – the idea seized my mind that perhaps it might in fact be occasioned by the disappointment of yr hopes respecting me – & I felt that if yr illness terminated as I then feared, from the accounts I heard, that I should never forgive myself; . . . [the] account of the state of yr mind interested & affected me & perhaps prepared me to receive more favourably than I should otherwise have done renewal of yr former proposals which the conviction of the depth & steadiness of yr attachment has aided materially – If I know my own heart it is warm & affectionate & unwilling to give pain to anyone.
>
> How much I was distressed at refusing a compliance with yr wishes on a former occasion, but I believed then that you would soon forget me & find that happiness in some other connection which I had it not in my power to bestow – I did feel at that time that I was hardly doing you justice in not permitting a correspondence, as a means of attaining a more thorough knowledge of yr character; but I had been taught to consider it in the same light as an engagement, & I thought that if I consented to it & after some time perceived no change in my own feelings towards you, that it would be trifling with yr best affections, & using you ill —[13]

She was right to be wary of a prolonged correspondence, or any correspondence, since written communication between men and women with no formal engagement subsisting between them was not acceptable. Martineau took full advantage of her tender indecision and she was eventually prevailed upon to marry him.

Refusing an attractive offer of marriage on the advice of a friend or relative, for whatever reason, risked long-term unhappiness. Anne Elliot relinquishes her power of self-determination to Lady Russell in cancelling her engagement to Captain Wentworth. Her father and elder sister's proud disdain of Wentworth's lack of status also influences her decision; she is made to feel isolated and at fault. Her joy in life and her bloom fade and at twenty-seven, after eight years of silence and obscurity, her life appears closed down by her loss. She cannot escape her environment nor her memories of Wentworth within it. The power of refusal, in effect exercised by others, almost puts an end to Anne Elliot's hopes and has the potential to push Wentworth into making an unsatisfactory match. Emma Woodhouse takes away Harriet Smith's right to accept Robert Martin and assumes the power to manipulate her into a match with Mr Elton. Harriet's confused silence enables Emma to introduce uncertainty into her mind:

> "I lay it down as a general rule . . . that if a woman *doubts* as to whether she should accept a man or not, she certainly ought to refuse him. If she can hesitate as to 'Yes,' she ought to say 'No' directly."[14]

How can poor scatty Harriet argue with such reasonable advice? Emma conveniently ignores the evidence of her friend's pre-Hartfield ease with the Martin family and the appeal of Robert Martin's character: he is good-natured, amiable and attached to Harriet, he writes creditable letters and he will suffer when he receives her rejection. If it were not for Emma's disapproval, Harriet would entertain no doubts about marrying him. Emma uses her position most unfairly and most dangerously – she does not consider the benefits of such a match for an illegitimate girl. She has no grasp of the stark reality of Harriet's uncertain position and despite her protestation of eternal friendship, she will not assume financial or emotional responsibility for her. Harriet may never receive another offer of marriage, despite her tractable nature and her prettiness. Mr Knightley's prediction of Harriet's impoverished future as the wife of the old writing master's son, when she might have gained a respectable farmer with good prospects and a comfortable house, is more realistic than Emma's ambitions for her protégé. As he points out, Emma has been no friend to Harriet Smith. She is driven to argue that '"it is always incomprehensible to a man that a woman should ever refuse an offer of marriage. A man always imagines a woman to be ready for anybody who asks her,"'[15] and while her claim holds some truth, it does not apply to all men, all of the time.

Emma herself certainly imagines that Frank Churchill will find her refusal incomprehensible as she runs the scene of his proposal through her head. In the meantime, she is quite contented to enjoy his company with no idea of a permanent attachment, fully aware that she is inviting speculation and gossip. Flirtation was just one aspect of initial attraction, of finding the right mate – it might lead to more serious courtship, it might lead nowhere, but society pronounced judgement on such behaviour if it produced no results. One of Jane Austen's Hampshire neighbours considered her a determined man-hunter after witnessing her willingness to stand up with anyone and everyone at the Basingstoke Assemblies. Women who were naturally high spirited and comfortable in men's company had to tolerate being labelled as flighty, or learn to curb their liveliness. This kind of flirting was not entirely safe, but it could be deliciously satisfying. Jane's cousin Eliza certainly thought so and admitted as much when she claimed that flirting made the blood circulate. Writing to inform Philadephia Walter of her marriage, she couldn't resist slipping in a reference to an earlier *amour* with Phylly's brother James:

> I suppose he is much grown since I saw him; I do not think we should either of us know one another again, I fancy we are both a little altered since the time he made verses on me in which he compared me to Venus & I know not what other divinity, & played off fireworks in the cellar in honour of my charms.[16]

Eliza revelled in admiration of any sort, she liked to be fallen in love with, at the same time professing that she was not likely to lose sleep or appetite for any man breathing. Like Henry Crawford, she did not mean to be in any danger of falling in love. Starched cousin Phylly commented on her 'dissipated' lifestyle in 1787, concluding, 'every woman is at heart a rake'.[17] Eliza saw a good deal of Henry Austen at this time and was obviously taken by his appearance. She wrote to Phylly of Henry's fashionable clothes and his imposing height. Both Henry and his elder brother James were fascinated by her and she must have been in her element. She and Henry planned to return to Paris together, but a place became vacant for him at St John's College, Oxford, which he could not defer. He was at this time seventeen, Eliza twenty-seven and married. A year later, she was still mentioning Henry in her letters to her cousin. In 1792, on the death of her mother, Eliza stayed with the Austens at Steventon for some time and Henry was still on the agenda, although the terms on which they existed were rather cool. Some kind of quarrel had been patched up, although it seems to have been up to Henry to apologise – 'and we are at present on very proper relationlike terms'.[18] Henry became engaged to Mary Pearson early in 1796, but by the end of the year she had broken it off. The now widowed Eliza saw him in London at the beginning of November and wrote to Phylly: 'he looks thin & ill – I hear his late intended is a most intolerable Flirt, & reckoned to give herself great Airs'[19] and this accusation from a woman who, in the previous paragraph, described the 'reasonable quantity of Beaux' she entertained each morning. James Austen was back on the scene too, his first wife having died in May 1795, but he had already given up thinking of Eliza as a second wife by the time she wrote to Phylly in December: 'I do not believe the parties ever will come together, not however that they have quarrelled, but one of them cannot bring her mind to give up dear Liberty, & yet dearer flirtation —'[20] She was not ready, she said, for 'sober Matrimony' with a parson, but Henry's new militia appointment in 1797 meant that *he* might be in with a chance:

> He is a very lucky young Man & bids fair to possess a considerable Share of Riches & Honours; I believe he has now given up all thoughts of the Church, and he is right for he certainly is not so fit for a Parson as a Soldier.[21]

That many readers and critics have drawn comparisons between Eliza and Mary Crawford is hardly surprising. In July 1797, in reply to Phylly's enquiries about her intentions regarding Henry, Eliza stated:

> the Lady is so well pleased with her present situation that She cannot find it in her Heart to change it, and says in her giddy way that independance and the homage of half a dozen are preferable to subjection and the attachment of a single individual.[22]

By September, despite all of her protestations to the contrary, Eliza left London for Lowestoft to be close to Henry and at the end of December, at the age of 35, she married him. Eliza's habit of flirting, what she referred to as 'trade', became less overt, but she still had a keen eye for a good-looking man:

> Captn. Tilson is remarkably handsome, and . . . Messrs. Perrott & Edwardes may be chatted with very satisfactorily, but as to my Colonel Lord Charles Spencer, if I was married to my third husband instead of my second I should still be in love with him.[23]

Acquiring a reputation as a jilt was something most women tried to avoid at all costs, but in facing the difficult task of finding a partner for life, mistakes were inevitably made. 'A young Lady who would wish to engage the affections of a Man of merit, should never sport with his Happiness, by trifling with the Sex for diversion',[24] stated one conduct manual, yet not all young women who changed their minds were Isabella Thorpes. Parson James Woodforde considered himself jilted by Betsy White of Shepton after she had broken a verbal agreement to marry him when his financial situation allowed. Fifteen months later, after seeing little of the parson, Betsy married a Devonshire man with a good income and expectations of property, who settled £300 per annum on her. '... she has proved herself to me a mere Jilt' complained Woodforde in his diary.[25] He believed she had given him up to marry a richer man, and he was probably right. Betsy had accepted a far better deal for herself than marrying, at some unspecified time in the future, a middle-aged clergyman on £400 a year, whose only recorded gifts to her were ripe peaches.

The Revd Thomas Gisborne, whose *Enquiry Into The Duties Of The Female Sex* Jane Austen had read and claimed to enjoy, took a more balanced view of the warm feelings a woman experienced when first singled out for special notice by a man:

> She beholds him with general approbation: she is conscious that there is no other person whom she prefers to him: she receives lively pleasure from his attentions: and she imagines that she loves him with tenderness and ardour. Yet it is very possible that she maybe unacquainted with the real state of her heart. Thoughtless inexperience, gentleness of disposition, the quick susceptibility of early youth, and chiefly perhaps the complacency which all persons, whose affections are not pre-occupied, feel towards those who distinguish them by particular proofs of regard, may have excited an indistinct partiality which she mistakes for rivetted attachment.[26]

Errors of judgement in matters of the heart were a painful fact of life, especially in a small, unvarying, country community, where choice was limited and the arrival of a prosperous or handsome stranger could challenge existing alliances. Anne Elliot recognizes as much when she hopes that Henrietta Musgrove will not keep Charles Hayter dangling if she has transferred her affections to Captain Wentworth. A distinction is made here between a genuine change of heart and the deliberate raising of hopes in order to disappoint them; the love lives of two of Jane Austen's nieces provided her with enough evidence to draw on.

Her brother James' daughter, Anna, engaged herself at sixteen to the Revd Michael Terry, a man with good prospects, but almost twice her age. For some reason, her father and step-mother viewed the relationship with displeasure and packed Anna off to her Uncle Edward at Godmersham, where she arrived on 23 November 1809. In the early spring of the following year, after another interview with Michael Terry, James Austen agreed to the engagement. Mr Terry duly arrived at Godmersham on March the 2nd, and although Anna's cousin Fanny had reservations – 'He is much younger looking and more shy than I had an idea of. *I* should not like him, but if Anna does, that does not signify' – she altered her opinion in his favour on a closer acquaintance. By May the 4th, the affair was over, Anna luckily having realized in time that she had misunderstood her own inclinations. 'What a girl!!! . . . Heavens! What will she do next?' recorded the astounded Fanny in her diary.[27] Unfortunately, the Terrys lived at Dummer, not far from Steventon, so it was thought politic to send Anna off to Chawton, where the immediate neighbourhood found plenty to gossip about, as her Aunt Jane soon discovered:

> She does not return from Farringdon till this evening, – & I doubt not, has had plenty of the miscellaneous, unsettled sort of happiness which seems to suit her best. – We hear from Miss Benn, who was on the Common with the Prowtings, that she was very much admired by the Gentlemen in general. —'[28]

A fairer interpretation of Anna's behaviour is provided by her daughter, Fanny-Caroline. She tells how the sixteen-year-old Anna lost her best friend and defender at home on her half-brother's removal to Winchester School:

> Being lonely & unhappy probably my Mother fretted more under the snubbing & fault finding than she had ever done before & perhaps had more to bear as his parents could not but miss the boy, as much as she did, at all events she was wretched & thought her life unbearable and while still in this mood she received an offer of marriage. The Gentleman was a young clergyman, the son of a neighbouring squire, tall & good looking & well connected with certainty

> of a comfortable family living if he did not already hold it. And she accepted him. I suppose because the warmth of the love & its sweet flatteries in contrast to the slighting & depreciation of home made her fancy that she did or could like the lover.[29]

When, three years later, in August 1813, Anna suddenly sprang her engagement to Ben Lefroy of Ashe on the family, Jane wrote to her brother Frank, expressing the whole family's concern. Anna was still suspected of emotional instability and the match did not hold out much hope of companionable happiness: Ben had an odd temperament and hated company, Anna was giddy and gregarious. Her Aunt Jane predicted only a slim chance of happiness for the pair if the marriage went ahead,[30] but despite the family's belief that the relationship could not last, Anna proved them wrong and married Ben a year later, her 'unsteadiness' only surfacing now and again in what her aunt considered to be the acquisition of unnecessary luxuries – notably a piano and a purple pelisse, both purchased with wedding-present money meant for towels and sheets.

Anna's habit of circumventing family disapproval by being secretive did her no favours with Aunt Jane; it certainly seems that she was more severely judged than Fanny Knight, who at sixteen was expressing her opinion of Anna's behaviour in exclamatory terms, at eighteen earning a reproof from Aunt Cassandra for idolizing the impossibly handsome George Hatton[31] and playing fast and loose with John Plumptre's affections at twenty-one. She encouraged him to a point where a proposal seemed imminent, then wrote in a panic to Aunt Jane about her rapidly cooling feelings for him. Jane had seen enough of the relationship to be an understanding judge of Fanny's feelings – 'Your mistake has been one that thousands of women fall into. He was the first young Man who attached himself to you. That was the charm, & most powerful it is.'[32] Just how flattering such attentions can be she explores in *Emma*, the novel she was working on at the time of Fanny's dilemma. '"I was tempted by his attentions, and allowed myself to appear pleased,"' Emma explains to Mr Knightley, regarding her flirtation with Frank Churchill. '"An old story, probably – a common case – and no more than has happened to hundreds of my sex before; . . ."'[33]

Jane Austen recognized the transitory nature of affection and in Fanny's case found it both serious and amusing: by all accounts, it was better to appear fickle than face a lifetime of misery committed to a loveless match.[34] Fanny recovered sufficiently from her worries to flirt openly with her Uncle Henry's surgeon, Mr Haden, a year later and Jane described to Cassandra how animated the pair were one evening in Henry's drawing room, sitting so close together that she could not be sure whether they occupied a chair each or were sharing the same one. Another year on and Fanny's fickleness flared up again, when John Plumptre became attached to someone else and Aunt Jane had to deliver a dose of strong medicine: Fanny was not in love with him, she never had been and now she must accept that he had transferred his affections to another woman.[35] In the same letter, James Wildman featured as a potential suitor and Fanny's 'fluctuations of . . . Fancy' and 'Capprizios of . . . Taste' left Jane Austen reeling in admiration. Fanny's appeal lay in her openness; this is what excused her – but no wonder she pretended that she couldn't find the letters her aunt had written to her, when her cousin James-Edward Austen-Leigh asked for material in the 1860s for his *Memoir*. The grand Lady Knatchbull that Fanny had become, with an unsteadier character in her younger days than her cousin Anna had ever exhibited, now had a solid Victorian reputation to protect.

Jane Austen herself refused one proposal of marriage, in December 1802, just before her twenty-seventh birthday. Jane and Cassandra were staying with their old friends Catherine and Alethea Bigg at Manydown Park near Basingstoke, when the Biggs' twenty-one-year old brother Harris asked Jane to marry him. He was plain and his awkwardness was heightened by a pronounced stutter, so presumably his proposal was as brief and to the point as he could manage. He apparently had little to recommend him beyond his size, his prospective property and his fortune, but Jane accepted him, then reconsidered overnight and said no the following morning. She did not love him and knew that 'the place & fortune which would certainly be *his*, could not alter the *man*'. She would not put her trust in finding love after marriage.[36] The advantages of the match to her family and to herself would have been considerable – here was a ready-made, familiar home and family for Cassandra and Mrs Austen when Mr Austen died, Jane would move out of Bath back to her beloved Hampshire, financial security was guaranteed and her brothers would be spared the future expense of supporting their mother and sisters. Her refusal was momentous; James' wife Mary – and probably other members of the Austen family too – were not best pleased and the two remaining Bigg sisters must have been disappointed that Jane would not be the future mistress of Manydown Park, securing their own place in it should neither of them marry. The whole affair caused much embarrassment and Jane and Cassandra cut their visit short, returning in haste to Bath, but the sisters at Manydown remained their firm friends and Harris married someone else two years later.

It is likely that Edward Bridges proposed marriage to Jane Austen three years later, or came very close to it, and that his mother Lady Bridges knew about it. Jane was staying at Goodnestone Farm in August 1805, when she was twenty-nine and Edward a twenty-six-year-old clergyman. They had known each other for nine years at least. In September 1796, while Jane was staying at Rowling, Edward Bridges chose her as his partner to open the ball at Goodnestone Hall. His interest manifested itself again in 1805, in his ordering toasted cheese especially for her one evening after a cricket match. Jane did not mention a proposal in her letters, it is something she would want to discuss with Cassandra face to face, but she either refused him or skilfully turned the conversation when she saw where it was leading. In the following letter three days later, it becomes clear that she was avoiding Edward's company. She stated that she could give no convincing reason for leaving Goodnestone before Monday, but since Edward had engagements which would take him away from home over the weekend, she might just as well stay.[37] Like Emma Woodhouse wishing to prevent Frank Churchill from making 'an absolute declaration', which could only lead to a painful conclusion, she did not wish to jeopardize a friendship. Rejection was inescapably embarrassing and few women wished to inflict pain or humiliation on men who had perhaps become their friends over the course of time, especially if that friendship had been interpreted as something more. Three years later, another reference to Edward and his mother appears to point to some kind of past experience which might have caused them to behave coolly towards her. She had seen neither Edward nor Lady Bridges since 1805 and felt uncomfortable about encountering them on this occasion, but all seemed to have been forgiven. Lady Bridges was her usual, friendly, smiling self and although there had been little opportunity for talking at any length, she and her son had given Jane the impression that their goodwill towards her was unaltered.[38] The final reference to the affair comes in a letter to Cassandra, who was staying at Godmersham in October 1808: 'I wish you may be able to accept Lady Bridges' invitation, tho' I could not her son Edward's.'[39] The following year, Edward Bridges married Harriet Foote, none the worse for being turned down by Jane Austen.

> It is too universal a maxim with novelists, that love is felt but once; though it appears to me, that the heart which is capable of receiving an impression at all, and can distinguish, will turn to a new object when the first is found unworthy,[40]

noted Mary Wollstonecraft, but it was no universal maxim for Jane Austen, either in fiction or real life. 'I suppose he has quick feelings —' she said of one dismissed suitor, 'but I dare say they will not kill him'[41] and her conviction that disappointment in love never killed anybody is carried through into her fiction. Despite the 'indelible' impression that Edmund Bertram's blighted hopes leave on his mind, it only takes from early spring until the end of the summer to cure his 'unconquerable passions' and effect 'the transfer of unchanging attachment'. Sitting around under trees all summer, talking confidentially with Fanny, Edmund on the rebound comes to value her character over Mary's.[42] Had Edmund married Mary Crawford, however, Jane Austen makes it clear that Fanny would have overcome her disappointment and married Henry. Captain Benwick is not likely to die of disappointment, either, however much he wishes others to think that he might. He deliberately feeds his loss by dwelling on poetry 'which imaged a broken heart, or a mind destroyed by wretchedness', yet Anne Elliot divines that, 'He will rally again, and be happy with another', and that this is how it should be.[43] Charles Musgrove marries Mary Elliot when he can't have Anne and in Anne's own case, after eight long years of disappointed hope and Wentworth now seemingly unattainable, she does not immediately discount the possibility of a relationship with James Benwick or Mr Elliot. Mr Elton disappears to Bath to find himself a wife within days of Emma's refusal of his proposal. He has no lasting feelings of disappointment, but his animosity towards both Emma and Harriet has inescapable consequences in such a narrow society. Emma must witness the effects of her meddling on an almost daily basis and it takes some time to persuade the deluded Harriet to cease dwelling on Mr Elton's perfections, her mournful preoccupation centred almost entirely on a piece of court plaster and a pencil stub. Remedies for disappointed love 'must vary much as to time in different people', but Jane Austen's message is always the same, that time will effect its cure in every case.

3

An Acquaintance Formed in a Public Place

The society within small towns and villages, where the majority of the population lived, was limited and limiting; a handful of families on an equal social footing provided little scope for choice, so how and where did single men and women find anyone to marry? Gentlemen's leisure pursuits mainly excluded women; the brave few who ventured onto the hunting field earned themselves the reputation of being 'masculine'. Groups of men met in the evenings to play cards, eat and talk; women sat at home, reading and sewing. Mr Darcy is not wrong when he comments on the confined and unvarying society in country neighbourhoods, yet eligible young men were not unknown to arrive out of the blue, to rent houses and make themselves available at balls and private gatherings. When the recently divorced Colonel Powlett and his brother moved into Southampton, Jane Austen claimed to have discovered a husband each for the two large-nosed Miss Maitlands, Caroline and Eliza.[1]

Men were more fortunate than women in being mobile, travelling independently where and when they pleased. Jane Austen reflects this freedom in her novels, sending her male characters all over England, from Devonshire to London, London to Derbyshire, Northamptonshire to Bath, raising hopes and disappointing expectations as they gallop through women's lives. In the late eighteenth century, the percentage of men with independent means who married within their own counties fell compared with the higher numbers earlier in the century, although lower down the scale, among the lesser gentry, the number of men marrying in-county stayed fairly static. Jane's sailor brothers, whose profession took them far and wide, found their wives beyond Hampshire, in Ramsgate and Bermuda, but of the remaining brothers, the three who were eligible to marry met theirs on home territory: Henry and James in Hampshire, Edward in his adopted Kent. The families of doctors, lawyers, clergymen, MPs, retired army officers, squires and aristocrats who lived within a twenty-mile radius of Steventon all mixed at social gatherings and Mr Austen took in the sons of some of these neighbours to prepare them for university. This is how his daughters came to develop lifelong friendships with the Fowle brothers from Kintbury and how Cassandra became engaged to Tom. At Christmas and New Year, relations from farther afield came to stay in the locality, adding to the number of participants at the seasonal festivities. It was not impossible to discover a Miss or a Mr Right on home ground and there are numerous examples of Jane Austen's neighbours doing just that. Two of the Terry girls from Dummer married a Digweed from Steventon and a Harwood from Deane; Ben Lefroy of Ashe found Anna Austen at Steventon and an elder brother married a Cottrell from North Waltham; William Heathcote of Worting chose Elizabeth Bigg of Manydown; the list goes on.

Mrs Radcliffe, Mary Brunton, Eleanor Sleath and a host of other contemporary authors solved the issue in more dramatic ways, whisking their heroines off to the Continent or across the Atlantic to experience unlikely adventures and captivate dashing heroes. And no wonder their novels proved so absorbing for female readers stuck at home with little congenial company and only an unpromising curate to look at. '... if adventures will not befall a young lady in her own village, she must seek them abroad'[2] pronounced Jane Austen, tongue firmly in cheek, but the furthest she sends any of her heroines in pursuit of a happy ending is Derbyshire. Elinor Dashwood, Elizabeth Bennet and Anne Elliot fall in love with men who come into their quiet, confined existences from elsewhere; Marianne does too, but eventually marries a man who lives just over the county border; Fanny Price and Emma marry men who are already part of the family. Her characters encounter realistic situations that readers would recognise from their own lives and only one heroine, Catherine Morland, actually meets her future husband away from home. At the age of seventeen, she has seen no one to fall in love with, which was more often than not the case for seventeen-year-old girls throughout England. Fortunately for her, she is whisked off to Bath by the Allens, but for the most part women stayed put, prayed fervently for their fathers to develop gout, or at the very least for an invitation to a ball at the local big house, and waited for suitable men, any men, to turn up.

The titles of popular dance tunes, 'The Handsome Couple', 'Haste to the Wedding', 'The Happy Marriage', 'The Private Wedding' and, perhaps played as a light-hearted joke, 'The Marriage Hater', registered the importance of balls in enabling young men and women to find marriage partners. Dancing in a large set inevitably involved a lot of standing around and interesting private conversations could be had under cover of the crowd. James Austen improved his dancing technique and performed enthusiastically at every venue he could get to, while he looked about him for a second wife: 'a Ball is nothing without *him*', claimed his sister early in January 1796.[3] By September, he had narrowed his choice down to two and Jane sent instructions from Kent that Cassandra must keep her informed of his progress at the next ball. To be fond of dancing might be a certain step towards falling in love,[4] as the prominent dance scenes in Jane Austen's novels illustrate, but male partners at private balls and public assemblies were often thin on the ground. The Bennet girls' excited anticipation before the Meryton Ball is tinged with disappointment when they learn that the women will outnumber the men and Jane Austen knew just how they felt. Girls desperate to dance had no option but to partner each other. Reporting to Cassandra on a ball at one of the large estates near Steventon, in November 1800, she revealed that out of ten dances she had sat down for only one, but four out of the remaining nine she had danced with Catherine Bigg. 'There was a scarcity of Men in general, & a still greater scarcity of any that were good for much,' she complained. 'There was commonly a couple of ladies standing up together . . .'[5]

Wealthy families had the means and usually the will to promote the social life of the neighbourhood in providing opportunities for young people to meet and dance at their grand houses. Not only rich couples like the Middletons in *Sense and Sensibility* perform this essential service – Mrs Philips in *Pride and Prejudice* invites all of the young ladies in Meryton to meet the visiting officers in her more modest home, clearing the furniture to the sides of the room and rolling up the carpet to create space for an impromptu dance. Only one musician was required; Mary Bennet reluctantly obliges at Aunt Philips' and Anne Elliot plays the piano one evening at Uppercross so that the Musgrove girls can dance with Captain Wentworth; a musical servant could be summoned from his quarters and any local tradesman with a violin sent for at will:

> Lady Winnington seemed in total absence of selfishness to lay herself out to make the young people happy. Often, when we dined at the Court, she would send for the miller, who played the violin, and set us all to dance . . .[6]

The Portsmouths at Hurstbourne Park, the Portals of Laverstoke House, the Harwoods at Deane, the Boltons at Hackwood Park and the Dorchesters at Kempshott Park all did their duty by their Hampshire neighbours in hosting regular balls. It was at a gathering at Deane early in 1796, followed by two others, at Manydown and Ashe, that Jane danced and fell in love with Tom Lefroy and barely noticed whether or not there were enough young men to go round. Several years later, at a ball in Southampton, where an older Jane did not expect to dance, she noted sympathetically the lack of dancing opportunities for dozens of young women, who could only stand by and watch the lucky few who had partners.[7] The shortage was a direct consequence of the war with France: after hostilities began in 1793, the Army increased its numbers from 45,000 to 100,000 men, and the Navy from 16,000 to 130,000. With so many eligible men out of the country, no wonder the presence of rich single landowners and army officers in Meryton animate the younger Bennet girls and their mother beyond the bounds of decorum.

Unmarried girls attending public balls were accompanied by a chaperon, either a married relative, or an older woman friend. Even at a dance in a private house, young women were under surveillance. Mrs Norris fusses around the ladies performing this role at the Mansfield Park ball and promotes a marriage between Maria and Mr Rushworth by ensuring that they dance together the required number of times at local gatherings to set the onlookers talking of an engagement. Mothers would usually act as their daughters' escorts at public assemblies, unless they were as indolent as Lady Bertram, but when young ladies went on independent visits to friends or relations, other women stepped in to assume the role. Charlotte Palmer offers to take Marianne and Elinor Dashwood into London society in place of their mother, who stays at home in Devon; Mrs

Forster is considered a fit chaperon for Lydia in Brighton and Mrs Younge for Georgiana Darcy at Ramsgate, until their unsuitability is discovered. In Bath, Mrs Allen proves an ineffectual guardian of Catherine Morland's reputation, allowing John Thorpe to monopolize her at the assembly rooms and drive her unaccompanied through the streets. Judging from Jane Austen's novels and letters, Mrs Allen was typical of many chaperons, gossiping on the edges of the action and not interfering with their charges' enjoyment of the evening. They derived as much satisfaction from the occasion as they could, predicting matches and catching up on the latest scandals and fashions, but there were dangers out there on the dance floor, many of them dressed in red coats.

In 1795, the South Devon Regiment, the Oxfords and the Derbyshires were billeted in towns around Steventon for the winter, their arrival swelling the number of eligible men at the Basingstoke Assembly Rooms and no doubt deranging the mind of every unmarried young lady in the area. The scarlet uniforms of the militia transformed the men who wore them into physical magnets and their company was invariably sought for balls and card parties, but little could be discovered of their backgrounds or characters if they were posted away from their own neighbourhoods, as Mr Wickham's regiment was to Hertfordshire. Captain Tilney's polished manners and military bearing facilitate his smooth operations in Bath and everywhere else he might chance to go. He fools both the inexperienced Catherine, who misinterprets his flirtation with her friend as serious courtship, and the more worldly-wise Isabella. It was not easy to ascertain motives in public places, where no real intimacy was possible and where budding relationships and flirtations rarely lacked a public audience. Elizabeth's interest in Wickham is noticed by Caroline Bingley, Charlotte Lucas, the Gardiners, Aunt Philips, Wickham's fellow officers, Elizabeth's sisters and parents and Mr Darcy. Various female onlookers in Bath speculate confidently on a future match between Anne Elliot and her cousin; similarly, Jane Austen's delight in Tom Lefroy was detected by a number of interested parties, including Mrs Lefroy, the Austen parents and John Willing Warren, a former admirer, who presented Jane with a portrait he had drawn of her new friend. Conversation could be frustratingly superficial, especially if starched notions of decorum were adhered to at more formal gatherings, which allowed only spiritless discussions on the state of the roads and the weather. In the limited time available for communication during the two permitted dances with the same partner at each assembly, good humour and a lack of discernment could easily be mistaken for good sense and a tractable nature. The opportunities for misrepresentation were numerous and many men and women must have been deceived on a short acquaintance made in a public place, yet even when ample opportunity for deeper conversation was available, duplicity could still go undetected. An appearance of sincerity, together with a handsome face, enable a liar like George Wickham to elicit the sympathetic affection of an otherwise intelligent woman.

The Revd Thomas Gisborne, in disapproval mode, warned young women against accepting 'improper' men as dancing partners, although he was unhelpfully vague about how to identify such undesirables, in fact, his condemnation makes them sound rather attractive than otherwise:

> Men of this description commonly abound at all scenes of public resort and entertainment; and are not seldom distinguished by fortune and birth, gay and conciliating manners, and every qualification which is needful to procure a favourable reception in polite company.[8]

Best to sit out every dance, he counselled unreasonably, than agree to partner a man whom every other woman in the room was falling over herself to attract. Few young women would have chosen to deprive themselves, especially when three ball tickets in Bath during the season cost as much as a guinea. The Revd James Fordyce was not against dancing as a female accomplishment, if exhibited only at private gatherings of friends and relations, but he refused to countenance 'a young lady's dancing often in public assemblies', which led, he argued, to immodest behaviour.[9] Typically, Fordyce attempted to thwart female enjoyment in any sphere other than the domestic. Jane Austen had little sympathy for his pompous pronouncements, putting many of them into Mr Collins' mouth and only her more subdued heroines, Fanny Price and Anne Elliot, are given no opportunity to dance at public assemblies. The introduction of the waltz into England around 1812, which, Byron noted, enabled the participants' hands to 'freely range in public sight / Where ne'er before'[10] would surely have brought on an apoplectic fit had Fordyce been alive to witness such indecency.

With every stage of courtship under intense scrutiny, from initial attraction through flirtation to love, the writers of conduct books made it their business to specify appropriate behaviour at each juncture. A young woman's dealings with members of the opposite sex in public or private was strictly laid down: if a man who was neither a friend nor a relative attempted to take her hand, she should 'withdraw it immediately with an air so declarative of displeasure, that he shall not presume to repeat the offence'. Shaking hands with strangers was likewise frowned upon, since 'A touch, a pressure of the hands, are the only external signs a woman can give of entertaining a particular regard for certain individuals' and this limited power of expression was not to be thrown away upon 'coxcombs'. Kissing was completely out of the question, and 'woe be to her' who yielded the 'lips of delicacy' to 'the stain of profanation'.[11] General disapproval is accorded, predictably enough, to the waltz, where 'none but husbands and wives can with any propriety be partners'.[12] Should any woman feel inclined to exhibit her charms in the wild excesses of a 'Spanish fandango' in the hope of attracting a husband, she is warned that:

> . . . there are few discreet men in England who will say, "such a woman I should like for my wife!" . . . she will hardly encounter one of a thousand who will venture to trust himself to the offering her the bond of a single gold ring.[13]

The fashion for plunging necklines and for damping down already clinging fabrics to accentuate curves and contours, obviously attracted notice, not all of it complimentary. Jane Austen was no prude, but she found plenty to criticize in the way of revealing female attire, especially when worn in public. In Southampton's assembly rooms, she noted the proliferation of 'ugly naked shoulders' and in Bath, at a private party, Miss Langley's 'exposed bosom'.[14] The author of *The Mirror of Graces* was moved to more high-flown finger-wagging at the 'modern fair' who scorned the 'mysterious involvements of, at least, three successive folds of drapery', in favour of low-cut gowns or other modes of undress to advertise their physical allurements:

> To correct this dangerous fashion, ought to be the study and attempt of every

> mother, of every daughter, of every woman; and I trust that the veil I would now throw over the bosom of modesty may never again be raised, to sate the voluptuous eye; may never be moved, but by the hand of nuptial happiness, to behold the revealed heart of love and virgin innocence.[15]

The writer's buttoned-up moralistic tone begins to waver, however, when she – if indeed the author is a she, since a number of men adopted female pseudonyms or hid their true identity in an impenetrable 'Anon.' – considers the 'well-proportioned foot', the '*je ne scai quoi* in a fine ancle, which seems to assure the gazer that the whole of the form of which it is a sample is shaped with the same exquisite grace'. This loving description extends to two whole pages before the writer appears to remember that such a provocative display, enhanced by the wearing of 'ornamented stockings' or 'unusually short petticoats', should be seen as contemptible, and, less convincingly, that men wouldn't like it.[16]

A visit to Bath supplied plenty of opportunities for the young of both sexes to mix socially – and not just in the assembly rooms. The concerts and firework displays, the Pump Room, theatre and Abbey, the parades, crescents and squares, provided a very public arena where everyone could see and be seen. A constantly shifting society granted a wider circle of acquaintance, but also comprehended a greater degree of vulnerability. Young women were relatively free to wander the city unaccompanied – Catherine Morland and Isabella Thorpe visit the circulating libraries, go shopping for hats and are driven about in carriages by young men who are not even their relatives; one of Isabella's sisters is spotted loitering in Bond Street with two new female acquaintances and gaggles of flirting girls throng the thoroughfares along which Anne Elliot and Captain Wentworth dawdle on their way to Camden Place. Opportunities existed for libertines to take advantage of youth and inexperience – Colonel Brandon's seventeen-year-old ward, ranging the streets of Bath and mixing with unsuitable companions, is an easy conquest for Willoughby. Given George Wickham's sexual proclivities, we can guess what he might get up to on his visits there without his wife. Not only the young and sexually active were potential predators: some mercenary parents, like General Tilney, were on the lookout for rich marriage partners for their children. Acting on less selfish motives, Lady Russell envisages a revival of Anne

Elliot's chances of being seen and admired in a larger social setting and perhaps Mr and Mrs Austen were considering their daughters' marriage prospects when they decided to move to Bath in 1801. Both Mrs Austen and her sister Jane had found husbands there in their mid-twenties.

In the absence of suitable opportunities for finding a marriage partner in all of the usual fashionable venues, a less than fastidious man, or woman, or parent for that matter, might scan the advertisements in the newspapers for most definitely unsuitable opportunities. The *Morning Post* in particular carried various heartfelt appeals: from a young man with a clear head and kind heart, but no fortune, aiming to devote himself and his virtues to a woman with a 'moderate' inheritance; from a guardian wishing to get a troublesome or physically unattractive heiress off his hands and from a young blood offering a sum of money to any gentleman 'or person in genteel business, who has good sense and resolution to despise the censures of the world', willing to relieve him of an ex-mistress by marrying her. Interested parties were instructed to address their replies to various coffee houses in the more dubious areas of London. Even though a respectable newspaper such as *The Herald* published advertisements in the late eighteenth century from men soliciting 'female friendships', it is probably safe to say that marriage was not the end in view; it certainly was not the intention of the 'Young Gentleman of the most liberal education and genteel address', who offered his 'services' to any rich, fashionable lady 'who may wish to have some particular deficiencies thoroughly supplied, without subjecting herself to any disagreeable restraint'.[17]

If only fox-hunting squires or card-playing parsons presented themselves in the immediate locality, then parents might go in for matchmaking by hawking their offspring around the numerous national marriage markets during the season. Society journals recognized this practice and lampooned it in various spoof letters from the parties concerned. One exhausted and demoralised communication from 'Biddy Willing' appeared in a copy of *The Lady's Monthly Museum* in 1798, describing how, over the past three years, her parents had whisked her from London to Brighton, from Brighton to Bath and from Bath to Cheltenham, in search of an eligible suitor, all to no avail, since 'no one has ever offered me any thing beyond a fashionable compliment'. Her parents' over-anxiety to catch a titled husband had scared off every man who showed the slightest interest in their daughter, leaving her convinced that she would be doomed to Rusty Hall for life, unless the tables were turned and some worthy man came into the neighbourhood to search for her.[18]

A real-life example of this kind of manoeuvring is recorded in a letter of 1810, from Mary Russell Mitford to Sir William Elford:

> The manoeuvrers, thank Heaven! are not quite so numerous; but we have one in our neighbourhood . . . She has two most charming daughters, who, though dragged to town every spring; to some watering-place every autumn; and to all the parties, plays, concerts, and balls within twenty miles of their home here, during the rest of the year: still remain in "single blessedness," to the indescribable mortification of their mamma, and to the great discredit of her inimitable talents for plots, schemes, and puffing, match making, and match-breaking . . . Nothing could account for the circumstance of two such very lovely young women having reached the age of twenty without attracting one serious admirer but the circumstance of their being the daughters of a manoeuvrer.[19]

Some accomplished young ladies went to great lengths on their own behalf to shine in public. In 1794, Miss Martha Butt, who became Mrs Sherwood, recorded her observations on the calculated posturing of two renowned Bath beauties:

> . . . the two Miss Gibbons who used to sing at public concerts, and go through all of the manoeuvres to attract notice . . . but they utterly despised common attentions, or attentions which, in some way or another, did not answer either of their purposes, one of which was to obtain for themselves splendid establishments, and the other to attract men to their mother's card parties.[20]

When Mrs Elton recommends the advantages of Bath to Emma, she has husband-hunting in mind, but a number of other spas and seaside resorts were recognised as good places for finding husbands and wives. Cheltenham, one of the spa towns in which Biddy Willing was exhibited by her parents, set out to rival Bath in the number of its entertainments and public spaces, including a Pump Room, Upper and Lower Assembly Rooms, Theatre Royal, billiard rooms, bowling greens and streets specifically designed for 'parading up and down' in daylight hours, accompanied by 'a band of music'.[21] In the north, Buxton with its good roads, healthy air and the medicinal properties of its spring water, became a fashionable destination from the early 1800s onwards. Visitors stayed in smart accommodation in The Crescent, where there were four luxurious lodging houses and two hotels, one of them housing the assembly rooms. Walking, riding, shooting and hunting comprised the daytime pursuits; the evening programme included theatre-going and dancing. While the gentlemen innocently amused themselves with shooting on the moors and fishing for trout and grayling, the women, suggests one travel guide, were intent on blood sports of a different type, 'assiduous in spreading *their nets* for the *game* in which they naturally delight'. Thus, each man could be unwittingly both captor and captive.[22] This particular witticism was clearly calculated to act as an incentive to male visitors rather than a deterrent.

Brighton had its encampments of soldiers and public entertainments and, like Bath, it had designated public areas where women and men could exhibit themselves in all their finery: '. . . look at the ladies, who walk, by dozens, up and down this red brick-walk. They smile, and fancy themselves still more charming than they really are; and the men are not a whit behind them in admiration.'[23] Back home in the countryside, there was no point in dressing up to trudge along muddy cart tracks, so it is hardly surprising that elegantly attired tourists took to the clean, raised walks in droves. Every seaside town worth visiting had a fashionable promenade; in Brighton it was The Steyne, where a small band of musicians performed each morning and evening for added amusement. The 1810 *Guide to all the Watering and Sea-Bathing Places* notes 2,000 houses, 12,000 inhabitants and 'more than an equal number of annual visitors, for the purposes of health or pleasure'[24] so there were plenty of opportunities for meeting interesting new acquaintances, who might become more than just temporary friends. At the Castle Tavern and Assembly Rooms, south of the Prince of Wales' Marine Pavilion, visitors would find a coffee room and a suite of assembly rooms, complete with a tea-room, card-room and an eighty-by-forty-foot ballroom. Balls were held here every Monday and Thursday evening during the season and on other days at the Old Ship tavern, which possessed a first-floor ballroom, card-room and tea-room. Everyone recognised the value of dancing as a way of forming alliances, but fears were voiced in the *Lewes and Brighthelmstone Journal* that Brighton was attracting the wrong sort of women: 'hoity-toity, bold, forward flirts of the present day . . . gadding about', their days 'taken up in preparing dress for the evening where they expose themselves in dancing the Irish wriggle with any fellow in a bit of scarlet and a feather'.[25]

If, after the previous evening's wriggling, partners felt the need to ascertain each other's characters and intentions more fully, they could meet in daylight hours in one of the two libraries, where 'The taste and character of individuals may be better learned . . . than in a ball-room' and where more 'rational' and 'permanent pleasure' may be enjoyed.[26] If all that the libraries offered by way of new publications, pamphlets, magazines, newspapers, perfumery, stationery and jewellery did not appeal, a quieter retreat could be found in Dorset-Garden, or more animated activity in Prince's Place, a circular range of shops rented by London tradesmen during the summer. In short, Brighton had everything necessary to turn the head of any Lydia Bennet fresh from a country existence, with the added incentive of the officers at the Barracks and Battery, only one mile from the centre of the town on the Lewes road.

Weymouth, unlike Brighton, was patronised by the older members of the royal family, particularly King George III, and considered rather staid and starched. The Campbells choose to take a holiday there, as does the serious Mr Dixon, who probably accompanied Miss Campbell to the 'elegantly fitted up' theatre, to the town's two libraries and to the Esplanade, where they would experience 'the invigorating sea-breezes playing around them'.[27] He has come to Weymouth armed with drawings of his estate in Ireland, to prove his credentials as an eligible landowner, although where he and Miss Campbell first met is unspecified. What is certain is that Jane Fairfax agrees to a secret engagement there and dances with Frank Churchill at the assembly rooms. The anticipation of a ball at The Crown in Highbury, where she will get the chance to be physically close to him again, is the only thing which breaks through her carefully maintained reserve.

In a scratchy exchange between Jane and Frank on Box Hill, the uncertain happiness attendant on attachments formed in public places is aired. There must have been couples who regretted committing themselves after only a short acquaintance, but Jane and Frank, once their difficulties are cleared away, are not of their number, and neither are Admiral and Mrs Croft, the most companionably married pair in all of Jane Austen's fiction. If the Admiral's memory is to be relied on, they agreed to marry after a matter of days rather than months, although his wife stresses that she had known something of his good character beforehand. On the face of it, an acquaintance of less than a month would not allow for any searching assessment of character on either side, yet there is no evidence to suggest that Jane's cousin Jane Cooper and her husband Thomas Williams enjoyed anything other than a happy union. The couple first met on 2 July 1792, when the Cooper and Lybbe Powys families were on holiday on the Isle of Wight. Ten days later the party visited Captain Williams' mother at Ryde and from that date on, the Captain accompanied them on delightful walks through woods and along cliffs to picturesque thatched cottages and romantic ruined abbeys, the ideal setting for acquaintanceship to blossom into love and opportunity enough for intimate conversation.[28] By 23 July, the final day of the holiday, Jane Cooper and Thomas Williams were engaged and their wedding date fixed.

Long engagements, where future prospects were uncertain, were considered unwise. Jane Austen's advice to twenty-one-year-old Fanny Knight was unequivocal:

> I should dread the continuance of this sort of tacit engagement, with such an uncertainty as there is, of *when* it may be completed. – Years may pass, before he is Independant. – You like him well enough to marry, but not well enough to wait. – . . . nothing can be compared to the misery of being bound *without* Love, bound to one, & preferring another.[29]

She has the sensible Mrs Croft speak against this kind of indefinite long engagement: '"To begin without knowing that at such a time there will be the means of marrying, I hold to be very unsafe and unwise, and what, I think, all parents should prevent as far as they can."'[30] Even so, looking back on the events of eight years ago, Anne Elliot can only regret not accepting Captain Wentworth, uncertain prospects and all. Although she takes heed of Lady Russell's warnings of the 'anxious, youth-killing dependence' that such an alliance would bring, Anne is a supporter of 'early warm attachment' and this is the other side of the coin. Left to decide for herself, she would have waited however long it took, but then Anne had no doubts of her own feelings, she loved Wentworth well enough to wait. Cassandra Austen too had faith in 'early warm attachment' and after Jane's death, wrote in the margin next to these words, 'Dear dear Jane! This deserves to be written in letters of gold.'[31] She had enough trust in the future to accept Tom Fowle's proposal in 1792, knowing that they would have a long wait ahead of them before Tom gained a living good enough to support a wife and family. Three years later, he left for the West Indies with his patron, Lord Craven, and Cassandra learned of his death from yellow fever early in 1797. All she had to show for an engagement of four years was £1,000 from Tom's will and a broken heart. Jane makes sure that fate treats Catherine Morland and Henry Tilney more kindly. They are kept waiting for the General's approval for a year and the delay is seen as a blessing in disguise, in that it enables them to reach a better knowledge and understanding of each other before marriage. Henry's financial position is sound and his comfortable living already in place.

The Morlands agree to a tacit engagement between Henry and their daughter and tactfully close their eyes to the letters that pass between them. Unmarried men and women who were not engaged were barred from writing to each other; Mary Russell Mitford at the age of twenty-three was suspected of a secret alliance with the sixty-four-year-old Sir William Elford merely on the evidence of a regular correspondence. Jane Fairfax has to walk into Highbury to collect her letters from Frank Churchill to avoid arousing the suspicion of her family and acquaintances; Elinor's suspicions work the other way – when Marianne receives no letter from Willoughby, she questions the existence of any formal pact between the pair. Lucy Steele's production of letters from Edward Ferrars puts their engagement beyond any doubt in Elinor's mind.

If long engagements were sometimes unwise, clandestine arrangements were always wrong and caused misery to all concerned, although the reasons underlying the arrangement might partly excuse the secrecy. Edward Ferrars is young and lacking both occupation and family affection when he engages himself to Lucy. The burden of his secret commitment makes him spiritless and dull and depressed about his future. Frank Churchill, on the other hand, enjoys all of the intrigue and deceit involved in blinding others to the true state of affairs. Frank, of course, is happy with his choice, whereas Edward bitterly regrets his. Uncertain prospects and enforced secrecy certainly hurt Jane Fairfax. She is forced to deceive those closest to her and suffers as a consequence. 'Misconduct' is the name Jane Fairfax applies to her actions – '"Pain is no expiation. I never can be blameless."'[32] The words Jane Austen gives to Emma apply to her own principles regarding relationships: '"Oh! if you knew how much I love everything that is decided and open!"'[33] Ironically, Emma predicts that her own engagement to Mr Knightley will be both long and secret, at least from her father. A certain amount of forward planning is involved before the news is finally broken, but no deceit. The two-year delay Mr Woodhouse talks of before the marriage can take place is done away with by the poultry thieves, who frighten him into welcoming Mr Knightley's nightly presence at Hartfield.

Eliza Chute recognized one advantage to women of a long engagement, even though hers to William Chute lasted only four months. In a letter to her niece, on hearing that she was to marry James-Edward Austen after an engagement of just two months, Eliza expressed surprise that she should not wish to prolong what she saw as:

> "the happiest time in a woman's life" . . . indeed, I almost feel sorry that it should be so short: for I think I am of the same opinion, that it is a happy time & looked back to always with the greatest complacency.[34]

Once a couple were committed to an engagement, they were allowed to spend more time together. Anna Austen and Ben Lefroy spent the summer months before their wedding dawdling in the meadows and lanes between Ashe and Steventon, although Anna's step-mother begrudged them even this short period of happiness, complaining ill-naturedly that they monopolized the shrubbery walk at the rectory and behaved in a 'foolishly devoted' manner.[35] Bingley becomes a daily visitor at Longbourne and he and Jane often escape into the garden to avoid other people. Elizabeth and Mr Darcy only find peace in each other's company at this stage; their encounters with Mrs Philips, Mrs Bennet, Mr Collins and Sir William Lucas cause a considerable amount of discomfort during their mercifully short season of courtship in Meryton. For most, however, this was a relaxed time when one's guard could be dropped. Mr Elton behaves very differently to the unmarried young ladies in Highbury when he is known to be an engaged man. His woodenness and 'parade of speeches' disappear, to be replaced by an easy, more natural manner once he is no longer fearful of raising expectations. Henry Crawford notes the more open behaviour of engaged women too and knows that he is safe flirting with one.

While the engaged pair were wrapped up in each other, hard-headed lawyers would be busy dealing with the financial aspects of the alliance and drawing up the marriage settlement. The woman's fortune was transferred to her husband and usually invested at 5% to provide a yearly income. Miss Grey's £50,000 would earn £2,500 a year for Willoughby, enabling him to maintain his foxhounds and hunters with a comfortable sum left over for other luxuries. The size of the jointure (how much the widow would receive from her husband's estate), also had to be agreed. The widow of a landowner had the right of dower, which entitled her to the income from one-third of her husband's land. A chunk of property, or money, might be set aside for such purposes. Mrs Jennings has a particularly generous jointure, which enables her to keep a London house in a fashionable area and travel as often as she pleases. The amount of only £5,000 is settled on Mrs Bennet and her five daughters by marriage articles, nowhere near enough to provide a comfortable existence or the financial incentives necessary for the girls to marry well. Mary Stanhope, in *The Three Sisters*, attempts to dictate the terms of her marriage settlement before she will consent to marry the dreadful Mr Watts. Apart from a 'great jointure', she specifies £200 a year personal allowance, a new carriage, a horse entirely for her own use, valuable jewels, two footmen, two maids, a conservatory, a private theatre, winter holidays in Bath, spring visits to London and autumn trips to fashionable watering places. In the end, one maid, a horse and the family jewels are written into the settlement, after a whole evening's quarrelsome deliberations. Mrs Wallis in *Persuasion* has completely different advantages in mind when she jokes that, as a condition of marrying Anne, Mr Elliot will have it written into the marriage articles that Sir Walter is not to marry Mrs Clay.[36]

The pre-nuptial agreement could be drawn up to entitle the wife to have a certain amount settled on her by her father during her lifetime, the money to be passed on to her children in her will. In this way, the children from the first marriage could be protected against the loss of income to any future half-siblings. The first Mrs Dashwood leaves the remainder of her fortune to her son John; her husband is entitled only to a life interest in the money. This arrangement would have been included in the marriage settlement. A similar benefit comes to Henry Tilney, in the shape of 'a very considerable fortune' secured 'by marriage settlements' which ensures his financial independence from his father, the General.[37] The addition to income occasioned by a good marriage settlement was just as important to families of the Morlands' social standing as it was to the class with expensive properties and lifestyles to maintain. The Morlands have no thoughts of the General contributing anything beyond his consent, but they are made easy by Henry's financial position. They are not guilty of mercenary motives here; they are considering Catherine's future comfort and security as a wife. Lawyers could set up a separate property agreement for heiresses, to prevent husbands getting their hands on every penny. Such transactions were overseen by the Chancery Court. A woman had access to all of her property, but only on application to a trustee. After Mr Hancock's death in India, Philadelphia Hancock's money was held in trust by her brother, George Austen, and the Woodman brothers, one of whom was a brother-in-law of Warren Hastings.

The time between the engagement and the wedding was often very short, sometimes only a month. There was no reason to delay, none of today's elaborate planning campaigns, waiting years for the availability of vicars and churches, hotels and caterers, or for invitations to be accepted or declined. Once the marriage settlement was signed, the ceremony could take place the very next day, provided that the banns had been called or the licence purchased, the wedding clothes ready and the items of the trousseau assembled. This was a woman's once-in-a-lifetime chance to be the centre of attention and while some handled the occasion with elegance and aplomb, those lacking taste and confidence failed to live up to expectations, their own and others'.

4

White Satin and Lace Veils

Emma begins with one wedding and ends with three, plus another for luck in the middle, but Jane Austen describes none of them in any detail. Wedding clothes are never a significant feature in her novels, nor in her letters, although there is no question that she saw plenty of weddings in her lifetime. Her father performed several marriage services at Steventon between 1780, the year when she would have started noticing such events, and 1801, when the Austens moved to Bath. She appears in the parish registers as a witness at the marriage of her cousin Jane Cooper to Thomas Williams in 1792 and of William Littleworth to Elizabeth Lovell in 1796. At some time in her teens, she created fantasy husbands for herself, filling in specimen forms in the church register announcing the calling of banns for Henry Frederick Howard Fitzwilliam of London and Jane Austen of Steventon; the marriage of Edmund Arthur William Mortimer of Liverpool and Jane Austen; then unassuming Jack Smith to Jane Smith,[1] a sharp reminder that most of her Steventon neighbours were labouring families. Mr Austen's experiences would have been similar to Parson Woodforde's in his Somerset and Norfolk parishes: 'Married my late Maid, Molly Peachman to one Js Shipley by Banns', or even

> married one Robert Astick and Elizabeth Howlett by Licence . . . the Man being in custody, the woman being with Child by him. The Man was a long time before he could be prevailed upon to marry her when in the Church Yard; and at the Altar behaved very unbecoming.[2]

Little wonder that the parson should find such forced alliances disagreeable. Nothing to describe by way of celebration, etiquette or finery here.

On any day of the week during the Austens' residence in Bath, as many as five couples might sign the marriage register in just *one* church. Over two thousand weddings were recorded in the parishes Jane walked through on numerous occasions, her thoughts barely disturbed by the sound of bells drifting down the nearby streets or the sight of a white-beribboned carriage bowling by. She mentions only two marriages in her thirteen letters from the city – those of the Revd Dr Gardiner of 10 Paragon Buildings, to Mrs Piersy '& her three daughters' on 10 June 1799, at St Michael's, when Jane was staying with her brother Edward in Queen Square, and of Mr Woodward to Miss Wroe on 9 May 1801, at St Mary's in Chapel Row.[3] Perhaps the first attracted her notice because Dr Gardiner lived near Uncle and Aunt Leigh-Perrot, but more probably because she was able to make a joke at his expense; it is more difficult to find any link with the second. She passed Stephen Terry, a former Steventon neighbour, taking a Sunday stroll with Miss Seymer in the field at Royal Crescent and noted that the lady was neither as dashing nor stylish as reported, but rather silent and dowdy and for some reason '*en Penitance*'.[4] Three weeks later, on 23 April 1805, they were married by licence in St Mary's, Chapel Row, Miss Seymer appearing in the register as 'a minor of this parish' – conceivably her subdued mood had something to do with the fact that Mr Terry was her senior by at least ten years – but Jane made no reference to the union in her communication to Cassandra on the same day.

At Chawton, wedding parties passing the Austens' cottage on their way to the church were rare enough to enliven the view from the sitting-room window, from where Mrs Austen no doubt called Jane and Cassandra to come and look, but any specific interest in bridal finery would be limited to those relatives and friends who were there on the day, or who were in some way personally involved, if absent. Rapturous accounts of bridal elegance can make for tedious reading and Jane Austen can never be accused of boring her audience, yet many contemporary female correspondents revelled in such details – 'what woman was ever brief in announcing a wedding?'[5] declared Mary Russell Mitford. She would not have relished the letter Emelia Clayton wrote to a friend about her sister Marianne's wedding in 1786: 'Her dress was a silver muslin night-gown [*evening dress*] trimmed with white sattin, a very fine muslin apron, and handkerchief [*neckerchief*] trimmed with beautiful lace, and white and silver shoes.'[6] Correspondence like this served its purpose in an age when costly and uncomfortable journeys often ruled out the attendance of friends and family members living at a distance. If James Morland had married Isabella Thorpe, Catherine would probably have had to rely on second-hand news of the wedding and there is no evidence that Jane herself attended any of her brothers' weddings.

Despite Jane Austen's reluctance to write herself into raptures over sarsenet, silver muslin, exotic plumage and white kid gloves, a keen interest in shopping for dress material, lace and hat trimmings enabled her to use her knowledge of shops in both London and Bath in her novels. While staying with Henry in London, Jane regularly endured the unbearable crush at Grafton House, with its crowded counters and inevitable queues, on the corner of Grafton Street and New Bond Street. Here she spent all of her money on coloured muslin and silk stockings. At Layton and Shears she admired the pretty English and Irish poplins, purchased a white silk handkerchief from Crook and Besford's and acquired a ribbon-trimmed cap from an unspecified source.[7] With so much on offer, it is entirely believable that Mrs Jennings should suspect Marianne Dashwood of being in London to buy wedding clothes, or that Mrs Bennet should fret over Lydia's ignorance of the best warehouses in which to spend Mr Bennet's money. In Bath, Jane Austen shopped widely, for artificial hat decorations, lace, gauzes and cloaks, and looked out for bargains in the cheaper outlets of Walcot Street. One visitor to Bath in 1788 marvelled at 'the beauty of the shops . . . I could not conceive how it was possible to invent all the wants, which here were professed to be supplied.'[8] Having lived in the city for five years, Jane Austen knew that Henrietta Musgrove would find a vast array of fabrics and trimmings for her own and Louisa's wedding dresses. On offer were Indian calicos and muslins, fine French cambrics and factory-produced cottons from Lancashire and Clydeside, ideal for achieving the perfect bridal gown in the latest style, falling from just under the bust to the floor in one simple, flowing line. Samuel Slack apprised the public of 'several hundred BALES OF MUSLINS' lately acquired from the East India Company's regular London sales;[9] Prynne and Collins supplied cheap fabrics at the Bengal Warehouse in the Marketplace, and Thomas Coward advertised 'India muslins' at his shop in Old Bond Street. At J. Isaacs in the Abbey Churchyard and Stall Street, fur goods, ornamental feathers and artificial flowers were on sale; Smith and Co. in Bath Street stocked fashionable millinery, embroidered shawls from Norwich and neckerchiefs from Barcelona; William Ashley's in Bond Street provided umbrellas and parasols. Haberdashers and hosiers, stay-makers and linen-drapers – the opportunities for spending money on wedding finery were endless.[10]

Some brides-to-be ordered by post if they felt exhausted by the thought of expending so much shoe-leather, or if there was no town or city with a decent range of shops within travelling distance. Miss Mary Curzon, in a letter to Miss Heber from Hagley, talked of 'writing for Wedding Clothes' for her sister's marriage. Maybe the Curzons shared Mrs Elton's opinion of their nearest city – 'not a place to promise much . . . One has not great hopes from Birmingham.'[11] A month later, Miss Curzon apprised her friend of the success of the order:

> . . . my Sister look'd beautifull. She was dress'd in a white figured sattin gown, a fring'd silk petticoat, white silk fring'd slippers, a beautiful white hat trimm'd with blond, a long figur'd white sattin cloak trimm'd with fur . . . and really you never saw a more elegant creature then [sic] she look'd.[12]

Her own bridesmaid's dress was made with the same white satin and 'Mama' was also 'all white'. Presumably, the silks, satins, fringes, lace and fur were delivered direct to Hagley, then made up by a local dressmaker, using patterns from existing stock, or original designs commissioned especially for the occasion. During the quieter summer months, top dressmakers in Bath went hunting for the latest designs in the London fashion houses and ordered fashion magazines from Paris, in order to reproduce the most recent trends in dress.

Dedicated warehouses in London, rather like large department stores, supplied fabrics and other items of the trousseau. Clark & Debenham set up as linen-drapers in Mayfair, close to Pearl and Co., bootmakers; B. Harvey and Co. – the modern Harvey Nichols – began as linen-drapers in Knightsbridge; Waithman & Sons supplied linens and shawls at 104, Fleet Street; G. Sutton manufactured silk goods in Leicester Square. From Bond Street to Cheapside, good-quality, well-lit shops displayed their wares with all the arts of seduction behind clear glass windows. Reeves Hosiery Warehouse in the Strand sold silk stockings and purses, while

Harding, Howell & Co.'s Grand Fashionable Magazine, a warehouse at number 89, Pall Mall, boasted four discrete sales areas, divided by glass partitions, each one resembling a large shop, with glazed domes in the roof to let in plenty of natural light, ceiling-high shelving with countless drawers beneath and polished wooden counters manned by sales assistants of both sexes. The four separate departments stocked furs and fans; huge bolts of patterned and plain silks and muslins, stored in large pigeon holes above tiered compartments of lace, buttons, ribbons and gloves; jewellery, decorative articles in ormolu, French clocks and perfume; and in the fourth, hats and dresses. The shop employed forty people on site to make up the orders and attend to customers.[13] It was just the place for Lucy Steele to purchase the latest in gloves and bonnets, before Robert Ferrars took her to Gray's in Sackville Street, where he had recently spent a morning inspecting every toothpick case in the shop. No doubt they would have found enough glittering rings and necklaces, enamelled snuff boxes and vinaigrettes to tempt them.

At Wedgwood's showroom in York Street, St James, Jane Austen, her niece Fanny and brother Edward chose a new dinner service from the large selection elegantly displayed on gleaming tables, where Jane could picture General Tilney purchasing a breakfast set on Catherine and Henry's marriage. Highbury might have Ford's, woollen-draper, linen-draper, and haberdasher's shop united, and Meryton its milliner's and draper's, but the chances are that Emma Woodhouse and Elizabeth and Jane Bennet would look in London for their wedding outfits, while Anne Elliot, Catherine Morland and the two Miss Dashwoods might have found what they wanted in Bath. The more fastidious Fanny Price would order her needs by post rather than risk the corrupting influence of the city, retreating to the nearest sofa with a headache after insisting on sewing the whole trousseau with her own needle. Many warehouses launched effective advertising campaigns by displaying the trousseaux of the rich and famous. When Miss Farren's coming marriage to Lord Derby became the subject of fashionable talk, Eliza de Feuillide reported to Phylly Walter from London in May 1797:

> A great number of simpletons have been to see her Wedding Garments which are superlatively magnificent – She has thirty Muslin dresses each more beautiful

> than the other, and all trimmed with the most expensive Laces, Her Wedding Night Cap is the same as the Princess Royal's & costs Eighty Guineas.[14]

Eliza said no more, evidently wishing to avoid being numbered among the vulgar hordes. Silly Charlotte Palmer in *Sense and Sensibility* knows which warehouse will exhibit Miss Grey's trousseau and dress-obsessed Mrs Allen gossips about the £500 Mrs Tilney spent on her wedding clothes in *Northanger Abbey*, but none of Jane Austen's characters, not even Miss Grey, would have spent over £1,000 on a trousseau, as the Spencer family did when their daughter married the Duke of Devonshire in 1774. The items included sixty-five pairs of shoes, forty-eight pairs of stockings, twenty-six pairs of gloves, hats with feathers and other trimmings, splendid ball gowns and dresses for a variety of occasions, cloaks, shawls and wraps.[15] When the Goodnestone Hall sisters Fanny, Sophia and Elizabeth Bridges all got married in 1791, the inventory of linen and clothes for each bride-to-be was extensive, if less ostentatious than Georgiana Spencer's, comprising thirty-eight shifts, twelve pairs of 'Drawers', twelve nightcaps, thirty-four pairs of stockings, fourteen under petticoats, sixteen upper petticoats, six cloaks, eleven gowns, four dozen gloves, three riding hats, two bonnets, three caps, fifteen pairs of shoes and various handkerchiefs, coats, corsets and nightgowns.[16] In Mrs Bennet's opinion, a marriage was scarcely valid without new clothes, but fitting out three daughters made quite a hole in the Bridges' family purse, as it did in Mr Bennet's pocket, despite his refusal to countenance any new clothes for the disgraced Lydia. The Bridges paid over £900 for three sets of wedding clothes; one consignment of linen came from Bath, another three from London. In less well-off families, the women would use their sewing skills to put together a trousseau, as Mrs Austen did when her granddaughter Anna became engaged to Ben Lefroy, making 'petticoats, Pockets & dressing Gowns' and decorating shoes.[17] Given that Jane and Cassandra were such deft needlewomen, they too no doubt made their contribution to Anna's stock of necessaries.

Some brides in the popular fiction of the time are shown to be completely absorbed by the trappings of the ceremony and concerns such as these must have been welcome to Maria Bertram, as light relief from the weightier consideration of her husband-to-be. On being asked how she felt before her marriage, one character in a well-known play, *The Belle's Stratagem*, replies:

> . . . exceedingly full of cares. I could not sleep for thinking of my coach, my liveries and my chairmen; the taste of clothes I should be presented in, distracted me for a week; and whether I should be married in white or lilac, gave me the most cruel anxiety.[18]

Such cares could take their toll and wreck the bride's appearance on the big day, notwithstanding the dazzle of an opulent bridal gown: 'Her dress was very rich with fine Lace and costly Trinkets but I thought I never saw her look Worse as she was quite disfigured with continual fretting and Anxiety.'[19] Another fright in an over-the-top outfit is described by a less-than-impressed attendant bridesmaid:

> Plenty of barouches and bridesmaids, cake and favours, kissing and crying! The bride, indeed, had amused herself with the last-mentioned recreation for a whole week, and . . . accumulated on her person so much finery in the shape of lace flounces, spensers, bonnets, veils, and scarfs that she looked as if by mistake she had put on two wedding-dresses instead of one . . .[20]

Social differences were reflected in conspicuous expenditure on dresses and accessories designed in the latest fashion, using the finest silks, satins, and lace. Silver and white had been popular for several years and many brides with money at their disposal chose this combination. One of the dresses in Mrs Elton's trousseau is a white and silver poplin and one bride's outfit which would have impressed her, given that she considered Emma's wedding clothes shockingly lacking in 'finery or parade',[21] was recorded in *The Ipswich Journal* in 1812: 'The bride wore a robe of real Brussels point lace over white satin . . . A cottage bonnet of Brussels lace with two ostrich feathers; . . . a deep lace veil and white satin pelisse trimmed with swansdown.'[22] Jane Austen's opinion of what she considered inappropriate display is expressed in a letter concerning a woman marrying her second husband: 'What an alarming Bride Mrs Coln Tilson must have been! Such a parade is one of the most immodest pieces of Modesty that one can imagine. To *attract* notice could have been her only wish.'[23] More to Jane Austen's taste, perhaps Emma Woodhouse's too, was Anna Lefroy's simple wedding dress, described at a later date by Anna's daughter,

Fanny-Caroline: 'a dress of fine white muslin, and over it a soft silk shawl, white shot with primrose with embossed white satin flowers and very handsome fringe, and on her head a small cap to match trimmed with lace.' Anna's daughter adds that the yellow tints in both shawl and cap 'must have been most becoming to her bright brown hair, and hazel eyes and sunny clear complexion'.[24] Mrs Elton's sister Selina would certainly have stared! It is probable that Fanny-Caroline saw her mother's wedding outfit, maybe folded carefully in a closet, but more likely worn on special occasions. Few women would dream of wasting a good frock by wearing it just once and since the style of the dress followed the fashion of the day, it could be given an airing at other weddings or evening parties. No doubt Mrs Elton parades some of her wedding finery at the dinners given for her in Highbury, and at the Crown ball she comments on the superiority of her own gown and pearls. Many of the white gauzy silk and satin evening gowns decorated with flowers, which feature in *The Ladies' Monthly Museum* for July 1820 and in countless other English fashion magazines of the time, could easily do double service as wedding dresses and probably did. One rare example of a wedding dress appears in *Ackermann's Repository* of June 1816. Actually labelled 'Bridal Dress', it is made of white satin with a transparent, striped gauze over-skirt, in a low-necked, high-waisted design, with short, ruched sleeves and flounced hem trimmed with Brussels lace; hardly distinguishable from a typical white evening dress of the period.

Fanny Price's white bridesmaid's dress with glossy spots, bought especially for her by Sir Thomas, is given a second outing to the Grants' dinner party. Maria is careful to ensure that both Fanny and Julia wear dresses 'duly inferior' to hers, but sometimes bride and bridesmaids chose such similar outfits that identification problems were often jokingly predicted: 'The Bride looked famously and dress'd in an Azure Sarsnet with white ribbons – Miss Blunden was dress'd the same way but for fear of Mistakes wore brown Ribbons . . .' Attending Miss Blunden's wedding as bridesmaid later in the year, Dorothea Herbert wore a white dress like the bride's, provoking one of the guests to pretend 'Great uneasiness lest Mr Matthews should mistake me for his Bride'.[25] Poor Dorothea hoped to make more of an impression at this event than she had done at the previous one, where she described herself as 'an Uninteresting Bridesmaid' swamped by 'the Azure throng' in her unassuming straw-coloured dress. At her half-sister Anna's wedding in November 1814, at Steventon, Caroline Austen, aged nine, and the six-year-old Anne Lefroy wore white bridesmaids' dresses, with straw bonnets trimmed with white ribbons.[26] Mary Lamb, acting as bridesmaid at the marriage of Sarah Stoddart and William Hazlitt in May 1808, insisted on buying her own dress, but agonized over the colour and fabric – spotted or sprigged muslin, or an oyster China silk. In the end, the China silk was rejected because, 'Mrs Hazlitt tells me that all Winterslow would be in an uproar if the bridesmaid was to be dressed in anything but white.'[27] Not only the bride and bridesmaids wore white: all of the female guests might choose to do the same, including the bride's mother, who sometimes also wore a veil. As the century progressed, white for bridesmaids became the exception rather than the rule, thus allowing the bride to stand out among her attendants and not be overshadowed. At Sarah Burney's wedding in 1821, the bridesmaids were dressed in green, which provided an attractive foil for the bride's white gown.

White dresses were commonly chosen by brides from the middle of the eighteenth century, but coloured gowns retained their popularity until white became an acceptable colour for everyday wear – acceptable as in washable. Sarsenet – a kind of thin silk – and the lighter cottons, cambrics and muslins essential for the softer, flowing, classical style of dress, were much more easily cleaned than the heavier fabrics which preceded them. Eleanor Tilney, as Mrs Allen points out, always wears white, even in Bath, where getting into and out of sedan chairs and carriages could dirty a clean gown in five minutes. In one particular print entitled 'The Wedding', dated 1794, the bride's fashionable day dress is blue with a grey jacket-bodice.[28] The colour blue symbolized constancy, yellow was the classic colour of Hymen, the god of marriage. William Thackeray's Amelia Sedley wears a brown silk pelisse and a straw bonnet with a pink ribbon, over which hangs a veil of white Chantilly lace, for her marriage to George Osborne, in 1815.[29] White bridal veils, occasionally worn before 1800 and usually made of Brussels or Honiton lace, became a must-have accessory in the nineteenth century. In 1785, Dorothea Herbert wrote in her journal: 'The bride was dressed in a white sarcenet and a white silk bonnet with a very long veil to it.'[30] Bonnets with veils were relatively common at this time and not worn exclusively by brides. Just into the next century, Eugenia Wynne described her own wedding attire, which featured a veil independent of a bonnet.[31] A fictional account in 1828 of a bride's blushes, glimpsed 'through the folds of the beautiful lace veil that hung all over her', confirms the changing fashion,[32] although veils *per se* remained in everyday use, as Jane Austen noted in 1814, when she saw 'several upon vulgar heads' in London.[33]

Many contemporary reports describe bridegrooms in light-coloured suits. Sarah Burney's bridegroom wore a pea-green coat to his wedding in 1821, whereas the man who gave her away wore black, provoking frowns from the bride's mother, who would clearly have preferred him to wear any colour but that.[34] By the end of the century, black clothing for men was *de rigueur*. A brother who gave away his sister wearing 'Scarlet faced with gold a very rich Dress', fared little better, since the colours did nothing to improve his complexion.[35] George Wickham in his blue coat might have been dressed the same as the bridegroom described in *The Ipswich Journal* in 1812: 'The bridegroom wore a plain blue coat with yellow buttons, a white waistcoat, buff breeches and white stockings.'[36] *Vanity Fair*'s George Osborne and William Dobbin also wear fashionable blue coats with brass buttons and buff waistcoats, instead of their army uniforms.[37] At the fashionably quiet wedding of Lady Charlotte Bertie and Lord Cholmondeley in 1791, the bridegroom and the male guests wore frock-coats and white waistcoats. Pale-coloured waistcoats were worn more often than not in the late eighteenth and early nineteenth centuries, although one report of a wedding in 1786 describes a more colourful example, netted for the groom by his bride-to-be and worn with a dark green coat.[38]

The custom of the bride buying the bridesmaids' dresses and the groom providing lockets, bracelets or brooches did not become common practice until the end of the nineteenth century, but gifts for relations, friends and others who attended the ceremony were customary, usually in the form of gloves or garters. The ribbons known as wedding favours, fashioned into decorative rosettes, hat bands and bouquets mixed with flowers or evergreens, were often given by the groom's mother. Some parents gave their daughters or daughters-in-law heirloom jewellery as wedding gifts:

in *Northanger Abbey* Miss Drummond received a beautiful set of pearls from her father when she became Mrs Tilney and in *Emma* Mr Churchill parts with all of his wife's jewels so that Frank can have them reset for Jane Fairfax. Engagement rings were not given as binding tokens to mark an accepted proposal – Mrs Bennet would certainly have agitated for such visible evidence of her daughters' marriage prospects if they had been – but Lucy Steele makes Edward Ferrars the present of a ring holding a plait of her hair at its centre, a ring which fulfils its purpose as a hair shirt when he visits Barton Cottage. This is the only reference to a ring given to mark a pre-nuptial alliance in Jane Austen's novels, but some lovers of the period did give and exchange rings, often inscribed with a sentimental message – *Amitié* and *Restez comme vous êtes* (Stay just as you are) were popular. Cleverly arranged gemstones formed acrostics, like 'Dearest' spelt out by a diamond, emerald, amethyst, ruby, emerald, sapphire and turquoise.[39] The sentiment expressed was usually innocuous enough to constitute no firm commitment, a safe option when a man could not honourably break an engagement, and might face an action for breach of promise if he did, and when a woman would be considered a jilt if she backed out.

Edward Ferrars' gift to Lucy to mark their secret engagement is a miniature portrait of himself, which Lucy uses to calculated effect when she reveals it to her rival. Although Lucy claims that the artist has not done him justice, Edward's features are instantly recognizable to Elinor, indicating that the work was evidently of good quality. It has scant value for Lucy when she runs off with Edward's younger brother, so she returns it. How Edward disposes of it, or of Lucy's ring, can only be guessed at; that Elinor would never be troubled with either again is certain. Henry Austen had a small likeness of his first fiancée, Mary Pearson, which Jane considered too flattering, fearing that Mrs Austen would be disappointed when she met the original.[40] It was not unusual for a future son- or daughter-in-law to be familiar at first only through the medium of a portable likeness. Henry's engagement was broken off in the summer of 1796 and three years later Jane was in the process of arranging with Miss Pearson an 'exchange of packets', probably the return of love letters and Mary's portrait.[41] A month before his marriage in December 1791, Edward Austen showed a picture of his intended to his cousin, Eliza de Feuillide. This time, the image told no lies, since Eliza described Elizabeth Bridges as 'a very pretty Woman' and the existing miniature validates her assessment.[42]

The popularity of these tokens is evidenced by the number of miniaturists practising in Bath and London between 1790 and 1820: no fewer than five in the former and more than fifteen in the latter, with one Bath artist charging 'from Seven and Sixpence to One Guinea LIKENESSES for Rings, Caskets, Braces, Toothpick-Cases, Etc —'.[43] Captain Benwick sat for a miniaturist at the Cape, planning to give his portrait to Fanny Harville on his return to England, only to find that she had died in his absence. On his engagement to Louisa Musgrove less than six months later, Benwick insensitively asks Captain Harville to get it set for Fanny's successor. A miniature of Frank Austen in his captain's uniform was executed in 1806, the year he could afford to marry Mary Gibson with the prize money gained in the St Domingo action. The medal he was awarded shines against two rows of polished buttons on his dark blue jacket. Soldiers as well as Navy men left miniature portraits with loved ones when they went off to war; one subject of a miniature painting, a lady in white with powdered hair curling over a white bandeau, wears an image of a red-coated soldier on a pearl necklace.[44] Long absences frequently prompted lovers to exchange likenesses and a number of eighteenth-century full-size portraits depict hopelessly lovelorn women contemplating miniature images of men. 'A Woman in Love', painted early in the century, has a reflective young lady gazing at an oval-framed portrait in her palm.[45] Another shows a kind of prototype Jane Fairfax, her lover's letter clutched in one hand, his tiny image in the other. No miniature of Frank Churchill appears in Jane's possession in the novel, but since he is capable of making the grand gesture in delivering a piano, he might equally have considered the small, in the shape of a tastefully framed version of himself, which Jane could conceal with his letters, or ease surreptitiously from a pocket in the few private moments allowed her.

Women whose alliances were openly acknowledged displayed their miniature lovers on their wrists and on chokers, ribbons, gold chains and pendants around their necks, a fashion promoted by Queen Charlotte, who always wore a ring and a bracelet holding images of her husband, George III. A miniature of her granddaughter Princess Charlotte Augusta, painted to celebrate her engagement to Prince Leopold in 1815, shows her wearing her fiancé's miniature on a long necklace. Men tended to wear such tokens less overtly, usually at the waist and often disguised as watches or seals. Oddly disturbing examples of the miniaturist's art depict a disembodied eye or mouth. On the reverse of the portrait the loved one's hair could be fashioned into plumes, plaits and circlets or twisted into the shape of corn sheaves, the more elaborate designs being reserved for the miniatures worn by women. Sometimes strands of the couple's hair were woven together and enclosed by seed pearls or thin gold wire. Jane Austen's parents and her Uncle and Aunt Leigh-Perrot exchanged miniatures on their engagements, but some couples waited until after the wedding to sit for husband-and-wife portraits, the perfect way for Mr Darcy to add a new pair of portrait miniatures to those hanging over the mantlepiece in his late father's favourite room at Pemberley.

Neither rings, portraits nor other gifts were seen as essential elements of matrimonial etiquette, but if time and finances allowed, a new carriage was a highly desirable requirement. Isabella Thorpe expects one and Mary Stanhope in *The Three Sisters*, written by Jane Austen in her teens, determines to marry the odious Mr Watts only if he promises to buy a blue coach spotted with silver, while he resists in favour of chocolate brown. Finally, dark brown with a silver border is settled on, to the satisfaction of neither party.[46] Captain Wentworth buys Anne 'a very pretty landaulette'; Mrs Weston has a carriage of her own on her marriage; John Willoughby orders a custom-made carriage for his union to Miss Grey and even the Eltons make an impressive entry into Highbury in a smart new equipage. *Vanity Fair*'s Amelia Sedley has a glass coach to deliver her to church and carry away the happy couple after the ceremony. Such carriages were covered, with large glass windows all round, and usually pulled by two or four horses. The whole package, plus postillions decked in wedding favours, would be hired for the occasion. Maria Bertram and Mr Rushworth are so impatient to marry after Sir Thomas' return from Antigua, that there is no time to acquire a new carriage, a fact noted by the whole neighbourhood. The year-old chaise which conveys the newly married couple and chief bridesmaid from the church is the only flaw in an otherwise outwardly perfect wedding.

5

Where N Takes M, For Better, For Worse

On the 11th of December, 1792, Jane and Cassandra Austen signed themselves witnesses to the marriage of their cousin Jane Cooper to Captain Thomas Williams. The newly ordained Thomas Fowle, an old pupil of Mr Austen's who became engaged to Cassandra at about this time, performed the service. Edward Cooper, the bride's brother, was the third witness and Mr Austen probably gave his niece away. The couple were married by licence, since neither was a full-time resident in the parish of Steventon – Captain Williams hailing from the Isle of Wight and Jane Cooper from Sonning in Berkshire, although she had been living with the Austens since the death of her father in August. The marriage service itself followed the usual form found in the Book of Common Prayer, but little else is known about what happened on the day. Eliza de Feuillide had written from Steventon to her half-cousin Philadelphia Walter two months earlier, as soon as she knew that the wedding was to be celebrated there, in high hopes of an entertaining diversion:

> I suppose you have heard long since of the Death of poor Dr Cooper, his Daughter came immediately here . . . At the Time of her Father's Death She was at the very brink of Wedlock, The Day being fixed, but the abovementioned melancholy Event necessarily occasioned a Delay of the [nuptials which] are now fixed for some Time in December and are to be celebrated in this [house so] that I suppose we are to be mighty gay; indeed, I am delighted with the Thoughts of it, for I never was but at one Wedding in my Life and that appeared a very stupid Business to me. I hope I shall be better amused at this . . .[1]

Apart from the immediate Austen family, Eliza and the brother of the bride, it is impossible to tell if other guests were invited. There is no evidence to suggest that any of Thomas Williams' family were present; long-distance travel was difficult and costly and since the couple left for the Isle of Wight immediately afterwards, the family members most likely considered their attendance at the wedding an unnecessary expenditure of time and money. The bride's appearance on the day was unrecorded, but given that her father had died only four months previously, she may have chosen to wear a very understated dress, together with the cloak sent as a wedding present by her Leigh relations from Adlestrop.[2] The class to which the Austens belonged, the social range encompassed by '3 or 4 Families in a Country Village',[3] tended to celebrate marriages in a subdued, private manner and Eliza's vision of a 'mighty gay' event may not have been realized. She could well have found this wedding as stupid a business as her own.

The ceremony at Steventon Church would still be familiar today, the bride standing on the bridegroom's left before the minister, a few Austen and Cooper relations in attendance. The form of words would be recognizable too, apart from the fact that Jane Cooper, in common with all brides at the time, had to promise to obey her husband, a requirement which had implications for women in cases of adultery in the divorce courts. As witnesses to the marriage, Jane, Cassandra and Edward Cooper would follow the couple to the vestry to sign the documents. With no music or hymn singing, the procedure would be over fairly quickly. Bells might have been rung at the end, if paid for. Parson Woodforde recorded two sets of ringers charging 10s 6d each at his sister's wedding in 1774. Marrying by licence ensured a degree of privacy not possible through the very public calling of banns, but it was not a cheap option. The licence cost £2 6s 6d (just over £100 in today's money) and the church fees, for entering the marriage in the register and conducting the ceremony, about £4 (£200 today).[4]

Wedding rings – given by women as well as men – varied from plain gold or silver gilt bands to finely engraved or chased designs. Some were inscribed with a message of love and called a posy (poesy) ring. The woman's ring could be protected by two other jewelled or diamond rings, one either side, known as keepers. In 1808, the magazine *La Belle Assemblée* described the new fashion of multi-coloured keepers; perhaps these are in Isabella Thorpe's mind when she imagines flaunting 'a brilliant display of hoop rings' on her finger. On her way back to Longbourne with her new husband, Lydia Wickham flashes her wedding ring at a former

Meryton acquaintance, to herald her arrival as a married woman in her old neighbourhood. Lord Byron claimed that the wedding ring was 'the damnedest part of matrimony', but married men wore them as often as not, engraved with the couple's initials and the date of the union. Lord Raglan was particularly attached to his. When his left arm was amputated at Waterloo in 1815, he immediately asked for his wedding ring to be put on his remaining hand.[5]

The Marriage Act of 1753 governed how marriages were performed in England and Wales. Better known as the Harwicke Act, after the Lord Chancellor who introduced it, the legislation aimed to prevent clandestine alliances, especially those contracted without the sanction of the Church of England. Up to this date, couples were considered legally married by simply declaring themselves to be so in front of witnesses, or by going through an informal ceremony conducted by a layman. Boys of fourteen and girls of twelve could be married without parental consent, which led to all kinds of abuses, especially where the forced marriages of heiresses were involved. After the Act, marriages could only be contracted in the Church of England by licence, or following the reading of banns in the parish church of both parties on three consecutive Sundays. One of the parties had to be resident in the parish where the wedding was to take place for at least three weeks and parental consent was required for those under the age of twenty-one. If a clergyman married a couple under the age of consent without parental agreement and without the publication of banns, he was liable for a fine of £100. Catholic rites of marriage were celebrated privately, followed by a Church of England ceremony for the sake of legality.

Marrying by banns cost less than marrying by licence, about £3 (approximately £150 today) for the three callings and the payment to church officials. Most genteel couples avoided the publicity involved in having their names called out in church by the curate, intoning the words specified in The Book of Common Prayer: 'I publish the Banns of Marriage between M. of – and N. of – . If any of you know cause, or just impediment, why these two persons should not be joined together in holy Matrimony, ye are to declare it.' It is to this form of words that Emma refers when she promises to use Mr Knightley's first name for the one and only time, on the occasion when 'M takes N' – a phonetic gloss on the names Emma and Knightley. The calling of banns was all very well for the lower orders, the Smiths and Browns Robert Ferrars gleefully imagines his brother joining together in wedlock, but anyone above that station in life bought licences. One particular father, however, was so determined to pin his daughter's illustrious suitor down that he opted for banns, as a letter from Mrs Bland to Miss Heber, in September 1791 illustrates:

> You'll see by the Papers the Wedding that is to take place today. Ld. Galloway, they say, lost no time for, as soon as the Marquess proposed to him (& 'tis believed before he had Consulted his own family) Ld. G. had them asked in the Church.[6]

The cost of banns was 2s 6d in Parson Woodforde's day and the same amount for the marriage service. If the marriage was called off, as it was in the case of Mr Flood, whom Parson Woodforde records as being 'forbid by the Girl', the half-crown was refundable.[7] At smarter weddings, the officiating clergyman might be fortunate enough to be paid generously by the groom. When Jas. Herring married Miss Peachman at Weston Church in 1788, Parson Woodforde received two guineas, which he considered very handsome.[8]

Special Licences enabled people to be married in fashionable or imposing places, such as abbeys and cathedrals, or at home, at a time of the family's choosing. This type of licence was obtained from the office of the Archbishop of Canterbury at Doctors' Commons in London and cost £14 12s in 1819 (about £700 today).[9] Mrs Bennet envisages that Elizabeth and Darcy will be married by special licence and we can make an accurate guess that Lady Catherine had anticipated the same arrangement for the marriage of Darcy to her daughter. A wedding to impress even Lady Catherine took place in 1806. Henrietta Bridgeman Simpson, heiress of Sir Robert Worsley, and the Honourable Charles Pelham, elder son of Lord Yarborough, were married by the highest prelate in the land, in particularly exalted surroundings. Lady Banks described the occasion to Miss Heber:

> We din'd at Lord Yarborough's in London, Augst. 10th, with a Party of Relations, all of which met & were present at the Marriage Ceremony on 11th, which was perform'd by the Archbishop of Canterbury at Lambeth Palace after which we had an elegant Breakfast in the Gallery at Lambeth. The Parties soon dispers'd;

> the Bride & Bridegroom went to Chelsea, where they staid. The rest of the Relations had a magnificent Dinner that day at Mr Bridgeman Simpson's, & we went back to Spring Grove that Night.[10]

Marrying by special licence also protected the bride's virginal modesty, such as it was. Contemporary descriptions dwell on blushes, awed expressions and visible tears. In November 1786, at Audley End, the marriage of Marianne Clayton and Colonel Henry Fox was celebrated. The bride's sister described with heartfelt satisfaction the highly charged emotions on the day:

> It is impossible to express what I felt holding her dear trembling hand . . . Her heart seemed quite to sink at first . . . What a variety of sensations I felt during the ceremony! surely nothing can be so awful? sweet angel . . . She trembled and had her eyes quite full, but she did not cry . . . *He* had his eyes quite full also, and looked agitated, which was just what I wished . . .[11]

Public weddings were more than such sensibilities could bear – 'I don't suppose anything can be so dreadful as a public wedding – my stars! I should never be able to support it' claimed Fanny Burney[12] – but the studied informality of some ceremonies went almost too far in the opposite direction. One such marriage took place after dinner, the ladies all sewing industriously when the minister arrived. The latter himself was baffled how to proceed, 'for he had never married anybody in a room before'. In the event, a table was moved to a different position, candles and a prayer book placed on it, and the service proceeded. Afterwards, the bride and groom set off for a friend's house and the minister and guests went to the theatre.[13]

Not all weddings conducted out of the public gaze were as relaxed and understated. One account by Dorothea Herbert of a private wedding in a grand house details a whole set of disasters. The bridegroom arrived at the last minute, having been late-night shopping for new gloves; the bride dropped her diamond watch, a present from the groom, and it smashed on the stone floor; the clergyman, Dorothea's father, lost his place in the prayer book at 'I take this woman to be . . .'; the ring rolled away at the height of the ceremony and could not be found; the four pet dogs in attendance in white ribbons and collars 'set up such a Yelling that my Father was forced to lay down the Book till they were turned out of the Room'. All of the guests expressed concern that such bad omens might augur an unhappy alliance, but the bride's angelic appearance and behaviour throughout the ceremony calmed their fears and at midnight they sat down to 'an elegant fancy supper'.[14]

Darcy and Elizabeth quit Meryton immediately after their wedding, leaving behind the bride's embarrassing relatives. Bingley and Jane follow them to the north of England a year later and the sisters live within thirty miles of each other, an achievable distance by carriage. Elinor and Marianne's marital homes are almost in sight of each other and their mother is a frequent visitor; Fanny moves to nearby Thornton Lacey with the cousin she has loved for most of her life, then to the parsonage within Mansfield Park's grounds. Emma returns to her own home with Mr Knightley. Catherine Morland is the only heroine who moves away from home *and* family on marriage, leaving nine siblings and much loved parents behind her. For many brides and their families, this wrench tinged an otherwise happy day with a sense of regret; perhaps in allowing most of her heroines to keep some companion from their previous home, Jane Austen recognized how keen her own sense of loss would have been had Cassandra married and moved to another part of the country. She stressed the desirability of marrying a man from one's home territory to Fanny Knight and reinforced in her novels how shared lives, shared memories, can create stronger ties between siblings than between husbands and wives. Miss Curzon's wedding, reported by her sister in a letter to Miss Heber in 1778, highlights the bittersweet emotions experienced by the bride's family on her departure:

> Sir G. & my Sister behav'd delightfully: both sides seem'd perfectly pleas'd with their choice. As soon as the ceremony was over, signing & witnessing done in the vestry, Sir G. handed his Lady thro' us all. They got in their chaise & four & drove away: they said not a word when they left us as that would have been more than we could bear . . . There were nobody but a few friends at the wedding.[15]

Parents and siblings felt the loss of a much loved daughter and sister acutely. Some mothers feared that they would be so overcome by grief that they did not attend the wedding. Lady Bertram expects to experience some agitation at Maria's wedding, but fails despite her best efforts, while Sir Thomas is described as feeling more anxiety than his wife. Emmeline Benson's mother in Caroline Lucy Scott's novel:

> betrayed her anxious agitation by the nervous twitching of the gold chain around her neck, to which was suspended her daughter's portrait, and the constant rearranging of her lace shawl . . . She was too fond a mother not to feel painfully the loss of her daughter.[16]

When Edward Cooper married Caroline Lybbe Powys on March the 14th 1793, the bride's mother stayed at home rather than go through the distress of giving up her beloved daughter, 'who till latterly I had never parted with for even one night'. The wedding guests mentioned in Mrs Lybbe Powys' diary are her husband, her youngest son Thomas, her eldest son Phil and his wife, Louisa. The family's inclinations were for a quiet wedding at Fawley, the living held by the bride's Uncle Thomas:

> . . . the ceremony was over before any but our own family knew that it was to be performed there. And Tom, who had been all the week before in parties in our large neighbourhood, was afterwards complimented at keeping a secret even better than a lady![17]

Anna Austen's marriage to Ben Lefroy at Steventon Church in November 1814, although not a closely guarded secret, was similarly understated. Not even the bride's grandmother and aunts travelled the eighteen or so miles from Chawton to attend the quiet ceremony and small celebratory meal. Anna's half-sister Caroline described the day:

> My sister's wedding was certainly in the *extreme* of quietness; yet not so as to be in any way censured or remarked upon – and this was the order of the day . . . we . . . had a slight early breakfast upstairs; and between 9 and 10 the bride, my mother, Mrs Lefroy, Anne and myself, were taken to church in our carriage. All the gentlemen walked. The weather was dull and cloudy, but it did not actually rain. The season of the year, the unfrequented road of half a mile to the lonely old church, the grey light within of a November morning making its way through the narrow windows, no flowers to give colour and brightness, no friends, high or low, to offer their good wishes, and so to claim some interest in the great event of the day – all these circumstances and deficiencies must, I think, have given a gloomy air to our wedding. Mr Lefroy read the service, my father gave

> his daughter away. The Clerk of course was there, altho' I do not particularly remember him; but I am quite sure there was no one else in the church, nor was anyone else asked to the breakfast, to which we sat down as soon as we got back.[18]

St Margaret's in London, where Eliza Smith married William-John Chute in October 1793, sounds crowded by comparison. Fifteen guests attended the wedding at half-past nine, then repaired to the Smiths' house in George Street for the customary breakfast. By noon, the newly wed couple had left for Mr Chute's estate in Hampshire.[19] James Austen, who held the living of Sherborne St John from the Vyne, was one of the first to greet its new mistress on her arrival, the rest of the Austen family from Steventon visited during the following month.

'The day on which Mrs Bennet got rid of her two eldest daughters . . .' implies that this particular mother had a more robust approach to weddings than some. It also suggests that Lizzie and Jane had a double wedding. Jane Austen's brother Edward married Elizabeth Bridges and her sister Sophia married William Deedes in a joint wedding ceremony at Goodnestone, as announced in the *Gentleman's Magazine* of December 1791:

> 27th December: – At Goodnestone, in Kent, Edw. Austen, esq. of Rowlin, to Miss Elizabeth Bridges, third daughter of the late Sir Brook B. bart. Also, at the same place, Wm. Deedes, esq. jun. to Miss Sophia Bridges, second daughter of the late Sir Brook B. bart.

Double weddings were not uncommon – if more than one couple wished to be married on the same date, they could be married in the same ceremony, especially if the participants belonged to the same family.

Many of the marriages in Bath recorded between 1801 and 1806 were witnessed by two church officials, indicating that the bride and groom were the only other persons present. The same witnesses turn up in the records for a number of marriages in different churches. In 1802, out of ninety-six marriages at St James', eighty were witnessed by Charles Russell and John Cole, who both did double duty as witnesses at the Abbey. Charles Russell also appears as a witness at St Michael's. Large celebrations in any case were considered passé, as Caroline Austen recognized in 1814: 'Weddings were then usually very quiet. The old fashion of festivity and publicity had quite gone by, and was universally condemned as showing the great bad taste of all former generations.'[20] Austen family marriages tended to be subdued affairs, attended by only a few closely related guests. All of Jane's brothers married in their brides' parishes. Mr Austen officiated at James' marriage to his first wife, Anne Mathew, at Laverstoke, in 1792, but whether any of the other Austens attended is unknown. Charles, away at Naval College and Frank at sea certainly could not be there. The same uncertainty applies to Edward's marriage to Elizabeth Bridges in Kent in 1791, and to James' second marriage, to Mary Lloyd, at Hurstbourne Tarrant in 1797. Henry's marriage to his cousin Eliza on 31 December 1797, although published in the *Gentleman's Magazine*, was exceptionally private. Eliza wrote to her godfather Warren Hastings five days before the wedding and the Austens were only informed afterwards. Mrs Austen, Jane and Cassandra were in Clifton on 24 July 1806, from where Jane wrote a poem to celebrate Frank's marriage on that day to Mary Gibson, at Ramsgate. Charles married in Bermuda in 1807 and his bride did not meet any of her Austen relations for another four years. This inclination for quiet weddings is replicated in *Emma*; Mr Knightley does not attend the marriage of his friend Mr Weston to Miss Taylor, neither does Mr Weston's son; Mr Knightley's own wedding is described as lacking in outward show. Neighbours were free to gather outside the church to watch the wedding party emerge after the service, but they were not invited to the celebrations. Mrs Elton's disinclination to wait outside the church with the Highbury hoi poloi means that she has to rely on her husband's description of the Knightley wedding, which is, predictably, critical.

Lydia and Wickham's subdued wedding in London, with only the Gardiners and Mr Darcy in attendance, takes place at eleven o'clock at St Clement's, the nearest church to the reluctant groom's lodgings, evidently chosen to reduce the chances of his beating a hasty retreat. No doubt Lydia would have preferred to make a show at the most fashionable venue in the capital for society weddings, St George's, in Hanover Square. Mary Crawford hints that Fanny should marry Henry there, '"Only keep your cousin Edmund from me at such a time, I should not like to be tempted."'[21] The location of this church, in the middle of Mayfair, was all-important. The parish covered an area spreading from Regent Street to the Serpentine and Oxford Street, where all of the most wealthy, fashionable people lived. Land owned by the church in Belgravia and Pimlico was developed later in the 1820s and '30s. In 1816, 1,063 weddings were recorded at St George's, about three a day on average and nine on Christmas Day. Some royals were married there, including the Prince Regent's brother Augustus, Duke of Sussex, at the end of 1793. He and Lady Augusta Murray had secretly married in Rome earlier in the year. Interestingly, they were married in St George's after banns were called. The living itself was worth £1,500 and the incumbent gained a fine house in Grosvenor Street. It was such a prestigious establishment that Dukes and Earls numbered among the vestrymen. Part of its popularity came from its patriotic response to the war with France. The St George's, Hanover Square, Volunteers were set up by parish subscription in 1794 and became the largest of all of the volunteer regiments in London by the time of King George III's review in 1798.

The law held that marriages in church without a special licence must be conducted between eight o'clock in the morning and twelve noon. An early start to the day had one advantage, in giving couples the chance to set out on their wedding journey in daylight, but even when the wedding took place later in the morning, the celebratory meal was still referred to as the breakfast. Unlike today, the church and vicar did not have to be booked months, or even weeks, in advance. At Ashe, in July 1801, Lucy Lefroy's marriage to Henry Rice was delayed for several days while the financial settlement was drawn up and the date remained unfixed until the papers arrived. 'Mr Rice & Lucy are to be married, one on the 9th & the other on the 10th of July', Jane Austen joked prophetically in a letter to Cassandra.[22] Mrs Lefroy's diary entries express no anxieties about this situation – she calmly continues to note visits and dinners, guests and deaths, inoculations for cowpox and excursions in the donkey cart.[23] With only a few local guests and the couple themselves to consider, weddings were much simpler affairs to plan – no transport to arrange, no hoteliers or caterers to worry about.

Wedding breakfasts were not always attended by the newly married couple – some chose to leave immediately on their wedding journey, or set out for their new home. The meal provided was not usually extensive, as Caroline Austen's description of Anna and Ben's wedding breakfast illustrates:

> The breakfast was such as best breakfasts then were: some variety of bread, hot rolls, buttered toast, tongue or ham and eggs. The addition of chocolate at one end of the table, and the wedding cake in the middle, marked the speciality of the day . . . The servants had cake and punch in the evening . . .[23]

Lydia Bennet takes a normal breakfast an hour before the wedding, with her uncle and aunt. Darcy accompanies Wickham to St Clement's directly from the groom's lodgings and the couple leave from the church door, arriving at Longbourne in time for dinner. Mrs Bennet promises the servants punch in the evening to celebrate the match. By Charlotte Lutterell's standards, both of these celebratory attempts would be classed as pitiful affairs. For her sister's wedding breakfast, she provides roast beef, broiled mutton, soup, cold ham, chicken, pigeon pie, turkey, tongue and numerous jellies, 'enough to last the new-married couple through the honeymoon', she boasts to her correspondent at Lesley Castle.[25] Surprisingly, there appears to have been no wedding breakfast laid on at Mansfield Park. The bride, groom and Julia leave for Sotherton from the church and the rest of the family return to the house to toast the couple with wine. Mrs Norris quaffs several glasses, but no food is mentioned. The extent of the post-wedding celebrations varied from family to family, regardless of rank, it seems. At Charlotte Blunden's wedding, where Dorothea Herbert had hoped to appear interesting in her white bridesmaid's dress, the young couple stayed to eat with their guests and more entertainments were planned for the evening:

> We had a most Sumptuous Entertainment of everything the Season afforded – In the Evening the Tenants Assembled and danced before the Windows – and were afterwards freely regaled and Money thrown to them – At night we had a Ball and Music . . . and the Day ended with a flaming supper and Concert.[26]

Wedding celebrations were not always sedate, well-managed affairs. One party attended by Mary Russell Mitford was decidedly raucous, as she detailed with great relish:

> The bride and her second sister set off to Brighton, and I and the youngest

> remained to do the honours of the wedding-dinner. Of course we all got tipsy – those who were used to it comfortably enough, and those who were not, rather awkwardly – some were top-heavy and wanted tying up like overblown carnations, some reeled, some staggered – and one fell, and catching at a harp for a prop, came down with his supporter and a salver of coffee which he knocked out of the servant's hands; such a crash, vocal and instrumental, I never heard in my life![27]

Wedding cakes were baked for most weddings and often featured in pride of place on the table. Dorothea Herbert remembered 'sitting in form for Wine and Cake' directly after the ceremony.[28] The remaining cake was usually parcelled up and delivered to neighbours and friends or served to the visitors who called to greet the bride. Two weeks before Catherine Bigg married Mr Hill, Jane Austen was making enquiries of Cassandra about the family's habit of distributing wedding cake:

> Do you recollect whether the Manydown family send about their Wedding Cake? – Mrs Dundas has set her heart upon having a piece from her friend Catherine, & Martha who knows what importance she attaches to the sort of thing, is anxious for the sake of both, that there shd not be a disappointment.[29]

Wedding cake is the first food mentioned in *Emma*; the newly married Westons share it with the visitors who arrive at Randalls to pay their respects to the bride. Parson Woodforde was treated to wedding cake and chocolate on a visit to a newly married couple in 1794 and the following year noted 'Very curious devices on the Top of the Cake' which was sent from London to the local squire. So decoration of some sort was used by the larger confectioners, perhaps in the form of fancy icing or maybe even tiny representational figures of the bride and groom.[30] Mr Woodhouse does his utmost to dissuade the Westons from having a cake at all, and when that fails, tries to prevent anyone from eating it, convinced that if such a rich concoction could ruin his constitution, it was likely to disorder the whole of Highbury. A typical eighteenth-century wedding cake recipe comprised:

> 4lb. fine flour, well dried; 4lb. fresh butter; 2lb. loaf sugar, pounded and sifted fine; 1/4oz. mace; 1/4oz. nutmeg; 32 eggs; 4lb. currants, picked over and dried well; 1lb. sweet almonds, blanched and cut lengthwise very thin; 1lb. each shredded orange and lemon peel, ½ a pint of brandy.[31]

All 32 egg whites and yolks were to be beaten separately by hand and after preparing such a time-consuming confection the cook and kitchen maids would need several glasses of strong punch to restore their strength. One custom regarding wedding cake was that pieces of it should be drawn through the ring, a messy business, and given to single men and women to put under their pillows to stimulate dreams of their future spouses. Mary Russell Mitford, at a wedding in 1816, regarded as unfortuitous 'our entirely forgetting to draw any cake through the ring, so that our fate still rests in abeyance'.[32]

The errant Lydia Bennet's marriage is announced in *The Times* and the local *Courier* as briefly as possible, in order to save the Bennet family further embarrassment. No mention is made of her father or place of residence and all of her relations, with the exception of her mother, must have hoped that the item would attract little notice. It was customary to publicize a marriage in a national and a local newspaper and considered odd not to: '. . . Miss Blachford *is* married, but I have never seen it in the Papers. And one may as well be single if the Wedding is not to be in print',[33] Jane Austen wrote to Anna about a cousin of the Bigg-Withers. Some announcements did not give the name of the bride, only that of her father and any titled connection: 'At St. James's Church, Lieut.-col Byng, of the 3rd Foot-guards, to the second daughter of Sir Walter James, niece to Earl Camden.'[34] Some added insult to injury and only mentioned the woman's fortune: 'At Wanlip, co. Leicester, Sir Charles Graves Hudson, bart. to the eldest daughter of the late Peter Holford, esq. one of the masters in Chancery, with 50,000l.'[35] A deceased father and a lump sum were obviously of more note than a live wife, and these kinds of entry in the marriage columns of newspapers and magazines were by no means uncommon. Occasionally, odd alliances were brought to the public's attention, the majority of them concerning considerable age gaps between the bride and groom: '*Marriage extraordinary*! – Lately was married, at Batley, Mr. G. Sheard, aged *seventy-two*, to Miss E. Cowling, aged *nineteen*! – The bridegroom has six children, forty-six grandchildren, and six great-grand-children, all living.'[36]

Jane Austen made her own inimitable observations on marriages she spotted in the press, some of them impenetrable jokes, understandable only to her sister. 'I must notice a wedding in the Salisbury paper, which has amused me very much, Dr Phillot to Lady Frances St Lawrence. *She* wanted to have a husband I suppose, once in her life, and *he* a Lady Frances.'[37] Both of these characters may have been known to the Austens, since they lived in Bath, and part of the humour might have come from Dr Phillot's age, fifty-nine, and Lady Frances' desperation to have a husband at any cost. Like her mother, Jane Austen loved wordplay and wrote punning verses on the names of a few married or engaged couples:

ON READING IN THE NEWSPAPERS THE MARRIAGE OF MR GELL TO MISS GILL, OF EASTBOURNE.
At Eastbourne, Mr Gell, From being perfectly well,
Became dreadfully ill, For love of Miss Gill.
So he said, with some sighs, I'm the slave of your *iis*;
Oh, restore, if you please, By accepting my *ees*.

ON THE MARRIAGE OF A MIDDLE-AGED FLIRT WITH A MR WAKE, WHOM, IT WAS SUPPOSED, SHE WOULD SCARCELY HAVE ACCEPTED IN HER YOUTH.
Maria, good-humoured, and handsome, and tall,
For a husband was at her last stake;
And having in vain danced at many a ball,
Is now happy to *jump at a Wake.*[38]

James Austen made alterations to this last piece; Jane refers to his changes as 'improvements' in a letter to Martha Lloyd, on 29 November 1812. 'Maria' was in fact Urania Wallop, niece of the Earl of Portsmouth, who married Henry Wake, an elderly curate, in March 1813. Jane had not in fact used Urania's name in the poem and had described her as 'merry and small'. Camilla, the name of Urania's mother, scanned more satisfactorily, but James presumably worried that if the verse ever got out, the Wallop family might recognize the identity of the 'middle-aged flirt', so he changed the name and the physical characteristics.[39]

Mrs Austen's brother, James Leigh-Perrot, also had a flair for writing epigrams. This one was written on the marriage of Captain Foote to Miss Mary Patton, on 24 August 1803:

Through the rough ways of Life, with a patten your Guard,

May you safely and pleasantly jog;
May the ring never break, nor the Knot press too hard,
Nor the *Foot* find the *Patten* a Clog.[40]

6

Wedding Journeys

Where newly wed couples went after the wedding depended on the money and time available, but for those who had never met their spouse's relations, the wedding journey became a necessity as well as, it is to be hoped, a pleasure. Before the 1790s, the Continent was a popular destination for the rich, but war with the French had closed down most forms of travel there, so choice was limited to home shores. English spa towns and seaside resorts, already thriving from an increase in tourism, became the places for the newly married to go and stopping off to see relatives on the way cut down on accommodation expenses. Some left immediately after the ceremony, as did Charlotte and Mr Collins. There is no mention of a wedding breakfast at Lucas Lodge, Mr Collins being in great haste to convey his new wife directly to Rosings, to be scrutinized by Lady Catherine. The arrangement suited Charlotte too; much better to put up with Mr Collins for a fifty-mile journey than spend an unrelieved week or more entirely in his company. She knew that her happiness as a wife would lie in her home and poultry yard, not in the irksome, unrelieved presence of her husband. Like Charlotte, a number of new wives only saw the property in which they would spend their married lives *after* the wedding and many of them would understandably have been eager to get there. This was the case with Harriot Wrightson, who wrote from Yorkshire to her sister in London, describing her feelings on first seeing Cusworth Park:

> — the place is indeed beautiful, much more so than I cd. have imagined. With the first sight of it I cd. but be highly pleas'd. But nothing cd. equal the impression I recd. from the affectionate wellcome my Dearest Wrightson gave me the moment after I enter'd his House . . . Yesterday even. my time was fully imploy'd. Mr Wrightson was showing me my room in the House & taking me round the Shrubery, &c, till it was late . . .[1]

Mrs Wrightson's experience was not unusual; if a future husband lived at a great distance from his fiancée, there would be little opportunity for her to visit his property before marriage. Jane Austen recognized the reality of this situation – she had faced a parallel experience when moving to Chawton, with only Cassandra's impressions to go on. In *Emma*, she gives Mr Dixon enough foresight to carry drawings of his Irish estate with him when he visits Weymouth, so that he can show Miss Campbell the house which she will inhabit as Mrs Dixon. Fanny Price, had she married Henry Crawford, would have shared Mrs Wrightson's ignorance, but Edmund must have made sure that she saw the more accessible Thornton Lacy before he began to carry out the necessary improvements which would make it attractive to his new wife. Jane Austen's heroines are fortunate creatures – Elizabeth Bennet falls in love with Pemberley almost simultaneously with falling in love with its owner; Catherine Morland is introduced to the homely comforts of the parsonage house at Woodston during her stay at Northanger Abbey and surely Elinor Dashwood would travel the easy distance between East Devon and Dorset before her wedding day to see Edward's Delaford living. Marianne is a regular visitor to the parsonage and is able to spend time in the property that will become her home, the Colonel's manor house. Anne Elliot's future home with Captain Wentworth is uncertain, since she is the only heroine to gain no property on marriage, but they can be imagined sharing the roomy Kellynch Hall with the Crofts to begin with, before the Captain purchases or leases a house of his own after peace has been declared. Emma remains at Hartfield to care for her father on her marriage to Mr Knightley, with the prospect of Donwell before her at some point in the future. Jane Austen reputedly told her family that Mr Woodhouse kept his daughter and son-in-law out of the Abbey for two years. Harriet Smith has spent a happy summer in Robert Martin's farmhouse and become acquainted with his mother and sisters, but some minor characters fare less well – Mrs Elton sees her husband's vicarage for the first time after the wedding in Bath and Jane Fairfax is removed from the familiar surroundings of Highbury and the Campbells' London house, to Enscombe, the Churchill estate in the far north.

It would be reasonable to assume that Eliza Smith travelled the manageable distance from London to Mr Chute's estate in Hampshire when she became engaged in June 1793, a journey of nearly six hours, together with her parents and perhaps her sisters. The family spent enough time that summer in carriages between London, Weymouth and Devizes, where Eliza's father was an MP, to make one more journey no hardship, but it appears that no visit to The Vyne was made before the wedding. Eliza was maddeningly circumspect in her journal and did not even risk any comment on her feelings for Mr Chute. Perhaps the whole idea of marriage troubled her to such an extent that she preferred to bury her head in the sand and pretend that the days left with her much loved parents and sisters were not numbered. So she arrived new to The Vyne in the late afternoon of her wedding day, having left London at a quarter to twelve and stopped off at Bagshot for twenty minutes to change the horses. Miss Curzon and her sister undertook a much longer journey from Hagley to Nottinghamshire to view no fewer than three houses belonging to her prospective husband.[2] A month later, she drove away from the church gate to become mistress of one of them.

Relatives with money and property were often generous in accommodating newly married couples in straitened circumstances. Frank Austen and Mary Gibson were married in Ramsgate on 24 July 1806, and, having little money to spare from a sailor's pay, left immediately to spend a long honeymoon[3] with Edward and Elizabeth at Godmersham. Cassandra, Jane and their mother did not meet up with Frank and his bride until October, when they all moved into a house in Southampton. Anna and Ben Lefroy were similarly circumstanced where ready money was concerned. Directly after their wedding breakfast at Steventon Rectory, they made the long journey to Hendon, where they were supported by Ben's bachelor brother Edward until the following August. The rich Knights of Godmersham needed no cheap bed and board at Steventon when they visited the Austens as part of their tour of relations, following their marriage in Kent in May 1779. Jane was just three-and-a-half and would not have remembered the couple's interest in her brother Edward, then eleven, but eight-year-old Henry absorbed everything and later described to a niece how the Knights took his brother with them on the rest of their tour, returning him to Steventon a few weeks later on their journey back home. Little did anyone at the time imagine that the future heir to the

Chawton and Godmersham estates would be chosen unconsciously on a wedding journey.

Strange as it may seem today, new wives often took a companion or two with them on their honeymoon, the prospect of total seclusion and dependence on just one person for conversation and occupation constituting a step too far, too soon. Most single women had led the kind of quiet, confined lives so eloquently evoked by Anne Elliot in the final chapters of *Persuasion*, their experience of men limited to fathers, brothers and perhaps cousins. New husbands, used to male society and outdoor activity, must have felt the constraints of continual female company and found the empty days of enforced togetherness difficult to fill. The honeymoon period constituted a very real shock to the system for both parties – 'and many a fondly devoted bride has . . . during the very first week, often wished for her usual occupations, as much as her lover has for his gun and pointers'.[4] A familiar presence eased the transition from the single to the married state for any couple unused to long hours in each other's company and viewed in this light, the inclusion of a third, fourth or even fifth party on a wedding journey appears eminently desirable. Parson Woodforde's niece went to Bath accompanied by her mother and a cousin and after only a few days alone together in Kent, Lord Cholmondeley and Lady Charlotte spent the remainder of their honeymoon with the bride's mother at a spa town in Belgium. One couple in 1770 seemed desperate to avoid conjugal isolation completely. After the wedding dinner at the bride's family house, coffee, card-playing and general chat followed until supper at ten. The bride and groom retired to bed well after midnight, but the succeeding month brought no privacy for the newly married pair, nor did they appear to desire it. The days were spent racketing about the county in carriages, the bride, groom and several family members in one, the rest of the wedding guests, including the clergyman, in others following on behind. Some time was given over to shooting and hunting by the men, while the women sat together in the drawing room, the sexes back in their comfortable, segregated coteries. The parson and his wife left with regret at the end of the month, but the house party seemed set to continue for several more weeks before the young couple were finally left to themselves.[5] The new-fangled notion of newly marrieds spending their honeymoon entirely alone was gaining ground at the time when Jane Austen was writing her novels, marking the final stage in a process of transition from the lengthy celebrations involving family and friends, through the journey undertaken with one or two companions.

Mr and Mrs Rushworth, plus the very necessary Julia, drive away from the church door, to spend their first night at Sotherton before setting out for Brighton, then London. The crowded, fashionable seaside town had plenty of amusements on offer for young married couples and their companions: exhilarating boating parties, where 'blue-trowsered fellows' charging extortionate prices for their vessels sailed at dangerous speeds out in the bay; opportunities to gamble on 'the loo-table, of notable celebrity' in one of the libraries, where trinkets could be gained for a shilling, plus all the thrills of the racecourse and carriage drives out to The Devil's Dyke and Lewes Castle.[6] Jane Austen herself wanted nothing to do with Brighton in person. The Prince Regent's liking for the place was enough to turn her against it and its appearance in her novels is associated with immorality and meaningless excess. In London, as well as choosing new furniture and opening the grand house in Wimpole Street for glittering private parties, the Rushworths would find abundant entertainment – and Maria would need all the distraction that she could get – at the British Museum, the theatre and opera in Covent Garden, the ballet at Sadler's Wells, the art exhibitions at the Royal Academy and the Menagerie at the Exeter Exchange, where Lord Byron had been entranced by an elephant stealing his hat.[7] Anyone spending time in London could revel in the 'Regions of Wit, Elegance, fashion, Elephants & Kangaroons',[8] and forget, for a while, the less-than-perfect qualities of a spouse.

Two couples in Jane Austen's novels go to the sea on their wedding journeys. Lucy and Robert Ferrars visit Dawlish, the only place he is aware of in Devon, as a result of its popularity with fashionable society. Jane Austen had visited this resort in 1802, and twelve years later she still remembered the paucity of books in the library there, but neither Lucy nor Robert would find this a drawback, being no doubt more interested in the Promenade, 'extending in a straight line across the strand' where they could exhibit themselves.[9] One family on the Isle of Wight entertained a honeymoon couple for a few days and found their restless need to see and be seen rather tedious: 'they seem to travel because (because what shall I say?) why because it is smart and fashionable to travell when first people marry . . . we did as well as we could with them . . .'[10]

Emma's lifelong wish to see the coast is realized on her honeymoon. Given that she and Mr Knightley have only two weeks' grace from the demands of William Larkins and Mr Woodhouse, they would not have travelled a great distance from Surrey, Emma's father probably maintaining a discreet silence on the advantages of Cromer on this occasion. A quiet spot like Bognor in October would have suited them, with its elegant accommodation, circulating library and assembly room, where Emma might persuade Mr Knightley to dance. The description of Worthing in the 1810 *Guide to All The Watering and Sea Bathing Places* would appeal to them too, its sheltered walks and rides, two libraries well supplied with newspapers and views out across the downs, providing the perfect occupations for gentle autumnal days. Jane Austen knew the resort well, having spent the autumn of 1805 there with her mother and sister, the Godmersham family and Martha Lloyd. Mrs Austen enjoyed walking down to the beach to buy fish each morning, Fanny and Elizabeth amused themselves in the sea and Jane won 17 shillings in a raffle. One other couple can be imagined at the sea – Anne and Captain Wentworth, driving into the fine countryside surrounding Lyme in their new landaulette, or simply strolling along the Cobb, with 'no necessity for making any inconvenient sacrifices to the support of style, or to the extravagance of exterior shew'.[11] The horrors of Portsmouth and the disturbing events of the previous year would have been enough to put Fanny off any further upheaval, so she and Edmund would be happy to spend the first night of their married life at Mansfield Park, moving on to the parsonage at Thornton Lacey in the following days, just as soon as Sir Thomas could be persuaded to let them go. Marianne and Colonel Brandon would surely have chosen somewhere craggy and romantic, like Wales, following William Gilpin's picturesque tour along the Wye Valley, where Marianne could indulge her love of rocky outcrops and, like Wordsworth, imagine a hermit living in the woods around Tintern Abbey. Lizzie and Mr Darcy, after calling in at Pemberley for a short stay, might turn to another of Gilpin's travel guides, tracing his route from Derbyshire to the Lake District, with Georgiana a welcome companion on their journey.

How long could a honeymoon couple spend away from home? Professional men must have had some restriction on their time, although Henry Rice talked of staying between a month and six weeks in Wales after his marriage to Lucy Lefroy in July 1801, before returning to Deane, where he had been curate for George Austen since the family's move to Bath. This long break from his clerical duties must have been covered by James Austen, with Lucy's father, The Revd Lefroy, perhaps stepping in to help out from the nearby parish of Ashe. Gentlemen of leisure could choose, if they so wished, to spend an even longer time away, leaving their estate business in the hands of trusted bailiffs. When Harris Bigg-Wither married Anne Frith at the end of 1804, their wedding holiday was passed at a dismal 'borrowed' house in the small hamlet of Quidhampton, while their house at Wymering was being renovated. Harris obtained leave of absence from his militia regiment for two months, but Mrs Lefroy, while looking forward to seeing a good deal of them, suspected that they would soon 'be tired of such a dull place —'.[12] Elinor and Edward Ferrars experience a similar situation, in that they move in with Colonel Brandon at Delaford Manor for a month immediately after their wedding, while necessary improvements are made to the parsonage. This couple, with plenty to keep them occupied in the way of superintending the alterations to their new home and making plans for the future, would be neither tired nor dull.

If no wedding trip was undertaken and the young couple retired to bed in the same house as the family guests, everyone would be eager the following morning to assess the appearance of the new wife. In many cases, the display of white satin and lace started all over again: 'Next Morning the Bride shone forth in All the splendour of Beauty – A highly Glazed white Linen Gown with white Ribbon and a large handsome French Night Cap . . .'[13] Such interest in the recently sexually initiated was only to be expected and probably hadn't changed much since earlier in the eighteenth century, when one female correspondent had reported wickedly on an exhausted wife's appearance in church, two days after her wedding:

> I happened to sit in the pue with them and had the honour of seeing Mrs Bride fall fast asleep in the middle of the Sermon and snore very comfortably, which made several women in the Church think the bridegroom not quite so ugly as they did before. Envious people say 'twas all counterfeited to oblige him, but

> I believe that's scandal, for she's so devout, I dare swear nothing but downright necessity could make her miss one Word of the Sermon.[14]

The bride's discomfiture at the breakfast table was much dwelt upon and not only by her female friends and relations. The brother of the groom, after speculating on 'who did or did not sleep' the previous night, comments on his brother's foolish demeanour the next morning and his bride's red face, but notes three days later, 'They go to bed with as little ceremony & blushing as other married people . . .'[15] Those newly-weds who spent their first night at a staging post on their way to a holiday destination, or in their own homes, would have thought themselves fortunate in escaping unwelcome attention from the strangers at breakfast the next day.

The whole neighbourhood's curiosity to see any new bride could be a daunting, embarrassing ordeal for those concerned, but Mrs Wrightson's experience sounds more pleasurable than otherwise. She describes

> our cheerful reception at Doncaster, thro' wch place our carriage was the whole way surround'd by people paying their compts: the Bells had been ringing the whole Day. I really cd. not help laughing to see how much I was the object of curiosity; every window was crowded with people . . .[16]

This kind of attention would have been very acceptable to Lydia Bennet on her return to Meryton as Mrs Wickham. She certainly makes an exhibition of herself, flashing her wedding ring at old acquaintances, parading her new status in the neighbourhood and in the servants' quarters at Longbourne and claiming precedence over her unmarried, older and more worthy sisters. Mrs Bennet's sense of her own importance is heightened by showing off her married daughter on visits to the neighbours and holding frequent parties in her honour. She could not have hoped to rival the spectacle organized by the Archer family in 1770, to announce their daughter's illustrious match to Mr Houblon. Two days after the ceremony, the newly married pair, dressed up in their wedding silver and white, were transported by a cavalcade of carriages and liveried out-riders, to process through the nearby town, setting the church bells ringing and drawing a large crowd of spectators. On the following Sunday, they treated the local congregation to another glittering display.[17]

Wherever they went, brides were noticed and given special treatment.

Etiquette demanded that visits be paid as soon as possible to the house of the newly married pair and Frank Churchill's five-month delay in paying his respects to his father's new wife is viewed severely by Mr Knightley. On an occasion like this, finely worded letters would not do. '"Not to wait upon a bride is very remiss,"' pronounces Mr Woodhouse[18] on his own reluctance to brave the corner into Vicarage Lane in order to visit the new Mrs Elton. In *Emma*, Jane Austen provides a comprehensive account of what such attention entailed. The Eltons' entry into Highbury in their specially ordered carriage, complete with bell-ringing, does not satisfy the neighbourhood's curiosity regarding their rector's new wife, neither does an unpropitious first sighting in church, where she could not be stared at. The formal rounds of visits are then paid and the new bride makes the most of what is due to her. Emma notes her fine clothes, over-confident manner and lack of elegance and forms no very good opinion of her. Mr Elton is less easy than his wife on the occasion, not surprisingly, given the circumstance of his proposal to Emma only a short while before and Emma's determination that he should marry Harriet. Jane Austen recognized the awkwardness of wedding visits for any couple, where the visitors had come to make their assessment regarding the suitability of the match and the degree of bridal beauty:

> All of you that are well enough to look, are now passing your Judgements I suppose on Mrs John Butler; & "is she pretty? or is she not?" is the knotty question. Happy Woman! to stand the gaze of a neighbourhood as the Bride of such a pink-faced, simple young Man![19]

Emma Woodhouse need not have wasted sympathy on the Eltons; they enthusiastically accept every invitation which comes their way, Mrs Elton flaunting her lace and pearls at dinner parties and evening gatherings and glorying in the precedence she can command over other women as a recent bride. Emma, sick of Mrs Elton's self-importance and the convention of treating a recent bride as the first lady at any social gathering, briefly considers marriage herself when she has to submit to taking second place at the Crown ball. Such attentions must have been a trial to James Austen's second wife, Mary, who was sadly pockmarked by smallpox. Following a bridal visit to the family at the Vyne, Eliza Chute described Mary as 'perfectly unaffected and very pleasant' but dreadfully 'scarred and seamed'.[20] Poor Mary was probably only too aware of her neighbours' pronouncements on her flawed face, but she must have felt some satisfaction on regaining Deane Parsonage, which she had quit five years previously to make way for James and his first wife.

The arrival of a new bride in the area did not always occasion unalloyed pleasure among the surrounding families. Charles Powlett's noisy party, held at the end of 1798 to celebrate his return to Steventon with his bride, pleased his neighbours so little that they wished imminent financial ruin on him. His wife bid fair to add to his problems, being 'everything that the Neighbourhood could wish her, silly & cross as well as extravagant.' Two years later, her expensive clothing and lack of sense were still the most striking elements of her character: 'Mrs Powlett was at once expensively & nakedly dress'd; – we have had the satisfaction of estimating her Lace and her Muslin; & she said too little to afford us much other amusement.'[21] What did amuse Jane Austen was Mrs Powlett's habit of referring to her husband as her '*Caro Sposo*',[22] an affectation which finds its way into Mrs Elton's terms of endearment. It is possible that her vulgar 'Mr E.' came from the same source. Mr Elton's fond 'Augustas' and doting pride in his wife had no appeal for Jane Austen either; she probably encountered this kind of sentimentality too often for comfort. Commending her niece Anna for her sensible letters about her new role as the wife of Ben Lefroy, Jane is pleased to note the absence of a '*parade* of happiness',[23] revealing that she had often been embarrassed by young married women writing too effusively about the joys of marriage. She found the more measured appreciation of her father's former pupil, Richard Buller, something of a welcome relief: 'I was afraid he would oppress me by his felicity & his love for his Wife, but this is not the case; he calls her simply Anna without any angelic embellishments, for which I respect and wish him happy.'[24]

7

Scandal and Gossip

Conventional engagements and marriages attracted interest enough, but so much more could be squeezed out of illicit goings-on. Gossip circulated at a rapid rate within small communities, then spread into all parts of England by letter and – if sufficiently scandalous – it found its way into the national press. Every neighbourhood had its spies and news travelled fast along a growing network of roads; nothing stayed secret for long. Seduction, elopement, adultery, the Press seized on every example of impropriety it could find, especially if it implicated the great and the good. Salacious reports of depravity in high places appeared in almost every newspaper and journal, national and provincial, in among the House of Commons reports, foreign news and agricultural sales. Sexually explicit cartoons by Gillray and Rowlandson were exhibited in print shop windows all over London and pamphlets giving the complete transcripts of celebrated divorce cases or actions brought for breach of promise were readily available. From the Prince of Wales down to the lower ranks of the aristocracy, no reputation was safe. Sniping against the ruling classes never went out of season and every example of vice or folly was treated as fair game. Under the headline 'Noble Marriage at a House of Ill Fame', *Bon Ton* magazine launched an attack in March 1819, that might have appeared in any magazine or newspaper of the time, on the kind of debauched education reputedly sanctioned by titled parents, to ensure that their children became 'learned in infamy'. The writer expresses no surprise therefore that:

> The heir apparent to an Earldom, one of the richest in Scotland, has, it is said, sacrificed himself on the altar of Hymen, to one of Mother B—ks's fair seducers. The young man is under age, and so likewise is the young lady, if report can be credited.[1]

The use of initials and dashes for full names protected editors from legal cases being brought against them – but this coyness was not usually in evidence where the intimate details of the scandal were concerned, revealed under the spurious concern for public morality. That such topics made fascinating reading is indisputable and Jane Austen herself was not above a delighted wickedness in retailing scandal and gossip to her correspondents, nor of including such behaviour in her novels. The newspaper paragraph reporting Maria Bertram's disappearance with Henry Crawford could have come directly from the pages of the *Morning Post* or *London Courier*:

> it was with infinite concern the newspaper had to announce to the world, a matrimonial *fracas* in the family of Mr. R. of Wimpole Street; the beautiful Mrs. R. whose name had not long been enrolled in the lists of hymen, and who had promised to become so brilliant a leader in the fashionable world, having quitted her husband's roof in company with the well known and captivating Mr. C. the intimate friend and associate of Mr. R. and it was not known, even to the editor of the newspaper, whither they were gone.[2]

The flighty Mrs Herbert's adulterous elopement with a Scottish Major in 1785 was just the kind of scandal the Press relished, and the case was pursued through the divorce courts to its final sordid conclusion. At the end of the tale of damage, disaster and intrigue, one follower of the hatchet campaign commented wryly: 'So the story Goes . . . but it all came to the Same thing for Mr Herbert lost his Wife and she her Character whilst every Newspaper echoed their misfortunes.'[3] There is no mention of either husband or lover losing his reputation. A similar report on the affair of Colonel Powlett's wife and Lord Sackville was spotted by Jane Austen in her brother Edward's newspaper in 1808 and communicated to Cassandra:

> This is a sad story about Mrs Powlett. I should not have suspected her of such a thing. — She staid the Sacrament I remember, the last time that you & I did. — A hint of it, with Initials, was in yesterday's Courier; & Mr Moore guessed it to be Ld Sackville, beleiving there was no other Viscount S. in the peerage, & so it proved.[4]

This branch of the Powlett family was known to the Austens in Southampton, and although Jane registers shock at the news, she is keen to solve the identity of Lord S— by checking in Edward's copy of the *Peerage*. The affair could hardly be called an elopement, since the pair met up at the White Hart in Winchester and were caught in bed together by the landlady, after which Mrs Powlett returned to her home in Southampton and Lord Sackville drove away in his carriage. The clandestine coupling was evidently revealed to the papers by the staff at the White Hart and the *crim. con.* case was brought fairly rapidly by the Colonel in the same year. *Crim. con.* was short for 'criminal conversation', otherwise known as adultery. Lord Sackville, a dapper little man who was popular with women,[5] succeeded his cousin as fifth Duke of Dorset, but did not take the final step of marrying his partner in crime. She was subsequently divorced by her husband and disappeared out of the public eye. The details of the newspaper coverage seen by Jane Austen is given in R. W. Chapman's collection of her letters:

> The scandal cannot be found in the London *Courier*, but see *Morning Post*, 18 and 21 June 1808. 'Another elopement has taken place in high life. A Noble Viscount, Lord S., has gone off with a Mrs. P., the wife of a relative of the Noble Marquis' (of Winchester). 'Mrs. P.'s *faux pas* with Lord S—e took place at an inn near Winchester.' Col. P. was awarded £3,000 damages.[6]

Practically all of Jane Austen's correspondence with her sister contains gossip of one sort or another, which is only to be expected, when she and Cassandra spent so much time apart. They kept each other up to date with the latest local news, wherever they were, and to justify the postage charge which had to be paid by the recipient, every page was filled with news of some sort in order to be cost effective. 'I wish I had 6 pen'orth of entertainment to send you, but fear 'tis an Article not to be had at this time of Year', wrote Mrs Bland from London to her correspondent in far-away Doncaster, in October 1791. The London season did not get under way until January, so the city was empty of the rich and famous who could usually be relied on to supply reams of scurrilous tittle-tattle. She did, however, manage to find a juicy minor scandal, with the exciting consequence of a duel, to justify the cost of postage:

> Gen. Gunning must think his family has not done enough to furnish discourse so he will assist by having Lately taken off a Mrs Duberly, Wife of an Army Taylor that has a house in Soho Square. They went Lovingly together to Kentish town . . . 'Tis thought Mr Duberly will take proper *measures* with the General.[7]

Much of Jane Austen's gossip gives news of forthcoming engagements or marriages, makes observations on happy and unhappy alliances, comments seriously or playfully on adulteries, elopements and divorces and describes balls at which young women fall woefully short of making the desired impression. The letter detailing the first ball of the season at Hurstbourne Park in 1800, is filled with wickedly sharp criticism of the participants – single ladies looking less beautiful than they supposed themselves and married women with husbands less prepossessing than their wives' fashion accessories:

> There were very few Beauties, & such as there were, were not very handsome . . . Mrs Blount was the only one much admired. She appeared exactly as she did in September, with the same broad face, diamond bandeau, white shoes, pink husband, & fat neck. — The two Miss Coxes were there; I traced in one the remains of the vulgar, broad featured girl who danced at Enham eight years ago; . . . I looked at [Sir Thomas Champney's] daughter & thought her a queer animal with a white neck. — Mrs Warren, I was constrained to think a very fine young woman, which I much regret. She has got rid of some part of her child, & danced away with great activity, looking by no means very large. — Her husband is ugly enough; . . . but he does not look so *very* old. — The Miss Maitlands are both prettyish . . . with brown skins, large dark eyes, & a good deal of nose . . . Miss Debary, Susan & Sally all in black . . . made their appearance, & I was as civil to them as their bad breath would allow me.[8]

It is to be wondered whether any of the single young ladies in this party, together with 'all the fat girls with short noses' mentioned in the postscript, were approached by dancing partners that evening, but the queer white-necked creature later found a husband, as did the Miss Maitlands and their noses. A letter from Bath a few months later describes the writer's perspicacity in identifying an adulteress at the Upper Rooms, and her amusement at the sight of a tipsy wife pursuing her even more inebriated husband through the onlookers at the same ball.[9] Adultery could be made entertaining if it did not touch one too closely and need not affect the sinners' reception in decent society, although adulterous women were not as readily countenanced as adulterous men. Henry's wife Eliza had recently met Lord Craven in Berkshire and found his manners impeccable, despite the 'little flaw' of his keeping a mistress at the family home.[10]

Jane Austen could laugh at such contradictions, but she knew the serious effects of moral laxity on the families who had to suffer it. The most vituperative tone in her letters is reserved for the Paget family, towards whom she felt a particular animosity, perhaps because the influential Henry-William Paget, the elder brother of Charles Austen's friend Arthur, had failed to secure Charles' promotion in the Navy. She knew of the elder Paget's divorce from his first wife, following his elopement in 1808 with Lady Charlotte Wellesley, the sister-in-law of the Duke of Wellington, and of Arthur Paget's seduction of Lady Borringdon, whom he married in 1809 when her divorce was finalized, six weeks before their child was born. Jane Austen described the younger son as unreliable and subject to the bad influence of Lady Borringdon, '— I dare say the House likes Female Government.'[11] The elder brother's indiscretions, however, were not so readily excused. He had abandoned eight children, Lady Charlotte four, and the subsequent divorce proceedings granted £24,000 to the wronged husband. In addition, Paget fought a duel with Lady Charlotte's brother.[12] Writing to Fanny Knight in 1817, Jane Austen refused to take an interest in a forthcoming Paget marriage, that of Lady Caroline, a daughter of Henry-William's first marriage, to the heir to the Richmond title:

> If I were the Duchess of Richmond, I should be very miserable about my son's choice. What can be expected from a Paget, born & brought up in the centre of conjugal Infidelity & Divorces? — I will *not* be interested about Lady Caroline. I abhor all the race of Pagets.[13]

In *Mansfield Park* she had already shown how Mary Crawford's skewed opinion of men and matrimony owed much to the fraught relationship between her aunt and Admiral Crawford, and how Mary was forced to leave the family home on Mrs Crawford's death, when the Admiral's mistress moved in. She understood, too, how Maria Rushworth's adulterous elopement with Mary's brother threatened the honour of the Bertram family: 'Whom would it not injure?' asks Fanny, pronouncing that the death of all concerned would be preferable to the disgrace of Maria's public exposure: 'it appeared to her, that as far as this world alone was concerned, the greatest blessing to every one of kindred with Mrs Rushworth would be instant annihilation.'[14] Fanny's is an extreme reaction which echoes Mr

Collins' inflexible advice to Mr Bennet on Lydia's elopement, but this is adultery. Maria has committed what Edmund refers to as '"the dreadful crime"', never to be expunged, even though she might have regained some shreds of respectability by marrying Henry Crawford. Maria's 'sin' must not be countenanced; she is to be damned forever.

The author herself shows a little more sympathy for Maria's plight through her comments on the inequality of the punishment meted out, 'she must withdraw . . . to a retirement and reproach, which could allow no second spring of hope or character', whereas Henry is free to re-enter society more or less untouched:

> That punishment, the public punishment of disgrace, should in a just measure attend *his* share of the offence, is, we know, not one of the barriers, which society gives to virtue. In this world, the penalty is less equal than could be wished . . .[15]

Henry Crawford, with his Norfolk acres, will still be seen as an eligible catch despite his past, but Maria's chances of any future relationship are nil. Other female writers recognized this unfair system of applied morality:

> . . . married women . . . have hardly a civil right to save them from the grossest injuries . . . the faults of women are treated with a severity and rancour which militates against every principle of religion and common sense . . . you know there is but one fault which a woman of honour may not commit with impunity; let her only take care that she is not caught in a love intrigue . . .[16]

One of the reasons that Maria's adultery is revealed is that she foolishly does not trouble to conceal her indiscretion from servants loyal to Mrs Rushworth senior, one of whom, with her mistress' support, exposes the affair very publicly, resulting in Maria's flight from her husband's house and the damaging paragraph in a London newspaper. Again, there were contemporary examples of servants tipping off their masters to their wives' adulterous activities, as in the case of Sarah Fozard, who visited her lover with the footman in tow. He told Mr Fozard of the lovers' place of rendezvous, where they were discovered, hiding in a cupboard.[17] The consequence was, of course, divorce.

The Bertram sisters' desire for liberty from family restrictions at any cost is imputed to the dangerous influence of amateur play-acting, a situation drawn from examples in real life, at least one of which Jane Austen would have been aware, since it involved a Leigh family connection. In September 1788, Thomas-James Twisleton, then only seventeen or eighteen and still a schoolboy at Westminster, had eloped with Miss Charlotte Wattell, opposite whom he had been acting in an amateur production of *Julia* at the Freemason's Hall in London. This 'imprudent step . . . blighted all his future prospects', claimed the writer of his obituary, thirty-seven years later. His wife proved extravagant 'and otherwise misconducted herself' and the union ended in divorce.[18] Not to be outdone, his sister, Mary-Cassandra, followed in his footsteps in 1790, eloping with the future Viscount St Vincent, at the age of sixteen. In 1799, she committed adultery with the MP for Wells and was divorced by her husband. Two years later, Jane Austen was congratulating herself on identifying her 'highly rouged' relative as the adulteress whom everyone had gone to ogle at a ball in the Upper Rooms in Bath.[19]

Mrs Sherwood recalled in her memoir meeting a recently married young couple, the Wolsleys, 'who had taken an airing during the autumn to Gretna Green and had come to Arley Hall to await the pardon of their friends'. Their precipitate elopement, and that of the lady's younger sister, 'who made just such a scampering match as her sister did', was blamed on their parents' dilettante passion for play-acting. Mrs Wolsley openly admitted that she did not much like her husband, and never had, but 'acting lovers together in a play . . . we said, "Suppose we really go off together"; and so we did, and here we are.'[20] The Revd Thomas Gisborne would not have been surprised. He firmly laid the blame for over-familiarity with the opposite sex and its dangerous consequences on private play-acting, especially among the rich:

> For some years past the custom of acting plays in private theatres, fitted up by individuals of fortune, has occasionally prevailed. It is a custom liable to this objection among others; that it is almost certain to prove, in its effects, injurious to the female performers [in destroying] diffidence by the unrestrained familiarity with persons of the opposite sex, which inevitably results from being joined with them in the drama.[21]

Jane Austen read Gisborne's treatise in 1805 and it appears likely that this section influenced her portrayal of the private theatricals at Mansfield

Park. Tom Bertram's self-reproach concerning the consequences to Maria of 'the dangerous intimacy of his unjustifiable theatre' bears this out. Novel reading also came in for its share of the blame in encouraging the heated fancies of the young: 'Of all the arrows which Cupid has shot at youthful hearts, the modern novel is the keenest,' claimed *The Universal Magazine* as early as 1772. 'In contempt of the Marriage Act post-chaises and young couples run smoothly on the North Road.'[22] Lydia Languish in Sheridan's *The Rivals*, an avid reader of sentimental novels and a despoiler of Fordyce's *Sermons* – she tears out the pages to use as hair-curling papers – is highly disappointed when her marriage plans become as unexciting as 'a mere Smithfield bargain', and she is done out of 'one of the most sentimental elopements! – so becoming a disguise! – so amiable a ladder of Ropes! – Conscious Moon – four horses – Scotch parson – . . . and such paragraphs in the News-papers!'[23] All of the sentimental conventions of elopement are listed here and the effect is humorous, but Jane Austen showed the darker, more serious consequences of such unrestrained conduct. The only elopement she condones in her novels is that planned by Colonel Brandon in order to save the woman he loves from a forced marriage to his elder brother, but she does not condemn either Lydia Bennet or Julia Bertram to remote farmhouses, to live out the remainder of their days far from polite society. She marries them off instead to unsatisfactory husbands.

Romantically inclined young couples denied their parents' blessing, or others – like Julia Bertram – with different motives, ran off to tie the knot in Scotland, where the Hardwicke Act did not apply. Scottish law only required two witnesses for every wedding and the bride and groom to be at least sixteen. Gretna Green was ideally placed to cater for clandestine alliances, being nine miles from the last English staging post at Carlisle and just one mile over the border with Scotland. A local blacksmith, Joseph Paisley, came up with the idea of offering marriage services in the 1750s. 'He is neither a clergyman nor a magistrate,' reported one foreign traveller to Scotland in 1810, 'but reads the English marriage-service to tranquillize the scruples of the lady, and persuade her she is rightfully married.'[24] He added that for the price of a glass of grog, tourists were allowed a sight of the illustrious blacksmith, but he was not the only tradesman who performed the rites, or took advantage of a good business opportunity:

> Here the young pair may be instantly united by a fisherman, a joiner, or a blacksmith, who marry from two guineas a job to a dram of whisky. But the price is generally adjusted by the information of the postillions from Carlisle, who are in the pay of one or other of the above worthies; but even the drivers, in case of necessity, have been known to undertake the sacerdotal office.[25]

So, even transport was laid on, and if the young couple were being hotly pursued by desperate relatives intent on prevention, the good offices of the drivers would prove invaluable. Joseph Paisley's death at the age of eighty-two, on 9 January 1811, was reported in most newspapers, together with the news that a young friend had taken over the role of 'coupler', so 'there is no fear that the business will fall off, as three weddings have already taken place since the interment of the old man,'[26] *The Lady's Magazine* reassured its readers. One of those matches had already been reported by the same magazine earlier that year: 'March 8. At Gretna Green, the Hon. Charles Evan Law, son of Lord Ellenborough, to Eliz. Sophia, sister of Sir C. Nightingale, Bart.'[27] It was not to their advantage for the parents of run-away couples to advertise the fact, so presumably Lord Ellenborough's son paid for the entry himself. Elopements attracted a degree of celebrity and he was probably keen to make public his fashionable disdain for parental interference, especially when his father was the Attorney-General. Many elopements involved the rich and the aristocratic, usually because parents with money and titles were the ones most likely to push their children into mercenary alliances, yet this was not always the case. The marriage of a considerable heiress to the eldest son of an aristocratic family sounds like a match made in heaven for the families concerned, yet Sarah Anne Child, the daughter of Robert Child the banker, eloped to Gretna Green with John Fane, tenth Earl of Westmorland, because her father opposed the match. The more down-to-earth viewed such behaviour as akin to madness: 'What say you to this elopement of Lady Charlotte Hornby?' asked Miss Iremonger. 'It occasions much talk & much speculation . . . & I incline to think that it partakes more of Insanity . . .'[28] In *Sense and Sensibility*, Jane Austen has the self-regarding Robert Ferrars, with more money than sense, elope with Lucy Steele, to pre-empt his mother's wrath and because it was a fashionable thing to do: 'He was . . . very proud of marrying privately without his mother's consent.'[29]

In early March, 1816, a flight to Gretna which would have interested the Austens was reported in Cheltenham. The woman involved was Anne Rachel Hicks, unattractive, unintelligent, but a niece of William Chute and heiress to two substantial properties. Her parents had paraded her at the Cheltenham assemblies, with the predictable outcome – she had fallen prey to an Irish fortune-hunter, the penniless heir to a baronetcy, William Lambart Cromie. Her parents forbade the match, so the couple ran off to Gretna Green, as the local press reported:

> A great sensation was excited in this town, last week, by the sudden disappearance of Miss H., daughter of Sir W.H. and sole presumptive heiress to more than one large fortune. The young lady took the road to Scotland, by a circuitous route, accompanied by Mr Cromy, to whom, according to a letter received from her, dated Carlisle, she has been united by the Gretna Green Parson . . . A pursuit was ineffectually instituted for the purpose of bringing back the fair fugitive.[30]

Presented with a *fait accompli*, most parents who did not entirely cast off their erring children arranged for a more conventional ceremony to be held in England on their return. Three weeks after their Gretna Green escapade, Anne Rachel and Cromie were formally married in London, as reported in the April edition of the *Gentleman's Magazine*: 'March 16. Re-married, W. – L. Cromie, esq. only son of Sir Wm. Cromie, bart. to Anne Rachel, only child of Sir Wm. Hicks, bart. of Whitcombe Park, co. Gloucester.' The couple were then dispatched to the Continent until the gossip died down, but Anne's first letter to her parents from Paris revealed that her husband had run off with her maid.

The Austen family itself came under the public gaze in 1826, when Edward Knight of Godmersham's eldest son, also Edward, eloped to Gretna Green with his sister Fanny Knatchbull's eldest step-daughter. They ran off on May the 13th, from the Knatchbull's London house, having encountered opposition to their alliance, mainly from Fanny's husband, Sir Edward Knatchbull, whom Caroline Austen held solely accountable for the young couple's desperate flight. He had objected to the close family connection, although in reality there were no blood ties, and the complications existed entirely in his head.[31] No doubt Sir Edward Knatchbull's anger on the occasion was heightened by anxiety about Fanny, who was pregnant with her second child. Edward Knight was worried too, but also understanding of his son's position. Although he described the elopement as 'a sad rash step with [sic] nothing can justify, whatever Degree of Palliation there may be', he had no intention of adding to the opprobrium, determining instead to 'restore tranquillity with as much propriety as possible'.[32] On the fugitives' return, they found shelter at Chawton, where they were welcomed by Cassandra and her mother and given moral support by other members of the Austen family in Hampshire. On June the 15th, they were married under the English system of law at Steventon Church, by the groom's brother, William. That summer, Edward Knight gave his eldest son and new daughter-in-law the Great House at Chawton as their permanent home.

Abductions, especially of heiresses and minors, decreased in number as a result of the Hardwicke Act, but plenty of examples still spiced up the plots of sensational novels, many of which Jane Austen read. She found Mary Brunton's *Self-Control*, published in 1810, particularly entertaining and read it more than once. The virtuous heroine is knocked senseless and abducted by the dastardly anti-hero who smuggles her away to Canada. Nothing daunted, she escapes by canoeing herself out of danger and back to England unsullied. No abductions feature in Jane Austen's fiction, but George Wickham's planned elopement with the fifteen-year-old Georgiana Darcy comes close. In real life, the occasional abduction was reported in the Press, as Parson Woodforde noted on 16 April 1791. One of the London newspapers was offering a reward of £100 for 'apprehending one Richard Perry . . . for running away with a Miss Clarke (about 14 Years of Age) from a boarding School at Bristol. Her fortune great, £6000 per Annum'.[33]

Couples determined to marry against their parents' will did not have to go to Scotland to effect their plans. Some disappeared into the anonymity of London and other large cities and lived together while they waited for banns to be called, or attempted to purchase a licence. Tom Lefroy's parents had married secretly in Ireland in 1765, the marriage being performed by Anthony Lefroy's regimental chaplain. Ann Gardner was the daughter of an Irish squire and Anthony was a twenty-three-year-old ensign with little money, which must account for their apprehension of family opposition on both sides. In 1774, they went through a public marriage ceremony at Limerick Cathedral in the hope that Anthony's rich Langlois uncles would smile on the alliance and Tom was the first boy to be born after this, in 1776.[34] He had five older sisters and found as a consequence that he was unable to follow his father's example and marry a girl with scant fortune. The whole family relied on Tom as the eldest son to make a good marriage and Uncle Benjamin Langlois, who had paid for Tom to train for the law, would countenance no further misalliances.

When families of runaways learned of their disappearance, they were as distraught as the Bennets were when Lydia left Brighton with Wickham. News like this always travelled fast, by way of servants and close neighbours, and the family's reputation teetered on the edge of respectability until a marriage came to light. Dorothea Herbert describes the reaction to her brother Otway's elopement to Dublin with Miss Russell, whose father had refused Otway's open request for his daughter's hand. Her descriptive style is reminiscent of the mock-sentimental tone of *Love and Freindship*, with enough fainting and running mad to convince Laura and Sophia of the family's laudable sensibilities:

> Next evening we were seated at Tea when Mr J O Donnels Servant came up to know if Miss Russel drank Tea with us — on being answerd in the Negative he swore by God then she was gone off — We ran to search for Otway but he too was Missing and we had soon enough to inform us of their Elopement together — We all ran about like people distracted — My Mother fainted away — the Girls and I were in hystericks and the Boys galloped about without knowing where to pursue the fugitives . . . We sat up all Night whilst the whole Neighbourhood was in an uproar and scouring the Country for the rash Pair, who, we at last heard, had taken the Road to Dublin — They got themselves married on the Road, and were remarried by License in Dublin.[35]

The couple subsequently wrote to obtain pardon from both families, but while the Herberts forgave them immediately, Captain Russell withheld his blessing and only relented on his deathbed. Elizabeth and Jane Bennet are only too aware that their youngest sister's thoughtless conduct has the potential to damage their marriage prospects, but it takes Mr Collins to air this uncharitable, but commonly held view: 'this false step in one daughter, will be injurious to the fortunes of all the others, for who . . .

will connect themselves with such a family?' Lydia's death, he states, would have been a blessing in comparison and Mr Bennet would be well advised to abandon her to her just deserts.[36] The Revd Fordyce had opinions on such matters, as one would expect, and although it was to his credit that he recognized the unfairness of condemning women alone, it didn't stop him going along with the common view:

> The world, I know not how, overlooks in our sex a thousand irregularities, which it never forgives in yours; so that the honour and peace of a family are, in this view, much more dependent on the conduct of daughters than of sons; and one young lady going astray shall subject her relations to such discredit and distress, as the united good conduct of all her brothers and sisters, supposing them numerous, shall scarce ever be able to repair.[37]

Lydia Bennet's elopement provides the 'spiteful old ladies' in Meryton with an endless supply of malicious speculation, and when their hopes that Lydia will either prove herself a common prostitute or be locked away from decent society 'in some distant farmhouse' are thwarted by the news of her marriage, they comfort themselves with the certainty that happiness with such a husband will be impossible. Mary Bennet's conduct-book pronouncements on the irretrievable loss of female reputation through such behaviour as Lydia's are challenged by Jane Austen's creation of an alternative outcome. The kind of husband Lydia acquires is punishment enough, but her reputation, and that of the whole family, is saved by her marriage and the local gossips will soon forget a discredited Bennet daughter once she has been removed to Newcastle. The likes of Lady Catherine and Mr Collins may regard Lydia's rescue as 'a patched-up business', and decry Mr Bennet's subsequent reception of the couple at Longbourne, but Lydia regains her footing in society and there is no long-term damage done to the Bennet family, nor, if the following newspaper paragraphs are taken at face value, to the reputation of a young female darling of society, although it is difficult to see how her situation would be improved by the writer's insinuations. The details were divulged in 1791, under the headline FASHIONABLE SCANDAL:

> One of the most beautiful of our young Ladies of Quality, whose person has been praised in poetry, and represented in painting, more frequently perhaps

> than any other . . . is at present the theme of fashionable scandal.
>
> Nothing less than an *elopement* from the house of her mother is imputed to her, and an absence of three weeks, just at the time that her *footman* was also missing!
>
> She returned, however, to her family, about a month since, and is now with them at a watering-place. The error being over-looked by her friends, she holds her station in the fashionable circle, and will probably, in a short time, find her repentance more remembered than her fault.[38]

Elopements were not exclusively the province of the rich and fashionable. In *Jack and Alice*, Jane Austen has the governess, after instructing her young charge 'in the paths of virtue', run off with the butler.[39] One of Miss Heber's correspondents bemoaned the fact that her cook had inconveniently absconded with a lover on a day when she happened to expect a party of gentlemen visitors and 'have only the Kitchen-maid to dress the Dinner'. The cook had apprised her mistress beforehand that she would be leaving the house at six the following morning, in order to be married in London:

> The scheme We thought very rash & hazardous . . . such a plan might be attended with great danger to herself as the young man is under age — & of course (as we suppose not having the Consent of his Guardians) cd not procure a Licence that wd stand good in Law — & that it would not be safe for her to remain wth him in London till they were three times ask'd in Church. Of these circumstances I inform'd her — & she assured me she determined to attend to all I said — but soon after, a New Gold *Watch*, Various *Great Coats*, Gowns, Riding Hats, Caps, etc, etc, sent by her admirer, proved more powerful arguments than sober prudence cd supply.[40]

The cook was risking her reputation, because she would have to stay in London, unmarried, like Lydia Bennet, until the banns were read on three consecutive Sundays. It is to be hoped that her young lover proved more trustworthy than Mr Wickham, since there would be no Mr Darcy to bribe him into fulfilling his commitments.

Gossip conducted at a distance carried its confusions and misunderstandings, rather like a game of Chinese whispers. The widowed Sir Thomas Williams, whose first marriage to their cousin Jane and Cassandra had witnessed back in 1792, was, according to Jane, drawing on a letter from her brother Charles in November 1800, looking every inch the lover and his chosen lady was one 'Miss Emma Wabshaw': 'handsome, accomplished, amiable, & everything but rich. — Perhaps the report of his being to marry a Miss Fanshawe might originate in his attentions to this very lady; the names are not unlike.' The confusion over names and fortunes continued for a month, until it was discovered by means of news from another quarter that the lady's name was actually Wapshire, and that she was tolerably well-off: 'I hope that I have now gained the real truth, & that my letters may in future go on without conveying any farther contradictions of what was last asserted about Sir Thomas Williams & Miss Wapshire.' Jane could not resist adding, 'I wish I could be certain that her name were Emma . . .'[41] Ironically, the lady's name was neither Emma, nor Wapshire, but Mary Wapshare. At least Captain Williams *did* marry her at the end of 1800.

Jane Austen understood very well how gossip could spread – how supposedly secret matters passed into the public domain. In an early letter, we find her at Rowling, retailing the gossip about a forthcoming marriage, which is 'a great secret, & only known to half the Neighbourhood, you must not mention it'.[42] Perhaps she remembered this occasion when she created the perfect way of ensuring that the news of Emma and Mr Knightley's marriage plans reached their neighbours – they tell Mrs Weston, knowing full well that her husband will be unable to keep the 'secret' to himself. From him it spreads to Miss Bates, then on to Mrs Cole, Mrs Perry and Mrs Elton, which is just what the engaged couple had been prepared for: 'they had calculated from the time of its being known at Randalls, how soon it would be over Highbury; and were thinking of themselves, as the evening wonder in many a family circle, with great sagacity.'[43] Mrs Bennet also pretends discretion where Jane and Bingley's engagement is concerned: 'Mrs Bennet was privileged to whisper it to Mrs Philips, and *she* ventured, without any permission, to do the same by all her neighbours in Meryton.'[44]

Gossip was not often so beneficial to its objects. Mrs Jennings openly voices her belief that Eliza Williams is Colonel Brandon's illegitimate daughter and encourages her maid to gossip about Willoughby and Marianne's visit to Allenham, news which she then retails to the twenty people at Sir John's dinner table. Marianne's unguarded behaviour with Willoughby leads to inevitable gossip about a forthcoming marriage, most of it spread by Mrs Jennings and her daughter Charlotte Palmer. Elinor's denials are not believed:

> "Don't we all know that it must be a match, that they were over head and ears in love with each other from the first moment they met? . . . did not I know that your sister came to town with me on purpose to buy wedding clothes? Come, come, this won't do. Because you are so sly about it yourself, you think nobody else has any senses; but it is no such thing, I can tell you, for it has been known all over the town this ever so long. I tell every body of it, and so does Charlotte."[45]

Marianne faces ridicule and a ruined reputation as a result of everyone's perception that she has thrown herself at Willoughby and been jilted. News of his engagement to Miss Grey and her £50,000 spreads in the same way: '"Mrs Taylor told me of it half an hour ago, and she was told it by a particular friend of Miss Grey herself . . ."'[46] The Dashwoods' own servant, Thomas, is maliciously duped in Exeter by the new Mrs Robert Ferrars into taking back the news to Barton Cottage that Lucy and Edward are now man and wife. Gossip in *Sense and Sensibility* is almost entirely hurtful, whether consciously intended or otherwise, whereas the news which reaches Anne Elliot's ears in Bath through her old schoolfriend is helpful to her. The invalid Mrs Smith in Westgate Buildings thrives on the entertaining gossip of Nurse Rooke, which includes the rumours circulating in Bath society concerning Anne and Mr Elliot. Mrs Smith learns from Nurse Rooke's intelligence from Marlborough Buildings that Anne and her cousin are frequently together and that their marriage is looked upon as certain and desirable. The gossip from this quarter extends to Mrs Clay's ambitions of becoming the next Lady Elliot and Mr Elliot's apprehension of her probable success. As well as serving its purpose of distracting Mrs Smith, Nurse Rooke's communications apprise Anne of Mr Elliot's real intentions towards herself and her family.

Common report often focused on family and fortune – as Mrs Drake pointed out to Miss Heber, in a letter telling of a forthcoming marriage: 'Her fortune is, I hear, £60,000 in the 3 p. Cents, and her Brother, who is in the Guards, has £150,000, but this I did not hear from any of the Family, only common report.'[47] In the same way, news of Darcy's fortune and extensive property is in general circulation within five minutes of his entering the Meryton assembly room and reports of Bingley's income and background precede his arrival at Netherfield. How did such precise information concerning annual incomes, the value of property and the inheritances of young ladies such as Miss King and Mary Crawford find its way into common knowledge? Servants boasted of their employers' fortunes and prospects, as Mr Elliot's valet did at the inn at Lyme and news of Mr Bingley's large income came from the letting agent for Netherfield. Wills were published and anyone might learn their contents. The type of property a man could afford to lease or buy was a good indication of his yearly income, also the kind of carriage he kept; invaluable information for mothers with marriageable daughters. Mr Bingley's chaise and four horses alone signify a disposable income of at least £1,000 and Darcy's house in London could not be considered on an annual income of less than £10,000.

Jane Austen's neighbours at Steventon and Chawton, like neighbours everywhere, foresaw financial collapse for those who were conspicuous spenders and certain ruin for anyone discovered flouting the rules of social conduct. Everyone was fair game. As Mr Bennet states in *Pride and Prejudice*: '"For what do we live, but to make sport for our neighbours, and laugh at them in our turn?"'[48] Cassandra, receiving Jane's gossipy news at Godmersham regarding Mrs Powlett's expensive fripperies, would have read aloud her communication to the family there, together with her speculation about a local romance and the marital prospects of the four unmarried daughters of a dead acquaintance, confirmation of two imminent marriages and the scandal of Lord Craven's live-in mistress.[49] A personal link with the subjects made the stories more piquant, but connections were not essential for the gossip to be relished. Letters served as newspapers, to be read and discussed and Jane Austen's were always packed with detail, some of it abusive, all of it colourful, despite her frequent complaint that she had nothing much to tell. As she grew older, more serious observations on the relationships between husbands and wives and the effects of continual childbearing were mixed in with the gossip. James-Edward Austen-Leigh in his *Memoir* found little in his aunt's letters to recommend to her novel readers. He remarked on the occasional vein of humour gleaming through what he considered to be the dead weight of domestic detail and concluded that there was nothing of interest, no political statement, no literary pronouncements, but he excised the juicier sections from the letters that he chose to include as examples of Jane Austen's epistolary style. His second cousin, Lord Brabourne, who published in 1884 the first collection of Jane Austen's letters inherited from his mother, Lady Knatchbull, followed the same practice. Names were replaced by blanks and the wording of the more disrespectful remarks altered to spare Victorian blushes. 'Scandal & Gossip;' Jane Austen wrote to one correspondent, '— yes I dare say you are well stocked;'[50] but that was not going to prevent her adding to the store.

8

A Contract of Mutual Agreeableness

The courtship successfully completed, the wedding ceremony over and the honeymoon period drawing to a close, conjugal happiness became the next, achievable goal for those fortunate enough to enjoy mutual respect and well-matched temperaments, qualities which would take any couple a long way down the road to marital accord. Jane Austen's heroes and heroines are evidently blessed with such sunny prospects and their future lives together – always active, always communicating, happiest in each other's company – are exemplified in the successful partnerships of two sets of minor characters, Admiral and Mrs Croft and Elizabeth Bennet's Uncle and Aunt Gardiner. The Crofts' marriage is the most companionate in all of Jane Austen's fiction; they are described as 'particularly attached and happy', interested in everything and everyone, but most comfortable when they could '"shut ourselves into our lodgings, and draw in our chairs . . ."'[1] Anne Elliot watches them with delight, as they walk the streets of Bath together, Mrs Croft as animated as her husband in conversations with old naval acquaintances: 'it was a most attractive picture of happiness', and illustrated in some detail, because this is the kind of easy companionship that Anne and Captain Wentworth will eventually enjoy. The link that is made between these two relationships in the early chapters of the novel establishes compatibility and sympathetic affection as the firm basis for married contentment. The strength of such an attachment distinguishes the Crofts from every other pair in the novel, apart from Anne and Wentworth:

> With the exception, perhaps, of Admiral and Mrs Croft . . . (Anne could allow no other exception even among the married couples) there could have been no two hearts so open, no tastes so similar, no feelings so in unison, no countenances so beloved.[2]

For Elizabeth Bennet, the example of her Aunt and Uncle Gardiner's companionable partnership provides a salutary contrast to that of her ill-matched parents. The Gardiners are well-suited in health and temper, cheerfulness and affection, intelligence and sense. With both examples before her, Elizabeth is sufficiently qualified to appreciate Darcy's potential compatibility as a husband, just as she thinks she must lose him:

> His understanding and temper, though unlike her own, would have answered all her wishes. It was an union that must have been to the advantage of both; by her ease and liveliness, his mind might have been softened, his manners improved, and from his judgement, information, and knowledge of the world, she must have received benefit of greater importance.[3]

The brief glimpse Jane Austen gives us into Elizabeth and Darcy's marriage bears this out. Elizabeth teases him, much to Georgiana's alarmed astonishment, into a more relaxed approach to life; he introduces her to a wider, more informed view of the world and provides the comfort and elegance which were lacking in her previous surroundings. Both bring something to the union, both gain emotionally and mentally from the alliance. 'Similarity of mind and principle is the only true basis of harmony',[4] stated Mary Hays, and Edmund and Fanny Bertram prove the point. Their marital happiness is rooted in their shared appreciation of domestic life, the countryside and books. Marianne Dashwood would have applauded Mary Hays, but pushed her assertion to its extreme: '"I could not be happy with a man whose taste did not in every point coincide with my own. He must enter into all my feelings; the same books, the same music must charm us both."'[5] What she settles for in the end is 'strong esteem and lively friendship' as the basis for her marriage to Colonel Brandon.

Most writers of conduct literature, from the radical Mary Hays to the conservative James Fordyce, agreed that happiness in marriage depended on a union of minds, strong affection and mutual respect, although a significant number stressed the expediency of wives accepting a subservient role in the relationship. The more traditional, but not exclusively male, writers adopted a patronizing tone, addressing their audience as 'Fair Readers', reminding them of their marriage vow to obey their husbands and promising that unquestioning obedience would be rewarded: 'they may be well-assured, that gentle and kind obedience to the wishes of their Husbands, is the surest means to subdue them to love, and to reign triumphant in their breasts.'[6] St Paul's much-quoted pronouncements regarding wives submitting to their husbands were invariably produced as biblical back-up.

The Revd Thomas Gisborne tried a variety of approaches to the issue. At first, his opinions appear rational, moderate and reassuringly sympathetic to women. He recommended himself by stating that marrying for love was essential, since, 'Where strong affection prevails, a spirit of accommodation will prevail also.'[7] So far, so good, but all too soon it becomes disappointingly clear that he envisaged this accommodating spirit operating more generously in women than in men. He fell back on the customary argument that for true marital harmony, the husband must be granted pre-eminence over the wife. If he was a religious man, then there would be no risk of autocratic cruelty; he would fulfil God's will and be a kind protector. In return, the grateful wife was to be endlessly good tempered, but not witty or satirical, to acquire only those accomplishments which were pleasing to her husband and to run the house. Even in this area of her duties, however, a wife was to assume no automatic authority, but act obediently, according to her husband's wishes. She was to stay at home as a rule and not wish to travel, which must be in her best interests, Gisborne counselled, since women were known and respected on home territory, more than they could ever be in other places. He deprecated the 'rage of rambling' and brandished St Paul – woman must be 'a keeper at home'[8] – as a big stick to beat wandering females back indoors.

James Fordyce, all too predictably, was an enthusiastic advocate of married women's limitation to the domestic sphere. For him, exemplary wives 'will love home, be attached to their husbands, attentive to their families, reasonable in their wishes, moderate in their expences, and not addicted to external show'.[9] Wives were to occupy their 'honourable station' through unquestioning devotion to their husbands, chiefly as soothers of the male brow:

> a kind of softer companions, who by nameless delightful sympathies and endearments, might improve our pleasures and soothe our pains; to lighten the load of domestic cares, and thereby leave us more at leisure for rougher labours, or

> severer studies, and finally, to spread a certain grace and embellishment over human life.[10]

A husband's concerns and happiness must invariably take precedence and his wife must be tireless in her strict adherence to Fordyce's list of commandments, the majority of which begin 'She will not', in pursuit of her man's ultimate well-being:

> She will not only return his love with equal affection, but endeavour to ensure and heighten his esteem by every engaging and respectable virtue. She will not only avoid whatever might provoke or displease, but study to deserve well of him by promoting his interest, and raising his reputation; . . . uniformly and constantly every day of her life.[11]

Mary Wollstonecraft was not the only woman whose hackles rose at such blatantly one-sided advice. 'Such a woman ought to be an angel – or she is an ass –', she remarked with asperity. Fordyce's portrait of a fulfilled wife was that of a 'house slave', she protested, a 'domestic drudge, whose being is absorbed in that of a tyrant's'.[12] Men did themselves no favours by demanding such unquestioning obedience and diffidence, she argued; a tractable, repressed woman rarely made a good companion, while wives with minds of their own were better able to understand and befriend their husbands. This is the impression Jane Austen gives in *Emma*: the relationship between Mr Knightley and his wife will be disputatiously healthier than that between John Knightley and Isabella. Emma's sister is a true conduct-book paragon, the worshipping wife, who has learned to ignore her husband's often impatient temper, rather than question and perhaps moderate it. As a consequence, neither husband nor wife enjoys the full benefits of a companionate marriage.

Eugenia Stanhope viewed Fordyce's recipe for conjugal felicity with a cynical eye, and while advocating wifely self-effacement as the best strategy for a peaceful life, she exposed male superiority as a sham. Far from believing in the existence of mutuality, she stated that there was only one path to happiness for a married woman and that involved 'conforming herself to the Sentiments of her Husband' and making no demands on his time or attention: 'To have your Husband always pleased with your Company, my Dear, the great Secret is to let him have it only when he pleases.'[13] While a wife would be well-advised to consider her husband a qualified judge of people and circumstances, she should, however, only accept his opinions on trifling matters; on issues of consequence, a trusted friend's view should be sought, privately. Her message was unequivocal and subversive – men were fallible, flawed creatures, requiring their own way in all things and every sensible wife knew it – but she drew back from a direct challenge to the *status quo*, however biased its application:

> Men have naturally great Obstinacy; the best of them have some of it: They all have Pride too; and the best of them some times the most of it. They do not love to be forced, nor even to be persuaded out of their Customs. They cannot bear to be led by a Woman to any Thing. They have a settled Opinion of us, as Inferior in Natural Authority and in Understanding . . . Endeavour not to get the better of this Opinion . . . 'tis not your Business to reform the World . . .[14]

Walking on eggs might be a tricky feat, but outright opposition was dangerous for a wife to attempt, given her economic and social dependency. Better to tread carefully, settle for a safe if circumscribed existence and accept that the contract of agreeableness connived at in many conduct manuals relied almost entirely on female submission and had very little to do with mutuality in any area of domestic life. This was the kind of advice given by woman to woman, in an attempt to highlight the double standards inherent in the marital state, but many married couples must have inhabited a kind of middle ground, where some happiness for both partners was available without too much of a struggle. The degree of marital harmony achieved by the Crofts and the Gardiners is as much a rarity in Jane Austen's fiction as it probably was in real life, but not all marriages of convenience or intellectual inequality led to domestic grief. The examples of Mr and Mrs Allen, Charlotte and Mr Collins, even Willoughby and his disagreeable Sophia, indicate otherwise. A tolerable shared existence could be achieved in a variety of ways and not exclusively on male terms.

Jane Austen had observed a sufficient number of marriages among her family and neighbours, and read enough of Gisborne, Fordyce and other conduct-book writers, to draw her own conclusions. Her mother and father's well-suited, equable relationship appeared to provide the Austen children with a workable model for their future alliances. James' daughter

Caroline remembered the companionable hospitality of the Chawton household from her childhood days and there is no reason to think the Steventon ménage any different:

> . . . it was a cheerful house — my Uncles, one or another, frequently coming for a few days; and they were all pleasant in their own family — I have thought since, after having seen more of other households, *wonderfully*, as the family talk had much of spirit and vivacity, and it was never troubled by disagreements as it was not in their habit to argue with each other — There always was perfect harmony amongst the brothers and sisters, and over my Grandmother's door might have been inscribed the text, "Behold how good — and joyful a thing it is, brethren, to dwell together in unity." There was firm family union, never broken but by death —[15]

The experience of domestic concord was carried through into the brothers' married lives and formed the basis of the enduring love and companionship between their unmarried sisters. Caroline's account of the Austens' family life has more than a touch of idealized retrospection – she was thirteen when her Aunt Jane died, and only four when the Austen ladies moved to Chawton – yet all of their dealings with each other seem marked by true affection and understanding. That family conflict did sometimes cloud the horizon is evidenced by a child's scrawl in the seven-year-old Jane's *Fables choisies*: 'Mothers angry father's gone out',[16] and who knows how strained family relationships might have been in the winter following Jane's rejection of Harris Bigg-Wither?

The Austen sons, excluding George, all achieved relative happiness in marriage, each in his own way. Twenty-seven year old James Austen met his first wife, Anne Mathew, while he was curate in the small vicarage at Overton. It was not an equal alliance as far as status was concerned, since she was the granddaughter of the Duke of Ancaster and daughter of a General, but James' future prospects as potential heir to the Leigh-Perrot property may have convinced her parents of the eligibility of the match. Anne was also thirty and James must have seemed like her final chance. They married on a joint annual income of £300 and lived beyond their means, Anne keeping a carriage and James a pack of harriers. There is nothing to suggest that the marriage was anything other than equable, but it lasted for only three years. Anne died in the spring of 1795, leaving a two-year-old daughter, Anna, who drove her father to distraction by wandering inconsolably around the house, calling for her mother. His first experience of matrimony encouraged James to look for a second wife just over a year later. His cousin Eliza declined his advances, but he had more luck with Mary Lloyd, marrying her in January 1797.

The relationship was not without its problems, particularly for other members of the Austen family, Anna especially, yet Mary and James seemed happy enough with each other. The connection with James' previous father-in-law was kept up and the General continued to grant his granddaughter an allowance of £100 a year, an amount not to be sniffed at, although Mary found the old man terrifying, if considerate towards her. Poor Mary must have had her trials, not least her pretty, clear-skinned step-daughter, who viewed her with Anne Mathew's beautiful dark eyes, a constant reminder of James' first choice and her own pockmarked face. Caroline Austen provides evidence of Mary's sensitivity, recording her mother's unwillingness to sit for a miniature portrait in 1811.[17] Mary's habit of wrong-footing Anna on the slightest provocation did not diminish with time either: 'Mary begins to fancy, because she has received no message on the subject, that Anna does not mean to answer her Letter; but it must be for the pleasure of fancying it,' remarked Jane in a letter from Godmersham, when Anna was fifteen.[18] Eliza de Feuillide, another beauty with whom James had fancied himself in love and to whom he had proposed in 1796, was not to be mentioned at all. Mary was not even second choice, then, but third. She avoided meeting Eliza, took every opportunity of speaking ill of her, and ensured that her two children and Anna were kept well away. Mrs Austen's early confidence in Mary's qualities as a loving daughter-in-law and substitute mother, were not wholly realized either, but James made himself completely happy, writing verses on her virtues as a wife, even if others noticed her lack of love for Anna, her sharp tongue and dogmatic opinions. More than his brothers, James had to learn the hard way how to keep the peace. He never spoke of his first wife, took scant notice of Anna, and allowed her to grow up feeling slighted and of little estimation to either father or step-mother.[19] Jane noticed her brother's seeming indifference and attempted to correct it by praising Anna's abilities and good taste, but with no visible success. James acknowledged her compliments with neither smiles nor words.[20] Little wonder that Anna developed a spirit of defensive intransigence, contracting secret engagements and rebelliously cutting off her hair at the age of fifteen.

It is from Jane's pen that the most incisive observation of James' second marriage is derived. As early as 1798, she was writing to Cassandra, noting Mary's attempts to monopolize their eldest brother's time: 'James seems to have taken to his old Trick of coming to Steventon inspite of Mary's reproaches, for he was here before Breakfast, & is now paying us a second visit.'[21] Another year's experience of Mary's ways and manners did not improve Jane's or Cassandra's opinion. After spending sixteen shillings on the present of a black lace veil in Bath, Jane remarked, 'I hope the half of that sum will not greatly exceed what You had intended to offer up on the altar of Sister-in-law affection.'[22] It is clear that the gift was an obligatory offering, rather than a voluntary one and all the more galling, since Jane had previously purchased a cheaper veil which proved dirty and ragged when she examined it more closely. Mary's irascibility drove Jane into making unfair comparisons between the situation at Steventon after the birth of Mary's first child and that obtaining at the much grander Godmersham. Mary's failure to make herself or her surroundings attractive is remarked on – her bedroom curtains are too thin, she has no dressing gown – whereas Elizabeth, in her spotless white dress and cap, is commended for her pretty appearance.[23] Mary did her best to keep up with Godmersham practices, turning one of the rooms in the vicarage into a nursery, hiring a nursemaid and begging patterns for children's clothes from her wealthier sister-in-law. She was still fretting about Elizabeth's childcare regime two years after Caroline's birth in 1805, pestering Cassandra to keep a note of how often Elizabeth fed her baby during the course of a day, and with what.[24] In her turn, Mary found some consolation in criticizing Elizabeth's children, expecting them to be troublesome on her first visit to Godmersham in the summer of 1808 and having to protect her small daughter against their boisterous teasing. Following Elizabeth's death at Godmersham later that year, the two eldest boys stayed initially at Steventon with Mary and James, travelling on to their grandmother's at Southampton soon afterwards. When they arrived, they produced a letter from Mary commending their behaviour, rare praise indeed, for which Jane had hardly dared hope.[25]

When the Austens moved to Bath in 1801, James and Mary acted as one in the scramble to get their hands on as much of the Steventon farm and household property as cheaply as they could; Mary was adept at pleading poverty. 'The whole World is in a conspiracy to enrich one part of our family at the expence of another,' Jane complained, when the valuations did not match her own idea of what items were worth.[26] 'Mary is more minute in her account of their own Gains than in ours – probably being better informed in them,' she stated bitterly.[27] She witnessed the familiar trappings of her past slipping away inexorably into her brother and sister-in-law's hands and pointedly declined an invitation to the couple's fourth wedding anniversary party on January the 17th, at which event Jane pictured her sister-in-law in true Mrs Norris style, finding 'all the festivity she can in contriving for everybody's comfort, & being thwarted or teized by almost everybody's temper'.[28] As a wife, Mary was reckoned a bad influence on her husband, making him a difficult guest to entertain whenever he stayed with his mother and sisters. He became a constant source of irritation, as he restlessly paced the rooms and sent the servants scurrying for endless glasses of water. Worse than this in Jane's eyes, he failed to fulfil his duty as a clever, conversable brother, he had absorbed too many of his wife's narrow opinions to make his conversation at all spontaneous.[29] James' happiness in marriage derived from agreeing with his wife on most matters and avoiding any intelligent discussion of literature which would exclude her. She was no great reader and perhaps felt overawed by her in-laws' enthusiasm for the written word: 'Mary, I believe, has little pleasure from that or any other book,' reported Jane on Mary's lack of interest in one evening's shared reading of a very entertaining novel.[30]

Mary comes across as the kind of woman who could make conjugal existence a misery if she was crossed and Jane certainly complained that she stirred up trouble in the family, by failing to exercise better judgement regarding what the elderly Mrs Austen should be told. When Ben Lefroy was causing problems on his engagement to Anna, Mary kept Mrs Austen up to date with his unsociable behaviour. Jane, having only recently persuaded her mother out of a lingering illness, wrote to Cassandra with unconcealed irritation: 'How can Mrs J. Austen be so provokingly ill-judging! — Now my Mother will be unwell again. Every fault in Ben's blood does harm to hers, & every dinner-invitation he refuses will give her an Indigestion.'[31] But the picture is not all negative – Mary was, by one account at least, generous with money and warm-hearted when it suited her to be.[32] Even Jane near the end of her life allowed Mary some praise, when arrangements were made to convey her to Winchester in James and Mary's carriage: 'Now, that's a sort of thing which Mrs J. Austen does in the kindest manner!' But she could not let Mary get away entirely with a spotless record, and she went on in the next sentence to say, 'But she is still in the main *not* a liberal-minded Woman . . .'[33] It is noticeable that none of the Marys in Jane Austen's novels is of shining character. The Musgrove family at Uppercross Cottage in particular seem to echo one aspect of James and Mary's relationship. Charles Musgrove is 'civil and agreeable; in sense and temper he was undoubtedly superior to his wife;' but 'a more equal match might have improved him; . . . a woman of real understanding might have given more consequence to his character, and more usefulness, rationality and elegance to his habits and pursuits.'[34] Nevertheless, they, like James and Mary Austen, 'pass for a happy couple' among their family and friends.

Eliza de Feuillide certainly recognized that 'unmixed felicity' was not to be expected in marriage, but if her letters to Philadelphia Walter constitute a true account of her life with Henry Austen, then the way in which she ensured her husband's compliance guaranteed her happiness and his too:

> Henry well knows that I have not been much accustomed to controul and should probably behave rather awkwardly under it, and therefore like a wise Man he has no will but mine, which to be sure some people would call spoiling me, but [I] know it is the best way of managing me . . .[35]

She refers to her husband as 'Austen' or 'my cousin', claiming an aversion to the word 'husband'; she would have laughed openly at Fordyce and Gisborne's stipulation of male superiority in marriage. Thirty-six-year-old Eliza was not about to relinquish her independence of mind to a man ten years her junior, but there is not much evidence to suggest that Henry suffered any serious check to his own autonomy. To her godfather Warren Hastings, Eliza wrote in more restrained terms of Henry's comfortable income, affection for her son and excellent heart, temper and understanding. At a low point, just before her son's death, she briefly entertained a romantic idea about moving away from fashionable society to Wales, with which Henry wisely appeared to agree, probably realizing that this particular whim would be short-lived. In the end, the pull of London life proved too strong and they continued to live in style at smart London addresses, hosting parties and private concerts. Jane and Cassandra sent presents to Eliza with none of the resentment which accompanied gifts to Mrs James Austen. Henry's wife knew how to value anything given by her sisters-in-law. Home-made fire screens and small items of jewellery, the kind of presents Jane and Cassandra could afford, pleased her enormously and she always made sure to acknowledge her gratitude.[36]

The Austens prized Henry and Eliza's company enough to share a holiday home at Lyme with them and Jane enjoyed her visits to their house in Sloane Street, shopping with her fashionable sister-in-law and visiting her London friends and neighbours – 'everything is smooth & pleasant', she reported to Cassandra. On Eliza's death in April 1813, Jane paid tribute to Henry's sincere attachment to his wife while she lived, but concluded that his active, independent spirit would soon overcome any sense of loss. He had, in any case, frequently spent long periods of time away from Eliza, on visits to Godmersham in particular, where he enjoyed the company of his Knight nieces and nephews every New Year and on flying visits whenever the mood took him. Perhaps their marriage, like so many, thrived on well-timed absences. Jane's assessment of Henry's rapid recovery from grief proved correct. By the summer of the following year, she had met three women in London who had taken her brother's fancy, but his bank failure put paid to any marital hopes for a few years. He did not marry his second wife, Eleanor Jackson, until 1820, when Henry was forty-eight. By all accounts, they remained a devoted couple over the thirty years of their marriage.

At Godmersham, Henry evidently basked in an atmosphere of domestic harmony, with a pretty sister-in-law to talk to, an easy-going brother with plentiful game on his acres and nephews and nieces to amuse with his quick wit. Anna's memories of her Godmersham relatives bears out this impression. She remembered Elizabeth Austen as a beautiful woman:

> highly educated, though not I imagine of much natural talent. Her tastes were domestic, her affections strong, though exclusive, and her temper calculated to make Husband and children happy in their home. Indeed my Uncle's own disposition was so sweet and yielding, his whole character so opposed to contention of every kind that he could never have been, under any circumstances, an irritable or discontented man —[37]

Unlike Henry and James, Edward had never shown much interest in academic pursuits and Elizabeth herself was not fond of reading or witty repartee, although she would listen with half an ear while sewing, if read to. 'I guess that Eliz:th works, that you read to her, & that Edward goes to sleep. —' Jane wrote to Cassandra, imagining the long December evenings at Godmersham.[38] Edward, a real pipe-and-slippers man, asked only a quiet, uneventful existence with 'somebody now & then to yawn with one',[39] the kind of contentment, perhaps, that Jane envisaged for easy-going Mr Bingley. There is certainly more than a hint of Elizabeth in Isabella Knightley, 'a pretty, elegant little woman, of gentle, quiet manners, and a disposition remarkably amiable and affectionate; wrapped up in her family; a devoted wife, a doting mother . . .'[40] Emma's less intelligent sister is everything Fordyce would have her be, given her delicate health and total immersion in domestic duties, 'a model of right feminine happiness',[41] observed Jane Austen sardonically. Despite the similarities, it would be wrong to think of Elizabeth Austen as a submissive, conduct-book wife, however. She, like Mary and Eliza, was a strong-minded woman, who used her husband's horror of contention to her own advantage. In her attempt to explain Jane's polite but cool reception at Godmersham, Anna noted that 'A little talent went a long way' with Elizabeth, '& much must have gone a long way too far.'[42] Elizabeth's 'exclusive' affections evidently did not wholly embrace her clever sister-in-law's wit and literary tastes, and it is significant that Edward did not offer his mother and sisters a permanent home until after his wife's death. Yet although Jane was sometimes bored in the company of Kentish ladies, and rather rueful that her poor-relation status was never entirely overlooked, she was, for the most part, happy staying with Edward's family. She appreciated eating fine food and drinking French wine with no consideration of the petty economies she was forced to practise at home, but she preferred the unconditional friendship, shared tastes and uninhibited exchange of views to be had in her sister's company. Her comment to Cassandra in September 1796 might be applied to all of her visits to Kent: 'I am very happy here, though I should be glad to get home by the end of the month.'[43]

Edward and Elizabeth's sixteen-year marriage certainly seems to have been a happy one. Their dispositions fitted them for domestic pleasures and they derived great joy from their many children. Their eldest daughter picked up on this at the age of ten: 'Godmersham was fast filling with a numerous and joyful race of children; all born to bask in the brightest sunshine that fond & wealthy parents could spread around them —.'[44] When Elizabeth died at the age of thirty-five after bearing her eleventh child, Edward sat distraught beside her body or drifted miserably from room to room. Jane did not predict for him, as she later did for Henry, a rapid bounce back to cheerful spirits and, unlike his other brothers, Edward never looked for a second wife – but then he had his large family and estates to engross him and his eldest daughter Fanny to take over Elizabeth's role in the house.

Frank Austen's happiness in marriage was of a different order to his older brothers'. Marriage for Army and Navy husbands and wives was a less settled experience altogether, the special situation of a service wife meriting attention from Thomas Gisborne:

> In time of war she is left to endure the anxieties of a long separation from her husband, while he is toiling on the ocean, or contending in a distant quarter of the globe with the bullets of the enemy and the maladies of the climate.[45]

In such cases, Gisborne recommended reliance on God and the life to come, which Frank Austen's wife Mary probably found comforting. Frank was a devout Christian – the only officer who was known to kneel in church – and would have looked for the same strong religious belief in a wife. With no prospect of a fixed home, and almost constant anxiety on her own and her husband's account, Mary remained largely cheerful through seventeen years as a Navy wife. 'Largely' is an apposite word to use in this context – Mary was usually pregnant after each of Frank's shore-leaves and dependent in a more pragmatic way on her in-laws during her confinements. Like Edward, Frank was happiest in the domestic sphere. He thought that Captain Harville's dexterity might have been modelled on his own love of fashioning toys and useful household contrivances; Jane records him making rabbit nets and a fringe for the drawing-room curtains. In the early years of his marriage, he welcomed his mother, sisters and Martha Lloyd into lodgings in Southampton, where they would provide company for Mary when he returned to sea. From lodgings, they moved to a more permanent residence in Castle Square, which had a garden and roomier accommodation, but by 1809 the Frank Austens were on the move again – of the eleven children produced between 1807 and 1823, one was born in Southampton, two in Alton, two in Portsmouth, one in Deal, three in Chawton, one in Ryde and one in Gosport. Jane expressed envy of the mobility of soldiers' and sailors' wives, on the occasion of the Austens' move from Steventon, although unlike Frank's wife, she didn't have the inconvenience of numerous children in tow:

> there is something interesting in the bustle of going away, & the prospect of spending future summers by the Sea . . . is very delightful. – for a time we shall now possess many of the advantages which I have often thought of with Envy in the wives of Sailors or Soldiers.[46]

She imagined Frank and Mary's contented existence on the Isle of Wight, living well on plenty of cheap fish, '& plenty of Engagements & plenty of each other.'[47] Frank and Mary's happiness lay in simple pleasures; they were very sociable, fitted in wherever they went and enjoyed playing charades and other games when old friends called.

Charles Austen, Jane's 'own particular little brother', married his first wife in Bermuda in 1807, when she was seventeen and he twenty-seven. Two of their children were born on the island before they moved to England, where lack of money meant living on board ship for the most part, broken only by visits to relations. On his first visit to his mother and sisters after an absence of seven years, Cassandra conveyed her impressions of the pair in a letter to Philadelphia Walter:

> His Bermudan wife is a very pleasing little woman, she is gentle & amiable in her manners & appears to make him very happy. They have two pretty little girls. There must be always something to wish for, & for Charles we have to wish for rather more money. So expensive as every thing in England is now, even the necessaries of life, I am afraid they will find themselves very very poor.[48]

Charles and Fanny visited the Chawton family again in the winter, then moved on board Charles' ship, the *Namur*, at Sheerness, the cheapest accommodation they could find which afforded tolerable comfort. In such cramped quarters, it must have been exhausting trying to keep their little daughters entertained or under proper control. Jane remarked on the unruly behaviour of the eldest girl, Cassy, concluding that if her parents would only exert themselves to discipline her, she would be an easier child to like.[49] The children enjoyed the rare opportunity of running around in the fresh air with their cousins when Charles and Fanny stayed at Godmersham in October 1813, and went home healthier and happier after their short holiday. Jane was there at Godmersham to welcome the disorganized pair on their late arrival: they had not allowed themselves enough time for the journey and to compound matters, had left home late. She was glad to see Fanny 'looking as neat & white this morng as possible', and 'Charles all affectionate, placid, quiet, chearful good humour.'[50] That his children took full advantage of their father's even temper and relaxed approach to life, Jane makes clear: 'Charles . . . will be as happy as he can with a cross Child or some such care pressing on him at the time.'[51]

Like his brothers, Charles preferred family pleasures, forgoing a game of billiards on his first night at Godmersham for a cosy chat with his wife, sister, niece and brother. The next day he went shooting with a nephew and the ladies spent the morning attempting to solve the problem of Cassy's sea-sickness. The Austen ladies had offered to have her at Chawton while the family were tied to living on board the *Namur*, but Cassy did not want to leave her mother and father and Charles himself was reluctant to part with her. Jane regretted that the girls had inherited Fanny's blonde and pink colouring, rather than Charles' dark good looks and probably held the Palmer nose in as little esteem as did Mrs Austen. The general feeling was that Fanny's physical features had too much influence.[52] Caroline Austen also remarked, but this time admiringly, on Fanny's 'very light hair' when she met her for the first time in 1811. Less than a year after the visit to Godmersham, Fanny died after giving birth to her fourth daughter on board ship at Sheerness. She and Charles had been married only seven years and the child survived less than a month. Charles' parents-in-law and their unmarried daughter, Harriet, took over the care of the three little girls in their London house and Charles sank his grief in a return to sea.

Not a great deal is known of his second marriage in 1820 to Fanny's elder sister Harriet, who had cared for his children for six years. Mrs Austen's trust in Harriet as a 'careful and attentive mother' to her sister's children echoes all of her earlier unfulfilled hopes concerning Mary Lloyd's care of Anna, but at least Harriet had proved herself a dutiful child-minder before she married Charles. What Mrs Austen reveals of her character, however, strikes a warning note:

> I hope they will be happy. She has good principles and good sense, and now that her heart is at ease (for she has suffered much for some months past) and that she has quitted London, which always disagreed with her, she will I trust have better health and in consequence better spirits and better temper.[53]

Significantly, Anna did not take to her – perhaps she detected more than one similarity to her step-mother – 'I cannot like Miss Palmer, do what I will,'[54] she confided to her step-brother, James-Edward. Compared with her pretty younger sister, Harriet appeared 'plain and sour countenanced';[55] perhaps having three undisciplined little girls foisted on her had taken its toll, but to Charles she was his 'Dearest Harriet' when they married at St Pancras Church in August.[56] Whatever the truth of the matter, she and Charles produced four more children between 1821 and 1826, after which Charles returned for several lengthier spells at sea.

None of Jane's brothers married fortunes, but there was money enough for comfort and happiness, for James, Edward and Henry, at least. Frank and Charles had to work long and hard in hazardous conditions to earn rather less than their brothers lived on. Their financial position was more akin to the Harvilles' – the money available had to be stretched to its limits, but with contrivance and common sense, happiness was possible. The importance of a good income to marital accord is reiterated throughout their sister's novels: Henry Tilney's independent means and Catherine's £3,000; Marianne's 'competence' of £2,000 per annum, realized by Colonel Brandon's estate and Elinor's £1,000 achieved by Edward's living and the lump sum bestowed reluctantly by his mother; Darcy's splendid £10,000 yearly income; Edmund's two lucrative livings; Mr Knightley's more than adequate means; Captain Wentworth's £25,000 prize money. Elinor and

Edward find everything they desire in each other, 'brought together by mutual affection, with the warmest approbation of their friends', but even though 'their intimate knowledge of each other seemed to make their happiness certain',[57] they are not prepared to marry on £350 a year, fifty pounds more than the income on which James Austen and Anne Mathew had married ten years before. Mary Crawford's belief in wealth as the best guarantee of marital happiness is treated as mercenary, but none of Jane Austen's heroines will be forced into practising stringent domestic economies.

That money and love could also breed exclusivity was part of Jane Austen's experience within her own family. Her Uncle James and Aunt Jane Leigh-Perrot were completely devoted to each other for life, almost constantly together and unhappy when apart. Even after forty years of marriage, the seventy-year-old James Leigh-Perrot wrote to his wife after a two-day absence: 'If I was able to say how much I love You and how much I long to be with You, perhaps you would not believe me.' He ends another letter several days later, 'Yrs faithfully, sincerely, lovingly & wholly.'[58] They spent half of each year in Bath for Mr Leigh-Perrot's gout, and half at their estate near Reading, where they passed their time contentedly, as Mrs Leigh-Perrot expressed in a letter after her husband's death: 'we were too happy in each other, to allow us to think our *retired* half year the least dull . . . whilst I had him, He was the whole World to me.'[59] A friend of Mrs Leigh-Perrot's cousin, visiting the couple in Ilchester, reported that she had never seen two people so attached to each other as they were.[60]

Their affection for each other did not have to be shared with children, neither did their money, yet Mr Leigh-Perrot's uxoriousness did nothing to soften his wife's parsimony. The Austen nephews and nieces were invited to Bath on several occasions, where Aunt Jane Leigh-Perrot's reluctance to part with money was noticed by Jane in particular. When James Leigh-Perrot died in 1817, he left his entire estate to his wife and very small legacies to his nephews and nieces, payable on her death. To his struggling sister, he left nothing and the Austen family did not benefit from his will until the following generation. His wife capriciously bestowed and withdrew allowances on a whim and kept her nephews dangling over who would inherit the Scarlets estate. Henry was not in the equation: he had never been forgiven for the £10,000 loss occasioned by his bankruptcy in 1816. Pleading poverty, she cancelled the £100 previously granted to James Austen, which enabled him to pay for Caroline's school fees, prompting James-Edward to write to his father: 'I have long thought too meanly of her, to be much astonished at any fresh instance of want of feeling or of hypocrisy.'[61] When James Austen died in 1819, she made the decision to leave Scarlets to Frank, but when he married Martha Lloyd, his aunt's outright opposition to the match ruled him out. Fortunately for him, her great-nephew James-Edward married a woman of whom she did approve, a woman with a comfortable fortune. First she doubled his allowance to £600, then hinted that she would leave her money and estate to him, if he would agree to its proper upkeep. The year before her death, she wrote to James-Edward in affectionate terms, but still with a maddening degree of unreliability: 'I think, *unless in my dotage*, I should never wish to leave this property from *You* – perhaps as I did change my mind you may be led to fancy I may again . . .'[62] James-Edward held his breath and expressed himself very properly and very carefully in his letters to her from that point on. He inherited Scarlets in 1846.

Her own brothers' marriages told Jane Austen that the married state was more than the sum of its parts, not a contraction into a private world of two, but an expansion, a widening of the ring to embrace siblings, parents, new connections. To marry was to participate in society, to adopt a pattern of social as well as familial commitments, and all of her novels recognize this, moving beyond the vision of dual harmony in the final pages, first to the family then into the wider community. Marianne Dashwood, on marrying Colonel Brandon, takes on a number of social as well as domestic roles, as 'a wife, the mistress of a family, and the patroness of a village'.[63] Her life at Delaford might also comprehend Brandon's ward and Willoughby's child, unless the girl is kept secluded in some distant country area, visited occasionally by her guardian. Marianne's responsibilities as the wife of a landowner extend beyond the family home, to providing food, clothes, advice and medical care for the needy, some form of education for the village children and the usual round of dinners and social gatherings for the local gentry families. The same fate is implied for Elizabeth Bennet, Catherine Morland, Fanny Price and Emma Woodhouse. Every

Austen household had its share of extended responsibility – relatives were accommodated for long periods of time and Jane was rarely the only guest in the various homes from where she wrote her letters. People in the neighbourhood called in for morning visits, for walks, for dinner, for evening parties.

Every heroine's marriage is seen against a wider background of friends and kin. Anne Elliot rejects the Elliots' narrow sphere of influence, adopting instead Wentworth's more hospitable 'family' of Navy friends. Edmund and Fanny remain indispensable to the happiness of Sir Thomas and Lady Bertram, their prime hope for the future and the restoration of their faith in humanity. Susan and William Price benefit and more financial help for the Price family is implied. Emma and Mr Knightley will continue to care for Mr Woodhouse and the wider communities of Highbury and Donwell. Elizabeth and Jane take some responsibility for the impecunious Wickhams and educate Kitty into a more sensible attitude. Pemberley comprehends Lady Catherine and Miss Bingley, which does not signal a very comfortable experience, but is preferable to outright schism. Mr Bennet feels able to drop in whenever he chooses, although Mrs Bennet's absence is probably necessary for the continuation of conjugal felicity. The Gardiners are welcome, despite their trade connections, Georgiana gains a sister and continues to live at Pemberley under her brother's protection.

Just as Jane Austen continued to consider the fate of her characters beyond the confines of the novel, she encourages her readers to imagine the happily married heroines in their homes. Somewhere in the narrative, there is always a description of the properties they will inhabit: Mansfield Parsonage, with its full-length windows and pantries, its evergreens and apricots; Delaford's stewponds and yew arbour; Donwell's sheltered meadows and strawberry beds; Pemberley's elegantly furnished rooms and picture gallery, its lake and wooded walks; Woodston's lawns and apple trees. We imagine Anne Elliot on the high seas, comfortably stowed away in Captain Wentworth's cosy cabin, or installed in a roomy country house, purchased with her husband's prize money. These fictional women and their spouses, like real-life wives and husbands who respected and loved each other, find their ultimate fulfilment in marriage, a true contract of mutual agreeableness.

9

Domestic Happiness Overthrown

In Jane Austen's novels, as in ordinary life, less than perfect marriages are an inescapable feature of everyday existence, with most married couples inhabiting a kind of second-best world to that enjoyed by the heroes and heroines. These grey-area marriages are not necessarily desperately unhappy – husbands and wives rub along somehow – but they are not what Jane Austen would have considered fulfilling or truly companionate. All of her fiction highlights the very real tensions between marrying for love and marrying for social or economic advantage, the moral obligation of resisting a loveless marriage, while never ignoring the necessity of a good income. Happiness in marriage should not be merely a matter of chance, but there were many unromantic Charlotte Lucases out in the real world who were willing to gamble on finding enough contentment from a home and a comfortable income, without loving or respecting the man who provided them, and plenty of men who chose wives for a variety of reasons other than affection. The Collinses and Hursts, Palmers and Middletons, Norrises, Rushworths and Grants were undoubtedly more numerous than the Darcys, Wentworths, Tilneys and Knightleys.

The bleakest marriage in all of Jane Austen's fiction is that of Colonel Brandon's brother to Eliza, in *Sense and Sensibility*, a match forcibly brought about by the Colonel's father, in order to secure the girl's fortune. Brandon's brother mistreats her, then divorces her for adultery. Abandoned by her lover, she produces an illegitimate child, passes from man to man, sinks beyond the pale of polite society and dies of consumption. This is the most extreme example of a disastrous marriage and its consequences that the author ever created and it illustrated a widely held belief, supported by moralists and proved by the scandals reported on a regular basis in the Press, that couples manoeuvred into marriage by mercenary parents would almost inevitably make adulterous alliances to compensate for the lack of conjugal affection. Despite Harriet Spencer's cautious optimism regarding her parents' choice of the Earl of Bessborough, he was rude to her in public and unfaithful to her in private. She married him in 1780, had four children by him, the last in 1787, then embarked on a long-term relationship with Granville Leveson-Gower, with whom she had two children in the early 1800s. Although she did not end her days facing ill-health and destitution, she never found lasting happiness in her relationships with men, and her experience found an echo in the fates of other women in a similar position. One of them, just four years older than Jane Austen, was forced into marriage at the age of fifteen to Sir Godfrey Webster of Battle Abbey. She had three children by him, but the marriage was a disaster. At twenty-one, she reflected on her position, which had driven her to consider desperate measures:

> This fatal day seven years gave me in the bloom & innocence of fifteen to the power of a being who has made me execrate my life since it has belonged to him. Despair often prompts me to a remedy within my reach . . . My mind is worked up to a state of savage exultation & impels me to act with fury that proceeds more from passion and deep despair than I can in calmer moments justify. Often times in the gloom of midnight I feel a desire to curtail my grief & but for an unaccountable shudder that creeps over me, ere this the deed of rashness would be executed.[1]

Fortunately for her, the cheerful Lord Holland rather than the arsenic provided the remedy for her misery and she married him in 1797. Mrs Sherwood provided a comprehensive picture of an upper-class marriage on the rocks from an onlooker's point of view, in 1793:

> Lord Valentia and his lady now met only at the six o'clock dinner, and at the card-table afterwards, the rest of their time was spent apart. My lord rose early, breakfasted at nine, had his hot luncheon at two, supped at six, and was in bed at ten. My lady breakfasted at two, dined at six, supped at midnight, and went to bed at three or four.[2]

No one in their social circle can have failed to notice this very public evidence of incompatibility, but at least embattled aristocratic couples had more space and often the financial wherewithal to indulge such discrete lifestyles. In ordinary families, couples were forced to rub along whatever the difficulties and learn to bear it. Mrs Aaron Stock, formerly the governess, Miss Weeton, had to stand cruelty and unreasonable behaviour from her husband. She had nowhere else to go. He married her for her shrewdly invested life-savings, ploughing them into his failing Wigan factory as soon as they came into his hands. Submission to his demands did nothing to prevent him turning her out of the family home, a home financed largely by her money. In 1814, she wrote to him, pointing out the unfairness of his behaviour:

> You required me to repair all your clothing, excepting shoes, and I dare say you remember how readily and good-naturedly I submitted to your wishes. I disliked exceedingly patching breeches, coats, waistcoats, and even neck-kerchiefs, besides darning stockings up to the very knees; but to please you, I did it cheerfully.[3]

She suffered blows to the head, often delivered unexpectedly, anxieties about being poisoned, imprisonment and starvation. In a letter to a married friend, she commented ruefully on the precept commonly peddled in conduct literature, that:

> if *one* of a married couple gives way to the wayward humours of the other, they are sure to be tolerably comfortable. Your experience has not shewn you, yet, the result of such a course of conduct. I have often read the experience of others, and have seen a few instances myself, where the accommodating spirit began, and remained, on one side, without having any softening influence on the other, but on the contrary, *increased* its *malignity* by *indulgence*; and where, likewise, an occasional *firm, judicious* opposition increased the comfort of *both parties* . . . The man who rules by tyranny, can never be obeyed by affection; he is submitted to from fear, and delights in abject submission . . . By way of experiment, I have acted on this principle for the last 10 months; and with so much success, that we have all much more peace than we had.[4]

Her spirit of resistance did not occasion any permanent change in her husband's tyrannical behaviour and at the end of that year, she wrote to her friend again, in envy of her kind, loving husband and in despair at the cruelty of her own. Finally, Mr Stock turned her out of the house onto the street. When she regained access to her home, he kept her in solitary confinement and attempted to starve her. So much for the idea that happiness in marriage would derive from the husband being recognized as the dominant partner. A husband had the power to divide his wife from her friends and family and severely curtail her movements, if he so wished. One of Eliza Chute's female correspondents knew of a man who had behaved in this domineering manner to a mutual friend, who had been very happy as a single woman, and concluded:

> What an awful and important change marriage occasions in the life of a Woman! ... When I reflect on this change and how often it happens, I am astonish'd Eliza how we found courage to marry. It is surely a very deep Game.[5]

Jane Austen knew how society more often than not condoned marriage for the sake of money and property alone and how problems arose as a consequence of conflicting family values – Mrs Bennet sees nothing reprehensible in conniving at a marriage between Lizzie and Mr Collins; Sir Walter Elliot and Lady Russell oppose Anne's engagement to Wentworth; General Tilney attempts to part Henry and Catherine. Mary Crawford's assertion that '"A large income is the best recipe for happiness I ever heard of"'[6] has more than an element of truth in it, but marrying entirely for financial gain, with little or no consideration of character or taste or affection, led to inevitable unhappiness. Maria Bertram's morally flawed justification of an alliance with Mr Rushworth hinges entirely on material gain – she will have money to spend and a large house in London. Reprehensible as this mercenary behaviour is, Maria's final commitment to Rushworth goes a step further. She marries in the end out of self-destructive pride – Henry Crawford must not think that he has destroyed her future happiness – contempt for the man she is about to marry and a desperate need to escape the restrictions imposed by her father. Once married, the Rushworths need the continual whirl of activity and company to distract them from the tedium of their empty relationship, but this solution is a very short-term one. Their alliance survives for barely five months. In a case such as theirs, the warnings issued by the conduct manuals were appropriate:

> ... if you give your hand without your heart for a title, a great estate, or any other consideration, expect that marriage to be comfortless, encumbered with more disappointments, troubles, and vexations than you can expect joys to flow in it, or proceed from it.[7]

Thomas Gisborne, in common with the majority of conduct-book writers, held that if wealth and status alone formed the basis for marriage, the relationship between husband and wife was not likely to be very satisfactory. All too often, he said, a 'good match' in the female mind meant that a wife would have enough money to triumph over other women in the locality, dress in a showy manner, live in an opulent manner and enjoy the giddy pleasures of London and Bath. Other conduct-book writers too, both male and female, had plenty to say about extravagance, particularly in women. A wife had better not expect many new clothes once she was married, warned Eugenia Stanhope: 'Your taste in this particular has been indulged to the extent in the Preparations for your Marriage; but do not look on these as the Standard of your future Appearance.'[8] The Revd Fordyce claimed that most sensible men's worst nightmares featured women who were inveterate spenders and served to put them off marriage for life:

> Some, I find, would like a sprightly companion in marriage, but not a dissipated one, and all of them, to a man, dread a woman of expence . . . men that are not very violent lovers, or very great fools, will not overlook it. Our sex of late years have been by many thought more backward than formerly to enter into the holy bands of wedlock; and what I hint at has been assigned as a principal cause.[9]

The Mirror of Graces agreed, advising its readers to practise the 'graces of economy'; in other words, dressing well on as little money as possible, a quality which would endear them to their husbands; 'for, though most of the money-getting sex like to see their wives well-dressed, yet, trust me, my fair friends, they would rather owe that pleasure to your taste than to their pockets!'[10] Mary Russell Mitford pointed out that women had been educated to think of little else but dress and marriage, so it would be very surprising if the habits of a lifetime were suddenly superceded by a conversion to wifely economy: 'They dress to marry and marry to dress; and so dressing and so marrying, there are, I fear, but small chances that they will make good wives . . .'[11] Little was said against men's expensive habits, beyond an obvious disapproval of obsessive gaming, but Jane Austen more than makes up for the omission. She does describe extravagant wives – the first Mrs Weston who missed her accustomed luxuries as the former Miss Churchill of Enscombe and drove her husband into debt; Mrs Allen with an incurable obsession for gowns; Mrs Elton and her lace and pearls – but she balances these examples with Sir Walter Elliot, who spends money like water to maintain his elevated position as a baronet; General Tilney, with his taste for conspicuous opulence; Mr Elliot who bankrupts his friends; George Wickham who runs up gambling debts and Willoughby who walks knowingly into an unhappy relationship in order to finance his estate, his stables and hounds. Marriage reformed none of them. Elinor recognizes that had Willoughby married her sister for love alone, the burden of economizing would have fallen on Marianne's inexperienced shoulders and he would have ended up regretting that he had married a woman with no fortune. One anonymous moralist got it exactly right:

> . . . it should seem very proper before all marriages, for both parties to know truly and fairly what they have to expect on this head; and seriously to consider with themselves, whether it will be sufficient so far to answer their desires, as to prevent further murmurings and anxieties, and allow them to enjoy life agreeably to their inclinations.[12]

Lack of money was, of course, a reason for unhappiness in any marriage. There was no lasting contentment to be gained in marrying for love alone, but that didn't stop some reckless couples from doing just that:

> Many there are, unfortunately, who marry, without one moment's consideration how or in what manner they are to live. Few, very few, of such Marriages are happy. A sufficiency, even though it be barely so, is a great promoter of Tranquillity . . . the connexion formed on PRUDENCE, is generally the most happy.[13]

Near poverty is the state Mrs Jennings predicts for Edward and Lucy, on only £200 per annum and probably a child year on year to support. No tranquil existence would be possible for them or for their family, they would live on half the income that the Price family had in their cramped accommodation in Portsmouth, and suffer the hand-to-mouth existence experienced by many poor curates and their families in Jane Austen's time. Mrs Jennings describes Lucy as a good manager of money, given her background, but Edward in particular would be denied the opportunity of mixing in better company. Fortunately for him, Lucy has no intention of suffering any financial hardships. The youngest Miss Ward in *Mansfield Park* had none of Lucy's experience of making a little money go a long way and when she married the uneducated, rough-mannered Lieutenant Price of the Marines to 'disoblige' her family, those who would suffer most from the lack of finance and judicious management would be their future children.

Men, or women, with bad tendencies were incapable of reform, despite the contrary message in plays and novels; so preached John Gregory and plenty of other moralists. They warned against reading novels and dramas and advised their readers to avoid the kind of sentimental material which 'warms the imagination, which engages and softens the heart, and raises the taste above the level of common life', since disillusionment was sure to follow. Husbands were far from perfect, Gregory pointed out, and the high expectations encouraged by romantic novels were doomed to be disappointed:

> Instead of meeting with sense, delicacy, tenderness, a lover, a friend, an equal companion, in a husband; you may be tired with insipidity and dulness; shocked with indelicacy, or mortified by indifference. You will find none to compassionate, or even understand your sufferings; for your husbands may not use you cruelly, and may give you as much money for your clothes, personal expence, and domestic necessaries, as is suitable for their fortunes. The world would therefore look on you as unreasonable women, and that did not deserve to be happy, if you were not so. — To avoid these complicated evils, if you are determined at all events to marry, I would advise you to make all your reading and amusements of such a kind, as do not affect the heart nor the imagination, except in the way of wit or humour.[14]

Amusingly, Tom Bertram speculates on Mrs Grant's need for a lover, given her dull life with a husband who sulks if his meat is not cooked to his liking and appears to need cosseting like a spoilt child. This cannot be the kind of marriage Mrs Grant envisaged for herself, but, being a sensible woman, she formulates a workable approach to the situation in which she finds herself:

> There will be little rubs and disappointments every where, and we are all apt to expect too much; but then, if one scheme of happiness fails, human nature

> turns to another; if the first calculation is wrong, we make a second better; we find comfort somewhere.[15]

Mary Wollstonecraft advised women to be content with less than the ideal man that existed in their imaginations: 'A woman cannot be reasonably unhappy, if she is attached to a man of sense and goodness, though he may not be all she could wish.'[16] This is what Marianne Dashwood settles for when she marries Colonel Brandon and his flannel waistcoats. In the end, 'strong esteem' and 'lively friendship', rather than a headlong fall into unrestrained passion, prove more realistic virtues on which to base a relationship. In Wollstonecraft's opinion, friendship and respect were more likely to be productive of happiness in marriage than a grand passion. Extreme feelings were transient and could not be maintained, and what was left when the intensity of desire had faded? Jane Austen gives us the example of Lydia and Wickham, 'brought together because their passions were stronger than their virtue'.[17] Sexual attraction is all that exists between them, and once that has worn off, indifference sets in on both sides. Lydia's experience of marriage is her mother's, but unlike Mr Bennet, Wickham does not find solace in innocent diversions; he disappears to Bath once a year to gamble and find more stimulating company. 'Passions are extremely transient and unsteady;' warned one moral essayist,

> and love, with no other support, will ever be short-lived and fleeting. It is a fire that is soon extinguished; and where there is no solid esteem and well-cemented friendship to blow it up, it rarely lights again . . .[18]

'Youthful infatuation' was Lady Elliot's failing when she made the mistake of marrying a spendthrift baronet. This 'excellent, sensible and amiable' woman was taken in by Sir Walter's good looks and title. She overlooked his vanity and self-absorption, probably believing that he would grow out of such habits, and had to live with the consequences when she realized that his character was fixed. She reined in his spending, but could achieve little else. Her error was the consequence of inexperience, as both Jane Austen and Wollstonecraft recognized: '. . . many women, I am persuaded, marry a man before they are twenty, whom they would have rejected some years after.'[19] Marrying an unsuitable partner was more dangerous for women than for men, as Mr Bennet warns Elizabeth:

> "I know that you could never be happy nor respectable, unless you truly esteemed your husband; unless you looked up to him as a superior. Your lively talents would place you in the greatest danger in an unequal marriage. You could scarcely escape discredit and misery. My child, let me not have the grief of seeing you unable to respect your partner in life."[20]

Mr Bennet does not only touch on his own unhappy marriage here; in fact, he appears to be implying that his spirited daughter will go off the rails if she marries a man she cannot look up to. Words like 'discredit', 'danger' and 'misery' certainly seem to imply it. That Mr Bennet himself had faced such dangers is briefly touched on when Elizabeth ponders her parents' dysfunctional relationship. Mr Bennet has no respect for his wife, having been initially 'dazzled by youth, vivacity, and beauty',[21] but very soon made painfully aware of her lack of sense and intelligence. He mistakes liveliness and humour for good temper, but he has not inquired too deeply into her true character, which is strange given that he is an intelligent man. It is implied that, had he not found consolation in books and country pursuits, he might have sought comfort 'in any of those pleasures which too often console the unfortunate for their folly or their vice'.[22] Rather than threatening the family's social and economic security by drinking, gambling or taking a mistress, Mr Bennet undermines it by exposing his wife to ridicule and neglecting the improvement of his younger daughters' minds, which might have made them more rational and respectable.

Considering the incompatible marriage of the Palmers in *Sense and Sensibility*, another instance of a clever man with a silly wife, Elinor reflects that many men are blinded by beauty to a lack of intelligence, but takes the optimistic view that 'this kind of blunder was too common for any sensible man to be lastingly hurt by it'.[23] Mr Palmer at least has the consolations of his newspaper and the cut and thrust of the House of Commons. Later, however, when she finds that the same fate faces Edward Ferrars, she is less sanguine – 'she wept for him, more than for herself', knowing that she would eventually recover her peace of mind, but that he stood little chance of ever being happy with an 'illiterate, artful, and selfish' wife. In the same way, Emma imagines a match between Harriet Smith and Mr Knightley in terms of unequal status and intelligence: 'Was it a new circumstance for a man of first-rate abilities to be captivated by very inferior powers? Was it new for one, perhaps too busy to seek, to be the prize of a girl who would seek him?'[24] Jane Austen reiterates this circumstance time and again. Captain Wentworth wonders at the disparity between James Benwick's scholarly cleverness and Louisa Musgrove's mere good temper and adequate intelligence, but Benwick has found someone to love and does not choose to enquire into Louisa's long-term suitability too deeply.

Closing one's eyes to potential incompatibility or character imperfections was not sensible, but might not end inevitably in grief. Edmund Bertram is so spellbound by Mary Crawford's beauty and wit that he blinds himself to her lack of moral fibre, yet despite Fanny's predictions that a marriage to Mary would ruin his happiness and respectability, Jane Austen hints that a more impartial judgement, 'would not have denied to Miss Crawford's nature, that participation of the general nature of women, which would lead her to adopt the opinions of the man she loved and respected, as her own'.[25] The author's view is not as black and white as her heroine's, but she does foresee problems for an alliance between Mary's brother and Fanny. Henry Crawford's vision of a happy marriage to Fanny Price, where he would parade her in London, and acquaint her with the Admiral, ignores Fanny's inflexible moral rectitude and retiring nature. His plans have little to do with her happiness. Their dispositions are so dissimilar, that in spite of his assertion that Fanny's mildness and piety are just what he is looking for in a wife, he would soon find himself plumbing unfathomable depths of boredom, reading aloud from Shakespeare every evening and attending to Fanny's raptures over stars and evergreens. Rather than Fanny reforming Henry, as Cassandra had urged in her attempt to change her sister's ending of the novel, his serious little wife would surely have driven him into the arms of someone more lively and amusing.

In the *Gentleman's Magazine*, usually reported under *Marriages of Remarkable Persons*, alliances between the young and the elderly appeared on a regular basis. How successful these matches proved is uncertain, but Thomas Gisborne cautioned his readers that, 'Great disparity in age between a husband and a wife', was 'liable to be productive of disquietude.'[26] In an early chapter of *Sense and Sensibility*, Elinor Dashwood agrees with this assessment, stating that '"thirty-five and seventeen had better not have anything to do with matrimony together"'.[27] Yet Marianne is eventually married off to a husband eighteen years her senior and only five years younger than her mother. Jane Austen is anxious to persuade the reader that this will be a happy match, with love on both sides, but are we convinced? The age gap is argued away by a mother keen to see only benefits for her daughter: '"His age is only so much beyond hers, as to be an advantage, as to make his character and principles fixed;",'[28] an important consideration for a girl who has previously been deceived in both, but it would seem to indicate widowhood and perhaps a second marriage for Marianne. Similarly, the age difference between Emma and Mr Knightley is sixteen years.

Despite glossing over significant differences in age between two of her heroines and their husbands, Jane Austen felt nothing but sympathy for women who married men much older than themselves. On the day before Catherine Bigg's marriage to the Revd Herbert Hill, she wrote to Cassandra, 'tomorrow we must think of poor Catherine'.[29] Poor Catherine was thirty-three, Mr Hill fifty-nine. Six years later, Jane visited her old friend, who by this time had three children: 'I had the pleasure of seeing Mrs Hill as well and as comfortable as usual; – but there is a melancholy disproportion between the Papa & the little Children. —'[30] Papa was sixty-six and more fitted to be a grandfather than a father.

For those trapped in less than satisfactory marriages, distractions were vital. Lady Elliot immersed herself in her children, Mrs Grant concentrates on her poultry and plants, Mr Bennet, all his hopes of domestic happiness thwarted, retreats to his library. Inner resources were more necessary for women than for men, since they had fewer opportunities for occupation away from the domestic environment. When he is forced to spend time at home, Sir John Middleton desperately seeks company to save him from the insipidity of his wife's conversation, which is entirely child-focused. On his side, there is no great attempt to widen his own or his wife's knowledge of the world. Lady Middleton's domestic insularity would have been approved by James Fordyce – her interest extends no further than her home and family, but she does not like reading, and is suspicious of those who do. It is clear that this is a marriage of convenience, like Charlotte Jennings' to Mr Palmer. Mrs Jennings has made matches for her daughters which take little account of their ultimate compatibility. Sir John presumably wanted an heir to his estate and someone to manage his home. Mrs Jennings' daughters were well provided for and he obviously chose the more elegant of the two. A house almost constantly filled with people is necessary to the happiness of both; their lives are too narrow to provide any scope for mutual interests. Sir John is a sportsman, Lady Middleton a mother – and that is all that can be said for them. Fordyce reserved his contempt and pity for women who found no entertainment in reading, conversation, 'ingenious works of any kind' or even just thinking, preferring instead 'to stifle reflexion in a tumult of pleasures, and to divert weariness in a crowd',[31] but men, too, could be just as restlessly empty-headed. This is not an unhappy marriage, but it is certainly not a satisfactory relationship, and not the kind that Jane Austen would condemn herself or her heroines to suffer.

With no inner resources, Mary Musgrove needs constant company in order to be happy. Left to her own devices, while her husband is out with his gun and his dogs, she invariably fancies herself ill and physically weak. Fordyce, and he was not alone, advocated female weakness as a stimulus to the male protective urge and promoted the sentimental cult of the frail woman, to which writers like Mary Wollstonecraft and Mary Hays were so opposed. Jane Austen knew women like Mary Musgrove, whose small stock of importance came from their imaginary ailments and she also knew that such tiresome ploys did not endear them to their husbands. Her old friend Edward Bridges, like Charles Musgrove, spent as much time as he could away from a wife who enjoyed being ill:

> They have been all the summer at Ramsgate, for *her* health, she is a poor Honey – the sort of woman who gives me the idea of being determined never to be well – & who likes her spasms & nervousness & the consequence they give her, better than anything else.[32]

Edward's journey between Ramsgate and his parish at Goodnestone took him past Godmersham, where he made a habit of calling in most Sundays to delay his reunion with his wife and probably to remind himself that life could be good: 'I think the pleasantest part of his married Life, must be the Dinners & Breakfasts & Luncheons & Billiards that he gets in this way at Gm. Poor Wretch!' Jane sympathised.[33] In the case of another acquaintance from Kent, Lady Sondes, she recognized the psychological link between unhappiness and ill-health and hoped that her second marriage, for love, would restore her to full vigour: 'provided she will now leave off having bad head-aches & being pathetic, I can allow her, I can *wish* her to be happy.'[34]

A husband's frequent absences and a wife's limited ability to spend time away from home were the cause of much marital discontent, but women were cautioned that any display of resentment would have the opposite effect to that intended: 'Never complain of the Hours which he spends from you; for, being uneasy at that, he will leave you the sooner; and expecting more of it at his Return, he will defer that Return the longer.'[35] Many wives faced hours of boredom, which was why inner resources were so essential in married life. William Chute of The Vyne was a kindly man, but an avid sportsman, who exercised his hounds at least five times a fortnight. He was MP for the area as well, which took him away from home, leaving his wife to occupy herself in his absence. As soon as he returned, she was expected to forget her own pursuits in favour of his needs and comfort. She wrote to a friend complaining of the unfair situation as she saw it:

> ... he seems to think it strange that I should absent myself from him for four & twenty hours when he is at home, tho' it appears in the natural order of things that he should quit me for business or pleasure; such is the difference between husbands & wives. The latter are sort of tame animals, whom the men always expect to find at home ready to receive them: the former are lords of the creation free to go where they please.[36]

Eliza Chute certainly baulked at conduct-book advice to wives, that they should sink their own concerns in those of their husbands. She was an intelligent, articulate woman and although Mr Chute was no crass Mr Rushworth, she might have felt, like Maria Bertram, 'doomed to the repeated details of his day's sport, good or bad, his boast of his dogs, his jealousy of his neighbours, his doubts of their qualification, and his zeal after poachers,—'.[37] Most of her diary entries record her husband's hunting pursuits, others are left blank and she comes across as a lonely woman.

Emma Woodhouse outlines the difference between herself and Mr

Knightley in terms of hours spent at home and her circumscribed existence at Hartfield will not alter to any great degree on marriage: '"[Mr] Knightley, who is absent from home about five hours where she is absent one – and who, when he is at home, is either reading to himself or settling his accounts."'[38] This is Mr Knightley's bachelor existence, of course, but is it likely to change that much when he has a wife? Parish business and his Donwell estate will still take up much of his time and the settling of accounts is a constant. His private reading habits will have to change, though; Emma and her father will require entertaining in the evenings. It is to be hoped, however, that Mr Woodhouse's valetudinarian habits take him off to bed early.

Women leaving their parents and the only home they had ever known added to the loneliness they faced when left to fill the interminable days with morning visits and embroidery, while their husbands followed their own separate pursuits. Perhaps Jane Fairfax's friend Miss Campbell found this out when she married Mr Dixon and moved to Ireland, since Jane reports to Miss Bates: '". . . till she married last October, she was never away from them so much as a week . . . and so she wrote a very urgent letter to her mother . . . to press their coming over directly . . ."'[39] Eliza Chute had married in October 1793, but a letter from her mother in the early days of the following year hints at the new wife's need for her mother's company and regret at the loss of a meaningful role within a loving family:

> Yes certainly, from other sources will arise the happiness of my beloved Daughter the self-improving mind the steady affection & esteem of a good Husband & the Duties of a family fulfilled; from these circumstances my Eliza will very soon find that rational happiness she now has in view all the past pleasures under the paternal roof will be only traced in her memory as some pleasing illusion, which will be reflected on with delight but not wished for as such for many years have appeared to me those days spent at Gatton before I was married; & like you I remembered, I thought myself when first I settled at home, a very idle being who seemed to have nothing to do, but eat, drink & sleep free from care, pleasure was all my occupation: but why should you condemn yourself for being of so little use, surely this is unjust you are now of much more consequence in life, & are engaged in duties much greater than ever: that of making an affectionate return to one who has given you the greatest proof of his love, may every succeeding year add to my Eliza's domestic felicity: believe me my love when I regret your

> society, I never feel any regret that I have resigned it to Mr Chute, I know you will mutually render this life a Blessing to each other, . . .[40]

Tears must have been shed on both sides over this obligatory attempt to loosen family ties, but another letter from mother to daughter the following month shows that Eliza was still not comfortable in her new role as a wife. What is implied in her mother's advice is her daughter's inexperience of sexual relations; she was twenty-three to Mr Chute's thirty-six. As early as Eliza's second week as a married woman, Mrs Smith had advised her daughter: '. . . a Woman should not give a husband any reason to think she is Cold or indifferent to his affection . . .'[41] and she continued this theme in a later note:

> . . . indeed my love I join with you in wishing you could get rid of some of your timidity, & be more at ease with Mr Chute. I am sure he tries to court you to familiarity; if you could see your friend Eliza Gosling, you would be ashamed of yourself she is so much at home . . . men are changeable, to please them we must vary the little advantages nature has given.[42]

Poor Eliza Chute's experience of miserable isolation and embarrassed bewilderment cannot have been unusual, and some enlightened conduct-book writers called on men to be patient with their new wives: 'The GOOD HUSBAND will never fail to reflect, that he has probably withdrawn an affectionate and confiding creature from her parental roof, from the asylum of natural and certain protection and tenderness . . .'[43] Both Jane Austen and Eliza Chute may well have seen the report in the *Hampshire Chronicle*, on 19 January 1810, which reported the case of a new bride who had left it a little late to decide that she did not, after all, wish to leave her parents:

> . . . no sooner was the ceremony over, than the fair one seemed to demur, and, strange as it may appear, she has not yet deigned to place herself in that situation in which a man's rib ought to be – in plaid [sic] English, she has not gone home!

Unhappy marriages surface regularly in Jane Austen's letters. She watched Mrs Badcock pursuing her drunken husband around the Upper Rooms in Bath and found the spectacle entertaining, but underneath her amusement is an awareness of marital incompatibility.[44] Her relation of Harriot Bridges' problems is more serious. Jane liked her sister-in-law Elizabeth's younger sister and worried about her relationship with her dictatorial husband. At twenty-six, Harriot had married the Revd George Moore, ten years her senior, after some initial reluctance to become his second wife. At first, Jane Austen showed scant sympathy for Harriot's hesitation: '. . . as to pitying a young woman merely because she cannot live in two places at the same time, & at once enjoy the comforts of being married and single, I shall not attempt it, even for Harriot.'[45] The Bridges were a close family and Harriot a much loved daughter, but at her age she was no doubt feeling pressured to marry rather than become a burden on her brothers' finances in years to come. Like Charlotte Lucas' brothers, the Bridges men probably breathed a collective sigh of relief when their sister finally accepted Mr Moore's proposal.

Jane began to observe the relationship with a keener eye when she witnessed at close quarters Mr Moore's cold manner and want of tenderness in his behaviour towards his wife. Although Harriot was careful to conceal any unhappiness, Jane picked up on her husband's irascibility: '. . . we sat quietly working & talking till 10; when he ordered his wife away . . . Mr M. was not un-agreable, tho' nothing seemed to go right with him.'[46] She hinted to Cassandra that Harriot was doing her best to put a brave face on her situation; it was too late to do anything else. Her elder sisters were all happily married: Fanny to Mr Cage, Sophia to Mr Deedes, Elizabeth to Edward Austen, and Jane knew that Harriot felt the contrast deeply: 'I really hope Harriot is altogether very happy – but she cannot feel quite so much at her ease with her Husband, as the Wives she has been used to. —'[47] Poor Harriot, admired ten years earlier by Jane Austen for being in no hurry to marry, probably expected to have her older sisters' luck in finding an undemanding husband. There would be no point in confiding her disappointment to anyone; she had married an ill-natured husband and had to put up with it. Jane Austen was not alone in finding Mr Moore a difficult man to like. His congregation at Wrotham hated him so much that 'when he made his first appearance at Church, on his marriage to Miss Bridges, to shew it the clerk put up & they sung the funeral hymn instead of the usual Nuptial Psalm'.[48]

For the middling ranks of society, to which the Austens and most of their friends and acquaintances belonged, there was no escape from a bad marriage. Wives suffered more than husbands, given that women did not enjoy the mobility and opportunity to mix in the wider society granted to men. Extreme care was essential in the choice of a mate, as one writer specified: '. . . to those virgins who hold a middle rank & station in the world. An unhappy marriage is by you much to be avoided, if you regard your happiness in this world.'[49] Divorce put an end to irredeemably unhappy marriages further up the social scale, but it was not a course to be undertaken lightly. Lengthy court cases cost money and the very public proceedings led to character assassination at best, sexual prurience at worst, all seized on joyfully by the Press and pamphleteers. Between 1670 and 1857, there were only 325 divorces in England, and all but four of these were obtained by men. Of the four obtained by women, two were for incest, two for desertion. Adultery was the most common cause for divorce in the upper classes of society, which is where it happened more often than not, an almost inevitable consequence of loveless alliances contracted for economic gain. Only men had recourse to the law in cases of adultery, for a variety of reasons, the foremost being the protection of property and fortune against spurious heirs. Challenges were made in an attempt to change this unfair system, but none were entirely successful until 1925, when women achieved parity with men under the law and could petition for divorce on the grounds of adultery alone.

Every attempt to alter the *status quo* provoked a battery of arguments in favour of the law as it stood. A common defence was advanced that a woman could not bring a suit of adultery against her husband, because *he* had not promised to obey *her* in the marriage ceremony:

> For, by *obedience* is universally known & understood, the acting in conformity to the known will of the person, to whom such obedience is due. So that if a husband does not, by some open concession or palpable connivance, permit the adultery of his wife, she must necessarily be supposed to act in disobedience to her husband; when she is guilty of violating the marriage-bed. For otherwise she can never conceive it to be consistent with her husband's will, that she should prostitute herself to other men, to get children for him to maintain, or to inherit his substance.

> Here then is a very essential difference between the terms of the vow, or matrimonial contract, on the side of the man and that of the woman. The man promises the woman no such obedience. He is not guilty, therefore, of conjugal infidelity, by disobeying her, or acting against her known will, either by conversing with other women, or any other act. He may be cruel, wicked and unjust; but, while he continues publickly to hold for better for worse, for richer for poorer, in sickness and in health, to love and cherish his wife; he may privately love and cherish as many other women as he pleases, without being guilty of conjugal infidelity, or breach of his matrimonial vow.[50]

The man's agreement to the injunction in the marriage ceremony 'and forsaking all other, keep thee only unto her, so long as ye both shall live', applied, said this particular apologist, to the forsaking of parents to take a wife and as such constituted no promise of fidelity. His fellow countrymen should, he said, in a final misogynistic flourish, tinged with more than a dash of xenophobia:

> reflect on what they owe to themselves, & the value they ought to set on the authority of husbands, both for their own sake and that of their posterity; that they may leave, to the fanatical French & emasculated Italians, the contemptible meanness, of being made slaves to the caprice, and dupes to the vanity, of a sex, which nature designed for the use, comfort and convenience of man.[51]

The economic basis for the law on adultery was, for most men, transparently simple. The law protected property above all else and upheld the rightful claims of inheritance. Such claims were threatened by a wife's adultery and a man stood to lose everything he owned to spurious offspring. Conversely, if husbands proved unfaithful, how could their wives consider themselves similarly disadvantaged? This, said Samuel Johnson, was argument enough to grant men recourse to the law, but not women:

> Consider, of what importance the chastity of women is. Upon that all the property in the world depends. We hang a thief for stealing a sheep; but the unchastity of a woman transfers sheep, and farm and all, from the right owner . . . Between a man and his wife, a husband's infidelity is nothing . . . Wise married women don't trouble themselves about infidelity in their husbands . . . The man imposes no bastards upon his wife.[52]

Most women gave the same advice to their friends and relatives. With the law as it stood, what, after all, could a wife do? The whole of society appeared to connive at a man's doing exactly as he pleased, no matter how unhappy he made his wife, or how often he infected her with venereal diseases. A suspicious wife should say nothing, do nothing, about a husband's unfaithfulness, but pretend blindness:

> Men bear Suspicion . . . but very ill, even when they are guilty; . . . A prudent Wife, even if she found her Husband false to her, would shut her eyes to the Discovery, knowing that to reproach is but to harden him . . . Many a one has relinquished a real Intrigue, from his Wife's avoiding to discover it. Many a one has thrown himself into a real one, by her Suspicion of such as were only Imaginary.[53]

The message was clear, if a wife complained, her husband would be sure to turn to other women and she would only have herself to blame. It was always the wife's fault if her husband found pleasure elsewhere, 'Nothing is so easy as to prevent, what it may be impossible to remedy.'[54] Recognizing the inflexibility of the system, most counselled silent acquiescence and steered well clear of admitting the pain involved in marital betrayal, but the radical writer Mary Hays attacked this unreasonable expectation head-on, exposing the discrepancy between what a loving wife suffered and how she was called upon to act:

> How great in some parts of their conduct, how insignificant upon the whole, would men have women to be! For one example – when their love, their pride, their delicacy; in short, when all the finest feelings of humanity are insulted and put to the rack, what is expected? When a woman finds that the husband of her choice, the object of her most sincere and constant love, abandons himself to other attachments, infinitely cutting to a woman of sensibility and soul, what is expected of a creature declared weak by nature – and who is rendered weaker by education?
>
> They expect that this poor weak creature, setting aside in a moment love, jealousy, and pride, the most powerful and universal passions interwoven in the human heart, and which even men, clothed in wisdom and fortitude, find so difficult to conquer, that they seldom attempt it – that she shall notwithstanding lay all these aside as easily as she would her gown and petticoat, and plunge at once into the cold bath of prudence, of which though the wife only is to receive the shock, and make daily use of, yet if she does so, it has the virtue of keeping both husband and wife in a most agreeable temperament . . .

> For, there are no vices to which a man addicts himself, no follies he can take it into his head to commit, but his wife and his nearest female relations are expected to connive at, are expected to look upon, if not with admiration, at least with respectful silence, and at awful distance.[55]

Double standards were in operation well before Victorian times. As well as voluntarily blinding themselves to their husbands' indiscretions, wives had to be particularly careful to avoid provoking their husbands' jealousy; it was best not to arouse suspicion by appearing to like other men's company: 'Your Civilities, although innocent, may be your ruin: Your Husband will lose his Peace; and after that, yours will be of no long Continuance.'[56] A woman who attracted notice through making the smallest of errors in her relationships with men, could never be pardoned, but must expect to be pointed at and avoided. One slip in her conduct, one stain on her virtue, made her a criminal forever in respectable society. Conversely, a man could lead the life of a libertine and still be welcomed as an agreeable addition to any social gathering. The Countess of Bessborough and other titled ladies might well escape ostracism within their own social circle, but their immoral behaviour attracted censure from those of Jane Austen's rank. Maria Rushworth is allowed no second chance following her adulterous relationship with Henry Crawford. In her full-blooded early twenties, she is banished from decent society, with no prospect of male company or love in the future, while Crawford, still a good catch although a known adulterer, with an estate worth £4,000 a year, can return to his flirtations with susceptible women.

That any of Jane Austen's heroes would indulge in extra-marital relationships is unthinkable; they have chosen as their companions affectionate, intelligent wives with independent minds, why would they look elsewhere? As Henry Tilney explains to Catherine Morland, marriage is formed for the advantage of both husband and wife:

> "and that when once entered into, they belong exclusively to each other till the moment of its dissolution; that it is their duty, each to endeavour to give the other no cause for wishing that he or she had bestowed themselves elsewhere, and their best interest to keep their own imaginations from wandering towards the perfections of their neighbours, or fancying that they should have been better off with any one else."[57]

10

The Simple Regimen of Separate Rooms

Companionate marriage implied healthy sexual relationships, which inevitably led in most cases to sizeable families. A spoof article written by James Austen in *The Loiterer*, purporting to criticize marriages of affection, pointed to 'the large families with which those who marry for love are commonly blessed, and the consequent increase in population . . .'[1] He obviously did not subscribe to the view that uncontrolled procreation spelled trouble, but some of his contemporaries would have considered his pronouncements short-sighted. Thomas Malthus published his *Essay on the Principle of Population* in 1798, stressing the natural tendency of population to increase faster than the means of subsistence and advocating 'moral restraint', by which he meant sexual abstinence and marrying later to cut the birth rate. With a population of under nine million in England in the 1801 census, it seems strange to us that population growth appeared to be a serious problem, but food production was still an imprecise science and bad harvests led to malnutrition and disease, especially among the poor, while those in the middle ranks had their own reasons for worrying about large families. Dowries for daughters and the means to launch sons into the world required considerable funds; Mr Austen with six sons and two daughters seemed always to be in financial straits. As early as 1772, on the birth of the Austens' fifth child, his brother-in-law Tysoe Saul Hancock had expressed anxiety: 'That my Brother and Sister Austen are well I heartily Rejoice, but I cannot say that the News of the Violently Rapid Increase of their family gives me so much Pleasure . . .'[2] The Austens declared themselves pleased at the birth of every child, but on a rational level they must have registered the extra financial burden. Mrs Austen's brother regularly lent them money and in 1776 they begged a loan from Philadelphia Hancock's lawyer. For all James Austen's wit on the subject of numerous children, he soon came to realize that bringing up just three was an expensive business, necessitating frequent injections of money from his ex-father-in-law and rich Aunt Leigh-Perrot.

Miss Iremonger was either taking a sideways swipe at Malthus or voicing anxiety about family size when she wrote to Miss Heber in 1800, congratulating her on the birth of her sister's sixth child – 'I am extremely glad to hear of Mrs Wrightson's doing so well, & congratulate you sincerely on her safety & the addition to her family, notwithstanding our population is found to be superabundant.'[3] From her early twenties onwards, Jane Austen expressed her views more candidly – she was weary of so many children coming thick and fast, one after another in an unstoppable torrent. Both James' and Edward's wives were 'in the encreasing way'[4] within a year of marriage and Frank's wife became pregnant on her honeymoon. Only six months after the marriage of her cousin to his second wife, Mary, Eliza de Feuillide confidently expected news of another pregnancy: 'I do not hear that Mrs. James Austen is breeding, but I conclude it is so, for a Parson cannot fail of having a numerous Progeny.' Five months later, on 11 December 1797, her prediction appeared to be accurate – 'James Austen has been v. near losing his second Wife'[5] perhaps after a miscarriage. Her first child was born on 16 November 1798, after some health problems – 'rheumatism, which she would be very glad to get rid of, and still more glad to get rid of her child, of whom she is heartily tired' – was the blunt report received by Cassandra from her sister two days before the birth. If Mary had suffered a late miscarriage the previous year, it would explain her mother-in-law's desire to be kept in ignorance 'before it should be all over'.[6] James' first wife, Anne, was ill enough during her pregnancy to be confined to her bed for whole days[7] and Frank's Mary also suffered through her many pregnancies, as Jane noted with saccharine grimness: 'Mrs F.A. seldom either looks or appears quite well. — Little Embryo is troublesome I suppose.'[8] On this occasion, Mary was two months pregnant with her seventh child, after ten years of marriage.

Elizabeth Austen kept pace with her sister Sophia Deedes in baby production after their joint wedding in December 1791. Between 1793, when the first child was born, and 1808, when Elizabeth died after producing her eleventh, Sophia gave birth to thirteen children. She went on to have six more and there is every chance that her sister would have done the same had she survived. Their elder sister, Fanny Cage, married in the same year as her sisters, was more fortunate in producing only two daughters, one in 1793, the other in 1799, but whether she breathed a sigh of relief or felt inadequate is unknown. Many marriages were broken by the death of a spouse – Fanny Cage died in 1805 at the age of thirty-four – but a subsequent alliance often meant that even more children were produced, as the second marriage of Sir Edward Knatchbull, who had six children by his first wife and a further nine by his second, Fanny Knight, proves. It didn't take multiple marriages, however, to produce an over-abundance of children, as a report in the *Bath Chronicle* of 6 February 1798 showed: 'Last week Mrs. R. Banting, of Little Riffington, near Stow-on-the-Wold, was safely delivered of a daughter, being her *thirty-second* child by the same husband.'

The term 'breeding' with its farmyard connotations of helpless fecundity, was in common use across all social ranks. 'I wish with you that I was not in the same way, as I have just as many children as I wish to have, but I am afraid that I am breeding again,' wrote Lady Napier to Lady Sarah Lennox. In 1818, another correspondent noted that the more refined 'in the family way' and 'confinement' were replacing 'breeding' and 'with child' although the stark reality could never be obscured – the inescapable child a year, interspersed with miscarriages.[9] Unlike women from earlier generations, young women from the late eighteenth century into the nineteenth were able to gain a little scientific knowledge about the workings of their own bodies. Exhibitions in London of waxwork models of the female reproductive system drew in the enquiring modern girl:

> Who 'ere for wedlock ripe, is wild to see
> What must its joys, and what its pains must be;
> How in the womb the foetus is reclined,
> What passage thence by nature is designed.
> With every other circumstance beside
> That may inform her 'ere she be a bride.[10]

This kind of sex education was useful as far as it went, but nothing could be learned from waxwork representations about the kind of options that might exist for limiting family size. 'Mrs Tilson's remembrance gratifies me . . . but poor Woman! how can she be honestly breeding again?'[11] asked an exasperated Jane. The tone implies that Mrs Tilson should have done something to prevent 'breeding again' but the writer recognized that the only reliable birth control was sexual abstinence. 'Good Mrs Deedes!' she wrote to Fanny, on the birth of her Aunt Sophia's eighteenth child. '— I hope she will get the better of this Marianne, & then I wd recommend to her & Mr D. the simple regimen of separate rooms.'[12] If a husband's separate room happened to be in his mistress' house, that could also be counted as an effective exercise in damage limitation. Perhaps a number of wives regarded sharing their husbands in this manner as a problem halved.

How much did Jane Austen, or any woman, know about the alternative methods of family limitation? She did realize that once breast-feeding ceased, the chances of conception increased. Her experience of the Steventon dairy cows would have told her that. On one of Anna Lefroy's visits to Chawton in the spring of 1817, the Austen ladies were quick to notice her pallor and predict a third child on the way, since she had just stopped breast-feeding her second.[13] Anna had produced two children in two years, but this suspected pregnancy must have resulted in a miscarriage, since her third child was not born until 1818, although at the end of March 1817, she still appeared to be pregnant and unwell, prompting Jane to write to Fanny Knight:

> Anna has not a chance of escape; . . . Poor Animal, she will be worn out before she is thirty. — I am very sorry for her. — Mrs Clement too is in that way again. I am quite tired of so many Children. — Mrs Benn has a thirteenth —.[14]

Poor women, poor animals, for whom there was no real option but to go on producing children until they were worn out, or dead. Most women knew that extended suckling, although far from foolproof, could increase the spacing between children and having become pregnant only two months after the birth of her first child, Anna chose to breastfeed the second for five months. Many conduct books instructed women to prove themselves tender, fully committed mothers by suckling their own children rather than employing wet-nurses, but failed to take into account their husbands' countering sexual demands. Men could resort to their mistresses, or to the growing army of prostitutes in every town and city, and some did, but they risked weakening their fertility through contracting sexually transmitted diseases. Frustrated spouses were not the only opponents of extended suckling: one aristocratic wife found herself at loggerheads with her in-laws because she chose to breastfeed her first child, a daughter. They wanted a male heir as fast as possible and knew that nursing might postpone conception.[15] It took Mary Wollstonecraft to put the well-being of women first and openly advocate breastfeeding as a means of birth control – 'For nature has so wisely ordered things, that did women suckle their children, they would preserve their own health, and there would be such an interval between the birth of each child, that we should seldom see a houseful of babes.'[16]

Of all Jane Austen's married brothers, only Henry produced no offspring. The simplest explanation might be that Henry himself was infertile, since neither of his two wives had children by him. It is highly unlikely that sexual abstinence would have featured on Henry's agenda; he had always been fascinated by women. His first wife Eliza had experienced all she needed to of the joys of motherhood, having tended a sickly son for nine years by the time she married Henry. Well versed in the ways of the world and still feisty at thirty-six, she perhaps chose to ensure – by whatever means she could – that no further children would sap her energies or threaten her love of flirting and personal liberty. Jane never had to regard her as a 'poor animal'.

The anonymous author of a widely read sex manual at least recognized that 'there are some that desire not to have children, and yet are very fond of nocturnal embraces' and although he then went on to describe the best ways of achieving conception, couples wishing to avoid such an outcome could do the opposite. Only the most credulous, however, can have been willing to trust in coughing and sneezing or sleeping on the left side after intercourse, or frequent 'amorous engagements' as efficient contraceptive methods.[17] The process of ovulation was imperfectly understood, but the relevance of the monthly cycle to the timing of conception was recognized, if wrongly applied. It was suggested that the week immediately after menstruation was the optimum fertile period, and that it was best to practise abstinence for the rest of the month. Couples following this advice would have unknowingly discovered one method of limiting family size, although others hoping to avoid conception by avoiding the 'dangerous' first week would soon come to grief.

As far as the withdrawal method as a main brake on fertility is concerned, it is unclear how prevalent the practice was, whether it was received knowledge or discovered by individual couples by accident. The method was well known enough by 1785, when it turned up in a popular slang dictionary: 'COFFEE HOUSE: to make a coffee house of a woman's ****, to go in and out and spend nothing.'[18] The habit was condemned by clergymen and medical quacks alike, who tried to terrify those who 'wasted' their seed by prophesying illness and debility. Barrier methods had been known since the sixteenth and seventeenth centuries and recipes for pessaries were passed from mother to daughter into the eighteenth and nineteenth. Castor oil and rue were common ingredients, also pepper and mint. Their purported effectiveness lay in the cooling of the reproductive organs, which makes pepper rather an odd constituent, rather than in the destruction of sperm. The more enlightened tried more effective barrier devices, such as douches, or contraceptive sponges soaked in vinegar, attached to a ribbon for ease of removal, both of which were widely known in France. To reduce the sexual urge and reinforce abstinence, men were advised to eat 'cold' foods such as lettuce and water lily roots and seeds. Condoms as a method of birth control were not in common use until the end of the nineteenth century; in the previous century their recognized use was in the prevention of transmitted sexual diseases. They were, in any case, clumsy and expensive and linked in the popular mind with prostitution and the excesses of the upper classes.

If all else failed, as it often did, abortion provided the second line of defence. Stories were told of seduced servant girls in particular, who were desperate enough to risk their lives in attempting to rid themselves of an unwanted child, rather than face losing their jobs or their reputations. Miss Weeton, a governess, wrote a letter to a friend in 1807 about a kitchen maid, whom she suspected of taking something to effect a miscarriage, which had not had the desired effect, but 'has light on herself. She has looked a bad colour ever since.'[19] Mary Wollstonecraft's fictional piece, *The*

Wrongs of Woman, or Maria: A Fragment, written in 1798, told the same tale of seduction and recourse to desperate measures, this time forcibly administered by the seducer. Dire warnings were issued by many writers of certain painful death, followed by God's wrath:

> My blood runs cold, and my hand trembles, in proceeding to describe the far more inevitable dangers that attend abortion brought on by artificial means. Ah! what a struggle between the emotions of pity for the sufferer, and of horror at the fatal cause! So wicked an outrage upon nature is sure to be punished with tortures and with death.[20]

The focus on single, lower-class women, whose plight was desperate and easily discovered, did not tell the whole story, however. Explicit advertisements aimed at women with unwanted pregnancies appeared in national and local newspapers throughout the country; even the Act of 1803 which made abortion illegal did not entirely put paid to such offers. One example concludes: 'Women labouring under obstructions from causes they are desirous concealing, would perhaps consult their own interest in an immediate application to the Doctor. The strictest delicacy, honour and secrecy, will, upon every occasion, be observed.'[21] James Austen could have had any one of a number of such advertisements in mind when he penned the following attack in his journal *The Loiterer*, published from Oxford between 1789 and 1790:

> In a corner of the same paper which contains the benevolent exertions of the supporters of the Bill for the Abolition of the Slave Trade, of Sir Joseph Andrews, Dr. Hawes and the Humane Society, for the comfort and preservation of mankind – the diabolical assassin of the human species in Embryo, to the eternal disgrace of the Police of Great Britain, is permitted to hold out an infamous temptation to the basest of murders; at the same time professing, that the *strictest honour, delicacy, and secrecy*, will, upon every occasion be observed.[22]

One particular advertisement appeared on a daily basis for twenty years, in newspapers up and down the country. The wording stayed more or less the same in each publication, promising a discreet midwifery service for pregnant women who wished their condition to remain a secret, 'their Infant put out to Nurse, and humanely taken Care of', but also offering for sale 'the Restorative Salo Pills, at £1. 2s. per Box; an effectual Remedy to remove all Obstructions or Irregularities.'[23] In modern day currency, the pills would cost about £50 a box. *The Morning Post* of 18 April 1780, carried an even more overt offer:

> TO THE LADIES.
> ANY LADY whose situation may require a temporary retirement, may be accommodated agreeable to her wishes in the house of a gentleman of eminence in the profession, where honour and secrecy may be depended on, and where every vestige of pregnancy is obliterated: . . .

Women who had been through pregnancy before would recognize the early signs and act quickly – miscarriages experienced by married women often passed without suspicion. The dangers of abortion were certainly frightening, but so were the ordeals of pregnancy and childbirth. Married women from all social groups took various potions and employed other means, often with the full agreement of their husbands, in order to prevent a further drain on the household finances and to protect their own state of health. Lady Caroline Fox wrote ruefully to her husband about her suspicions of a third child on the way, following hot on the heels of the second: 'I am in a great fright, and if my fears prove true, I shall be vastly angry with you . . . for 'twould be very hard for me as I have not yet recovered my strength from the last lying-in.'[24] Her husband had evidently insisted on his conjugal rights at a dangerous time. 'I'm certainly breeding,' she reported several days later. 'I took a great deal of physic yesterday in hopes to send it away, but it has only convinced me my fears prove true.' Luckily for her, the 'physic' eventually proved effective and she wrote again in improved spirits: 'I am not breeding (is not that clever).'[25] Such references are rare, but another comes to light slightly later, in 1847. Lady Henrietta Stanley, who had nine children already, wrote to her husband Edward about a suspected tenth. Her last child had been born three years previously and Lady Henrietta was now approaching forty, which accounts for some of her anxiety and her husband's comments about 'juvenile' proceedings. Why he should hold her entirely responsible is not so readily understood:

> This your last misfortune is indeed most grievous & puts all others in the shade. What can you have been doing to account for so juvenile a proceeding, it comes

> so opportunely to disturb all your family arrangements & revives the nursery & Williams in full vigour. I only hope it is not the beginning of another flock for what to do with them I am sure I know not. I am afraid however it is too late to mend & you must make the best of it tho' bad is best . . .

The following day, Lady Henrietta expressed her relief: 'A hot bath, a tremendous walk & a great dose have succeeded but it is a warning . . . I feel not too well which makes me idle.' Her husband then voiced his fears about the methods she had employed to bring about the miscarriage:

> I hope you are not going to do yourself any harm by your violent proceedings, for though it would be a great bore it is not worth while playing tricks to escape its consequences. If however you are none the worse the great result is all the better.

She replied: 'I was sure you would feel the same horror I did at an increase of family but I am reassured for the future by the efficacy of the means.'[26]

What the 'great dose' comprised, Lady Henrietta did not say, but there were plenty of easily procured herbal abortifacients, most of them common in English gardens and fields: black hellebore, mugwort, rue, pennyroyal, angelica, bistort, chervil, feverfew and the most powerful of all, savin. 'To describe a plant so well known is needless,' wrote Culpeper in the 1835 edition of his popular herbal, 'it being nursed up almost in every garden.' A number of recipes in herbals and in medical books of the time were described as useful for 'restoring the menses' or 'provoking the terms' or clearing 'obstructions' and although the writers of herbals protected themselves against suspicion by condemning the use of abortifacients, these recipes could obviously be effective in causing miscarriages. Women at this time did not consider the foetus alive until movement in the womb was detected, about forty to fifty days after conception, and doctors' ability to diagnose pregnancy in the early stages was hardly more advanced than their patients'. The concept of 'quickening' was upheld by the law even after 1803, when abortion became illegal, which allowed women to consider legitimate any remedies for reinstating menstruation. Most doctors, however, did not recognize such a concept, claiming that the foetus was alive from the time of conception.

Natural remedies used to expel the afterbirth or dead child could also be tried to effect miscarriages, referred to euphemistically as 'accidents'. That Jane Austen was aware of such stratagems is seen in a letter to Cassandra in 1801. In reply to her sister's sly intimation that the widowed, forty-seven-year-old Mrs Knight had recently given birth, she stated:

> I am happy to hear of Mrs Knight's amendment, whatever might be her complaint. I cannot think so ill of her however inspite of your insinuations as to suspect her of having lain-in. — I do not think she would be betrayed beyond an *Accident* at the utmost.[27]

At the end of the eighteenth century and into the nineteenth, savin was recognized as one of the most powerful abortifacients, as was ergot of rye. Controlled doses of the latter were used to stop maternal bleeding after childbirth; the danger lay in the convulsions and hallucinations, constriction of the arteries and gangrene which an inexperienced user could induce by taking too much. Earlier herbals listed savin as 'a powerful Provoker of the Catamenia, causing Abortion, and expelling the Birth . . .'[28] John Burns, a renowned lecturer on midwifery in Glasgow, certainly recognized savin as an effective abortifacient, but also repeated the warnings regarding violent exercise, physical shocks such as tooth-pulling and any 'strong passion of the mind'. At least he was enlightened enough to promote the idea that 'when the safety of the mother demands this interference abortion is justified'.[29]

Recipes for menstrual 'obstructions' were given in many widely available family medical books: William Buchan provided one for a 'Deobstruent Pill' comprising 'salt of steel; succotrine aloes; myrrh in powder; of each a dram.' He indicated the common causes of miscarriage, with the aim of prevention, but his list was also helpful to those who wished to terminate a pregnancy: '. . . violent exercise; raising great weights; reaching too high; jumping, or stepping from an eminence . . . coughing . . . falls . . . high living . . .'[30] Buchan himself spoke out against abortion by any means and castigated 'Those wretches who daily advertise their assistance to women in this business',[31] warning his readers that:

> there is not known nor ever was, either in the regular profession of medicine nor among quacks or midwives, any drug or combination of drugs, which will

> have the certain effect of procuring a miscarriage; and those who pretend that there are such things, do so with the knavish design of making money of the ignorant . . .

He implied that the 'restorative' pills supplied by dubious sources contained cantharides, powdered blistering flies. He described in graphic language the effects of taking such a dangerous drug, frightening enough to deter any but the most desperate:

> . . . burning heat of the stomach, vomiting more or less bloody, intolerable griping pains of the belly and bladder, great pain in making water, which is usually bloody. These distressing symptoms often end in delirium, convulsions, and death. Violent however as these effects are, there is not commonly produced any tendency to miscarriage when cantharides are given with that view . . .[32]

If the dangers inherent in limiting family size by artificial means were potentially lethal, the rigours of childbearing were equally fraught. In the early nineteenth century, the average age of puberty was fifteen, while the menopause kicked in between forty-five and fifty.[33] When, at the age of thirty-seven, her sister had only two children to her credit and there were no signs of any more, Mrs Austen wondered if she had 'done'.[34] Women faced extreme physical wear and tear, especially if they had started producing children while still in their teens, turning motherhood into an all-consuming task when the older children's concerns in the wider world coincided with later pregnancies and infant feeding. The Morland family in *Northanger Abbey* is a case in point. With ten children, Catherine's mother is so overwhelmed by the demands of lying-in and teaching the younger of her brood, that she barely has time to consider the education of the older ones. Jane Austen saw this happen to so many women of her acquaintance that she warned Fanny Knight against marrying too soon: 'by not beginning the business of Mothering quite so early in life, you will be young in Constitution, spirits, figure & countenance, while Mrs Wm. Hammond is growing old by confinements & nursing.'[35] Fanny was twenty-three and not what most people would have considered too young to marry and start a family, but she would have at least twenty-two fertile years ahead of her. When she wrote this advice, Jane also had in mind the death at thirty-five of Fanny's mother Elizabeth, after producing her eleventh child, and of Charles Austen's wife Frances at twenty-four, on the birth of her fourth. Both had started producing children before they were twenty. It is no coincidence that the heroine of *Persuasion* is married off at the relatively late age of twenty-seven, allowing her fewer than twenty years in which to reproduce.

Concern for female friends and relations is evident in other letters written by women at the time: 'Sunday we dined at Mr A. Drummond's and met with Mrs John Dd. She has lost her beauty and seems very indifferent, I fancy she has bred too fast having had 7 children . . .' confided Lady Northampton to Eliza Chute, adding, 'Mrs W. Gosling is very indifferent but as she is not with Child I hope she will recover her strength.'[36] Eliza herself was worried enough to give this last-mentioned friend a direct warning: 'I hope you are not likely to add a sixth bambino to your nursery; five is enough to have the charge of, & Me. De Sévigné our old friend, would tell you how necessary rest is to your health.'[37] What Madame de Sévigné also told the women who read her famous letters to her daughter was not to trust in the efficacy of merely sleeping separately: 'I pray you, my dear, don't pride yourself on two beds; it is only a temptation; have someone sleep in your room.' Many mothers warned their daughters to protect themselves against the inevitable effects on their bodies of almost continual pregnancy: 'I don't know whether I shall make any court to you in saying it, but I own I can't help thinking that your family is numerous enough . . .' wrote Lady Mary Wortley Montagu to her daughter.[38]

Lack of adequate medical skill and care resulted in mother and child fatalities. At the end of the eighteenth century, nine in every one thousand births were fatal to the mother. Inadequate knowledge of hygiene on the part of some rural midwives led to infection and one baby in every four was stillborn. Mrs Hall of Sherborne gave birth to a dead child within a few weeks of full term, as a result of a sudden shock. The news reached Jane Austen the following day and rather than express horror at the awful event, with James' wife eight months into her first pregnancy, '& uncommonly large', she reports several lines earlier in the letter, she makes a savage joke: 'I suppose she happened unawares to look at her husband.'[39] Better to defy death with a cruel jibe rather than allow it to overshadow life, when even those mothers who received the best that was available in medical care were subject to miscarriage and physical exhaustion. Three daughters of the second Earl of Ilchester lost several babies this way; one of them wrote: 'I am going to try what profound quiet will do . . . My repeated miscarriages have so weakened me, and I have so little recovered my strength from the last, that I feel nothing but great care will make me go on now.' Her sister suffered three miscarriages in one year and another the following year.[40] Mrs Austen was one of the lucky ones. She had eight children, all of whom survived, and she remained strong, despite occasional bouts of unspecified illness. She lived to eighty-seven and was still digging potatoes in her seventies. Her robust constitution is reflected in Jane Austen's description of Mrs Morland, a healthy mother of ten and to a lesser degree in the active Mrs Gardiner. Mrs Austen herself might have wondered how Lady Bertram ever exerted herself enough to produce four children, however much she languished on the sofa afterwards.

It is hardly surprising that none of the childless married women in Jane Austen's fiction voices any regrets about a lack of offspring. Mrs Smith must have experienced nothing but relief that she had escaped a greater weakening of her health; Mrs Allen spends her time and money on clothes instead, and Mrs Croft, the happiest married woman in all of Jane Austen's fiction, is able to accompany her husband wherever he goes. It is not easy to imagine Mrs Norris as a sexual being at all and considering Fanny Dashwood's cold self-regard, her withdrawal from the marital bed after the birth of her only son would be entirely credible. A chilling portrayal of their fortune depleted by a surfeit of children and little Harry's certain impoverishment would be enough to freeze her husband's ardour.

We speculate at the end of every novel how the heroines will manage their married lives, how they will overcome their biological destiny when so many women failed. We are unwilling to imagine Anne Elliot denied the freedom of a child-free Mrs Croft, or Catherine, Elinor, Marianne, Lizzie, Fanny and Emma overwhelmed by the physical and emotional demands of husbands and innumerable children. The closing pages of *Sense and Sensibility* and *Mansfield Park* make it clear that Marianne and Fanny begin to produce children almost immediately, but if 'It is impossible to imagine Darcy inflicting a yearly baby on Elizabeth'[41] it is equally impossible to imagine voluntary sexual abstinence for any couple who marry for love.

The best we can hope for is low fertility, frequent separation, enlightened advice on family limitation and, given the age difference between them and their wives, the early deaths of Mr Knightley and Colonel Brandon. Jane Austen wisely put down her pen and left her readers to conjecture what happened next, not because she knew nothing about the consequences of married love, but because she knew too much.

11

The Years of Danger

Twenty-five per cent of gentlemen's daughters in Jane Austen's lifetime never married, either through choice or, more commonly, lack of opportunity. Females outnumbered males throughout the eighteenth century and the gap widened gradually until, in 1851, there was a surplus of 365,000 women over men in England and Wales.[1] How many hopeful years did single women have before they gave up looking for a husband, or potential husbands gave up considering them? At twenty-nine years of age, Sir Walter Elliot's eldest daughter, with her heart firmly set on marrying a baronet, experiences a growing apprehension that she is 'approaching the years of danger'. Once into her thirties, her chances of marrying will be drastically reduced. Given that the average age on marriage was twenty-four for women in the late eighteenth century, she is five years past her sell-by date, but because her face has worn well, she has not entirely relinquished all hope of finding a titled mate.

As a general rule, women expected to be married by the age of twenty-six, although there were a number who became wives beyond this age. Anne Mathew married James Austen when she was thirty; Catherine Bigg was thirty-three on her marriage to Mr Hill; in the novels, Charlotte Lucas and Anne Elliot are rescued from spinsterhood at twenty-seven. Childbirth was always a dangerous process, but the risks faced by women bearing their first child beyond their late twenties were even more considerable. On the other hand, the later a woman married, the fewer the childbearing years she had to endure. Older men choosing second wives might settle for women who were considered to be past their prime. Frank Austen's second wife, Martha Lloyd, was sixty-three; Emma's companion Miss Taylor is in her mid-thirties when Mr Weston chooses to marry her. While bachelors could fare relatively well without ever considering marriage, especially those with independent means or a sufficient income from their professions, the position of single women, whether spinsters or widows, was a very different matter. Compulsive husband-hunting had an economic basis: a single man with money might choose to have a wife, but he was not in want of one; a single woman with neither fortune nor the means of earning her living, needed a husband for financial security, especially if she had no brothers.

The plight of the impecunious single woman was dire and almost anything was to be preferred to the ridicule spinsters had to tolerate. They were the rejects, the women left over after men had chosen their wives, each one a potential threat to the financial health of the nation. Society in general mocked what it feared, as Jane Austen has Emma explain to Harriet Smith. A woman with money who chooses to stay single will always be respected, because she has the means to support herself and maintain her position in society: '". . . it is poverty only which makes celibacy contemptible to a generous public! A single woman, with a very narrow income, must be a ridiculous, disagreeable, old maid! the proper sport of boys and girls."'[2] This is the 'generous public's' opinion, not Emma's, but she does recognize that straitened circumstances meant the closing down of social opportunities, which in turn led almost inevitably to envy, resentment and crippling insularity. Miss Bates is an exception; poor as she is, her mind is open to receive any and every impression and when Emma stoops to make sport of her on Box Hill, Mr Knightley administers a stern reprimand. There are no men in the Bates family to provide any kind of financial support to enable Miss Bates and her mother to maintain the genteel position to which they were born. And even where there were brothers, their generosity was not guaranteed. One contributor to the mass of articles on the helpless dependency of the unmarried woman, a subject aired regularly in periodicals of the time, accurately envisaged the misery of her contracted life:

> . . . it is probable, that after having passed the sprightly years of youth in the comfortable mansion of an opulent father, she is reduced to the shelter of some contracted lodging in a country town, attended by a single female servant, and with difficulty living on the interest of two or three thousand pounds, reluctantly, and perhaps irregularly, paid to her by an avaricious or extravagant brother, who

> considers such payment as a heavy encumbrance on his paternal estate. Such is the condition in which the unmarried daughters of English gentlemen are too frequently found.[3]

A spinster sister who had filled the useful role of housekeeper for a bachelor brother might find herself in this position when that brother married. Unfitted by her scant education to become a governess and prevented by society from taking other paid employment – 'unable to work and ashamed to beg' – she could find herself forced out of the family home by an unsympathetic sister-in-law, and grudgingly granted only a small allowance to supply her needs. Mary Wollstonecraft's description of such a hard-hearted interloper fits Fanny Dashwood like a glove, and although the circumstances of her step-in-laws' removal from Norland do not exactly match Wollstonecraft's example, they are close enough for comparison: 'jealous of the little kindness which her husband shews to his relations . . . she is displeased at seeing the property of *her* children lavished on an helpless sister.'[4] Fanny puts a stop to all of her husband's intended little kindnesses before his hand reaches his pocket, thus condemning Mrs Dashwood and her daughters to an existence circumscribed by what they cannot afford: they can keep no carriage, no horses, no company and few servants. Their lack of money restricts the girls' chances of meeting potential husbands, unless men come to them and, even then, those men will need to be highly altruistic to ignore the absence of fortune. Jane Austen created such men for Elinor and Marianne, but many single women in reduced circumstances were not so lucky.

The Austen women were fortunate that the men in the family contributed towards their financial support without question on Mr Austen's death in 1805. His pension of £600 per annum expired with him and with no welfare state, Jane, Cassandra and their mother were left with very little to sustain them. There was no grudging acceptance of responsibility in the Austen men's immediate response, but Henry's letter to Frank on the occasion carries a surprising echo of Fanny Dashwood's insensitivity when she considered the plight of her husband's kin: '"Altogether, they will have five hundred a year amongst them, and what on earth can four women want for more than that? They will live so cheap! . . . Only conceive how comfortable they will be!"'[5] A complacent Henry reassured Frank that the Austen ladies would survive very comfortably:

> & as a smaller establishment will be as agreeable to them, as it cannot but be feasible, I really think that My Mother & Sisters will be to the full as rich as ever. They will not only suffer no personal deprivation, but will be able to pay occasional visits of health and pleasure to their friends . . . [6]

The sum on which the Austen ladies were expected to live was £450 a year, which reduced them to one female servant and furnished rooms in Bath's Gay Street, a definite slide down the property scale from three servants and a whole house, affordable on Mr Austen's pension of £600. At least their social circle did not contract; unlike the Dashwood women in the depths of Devon, the Austens could get around the streets of Bath on foot to repay visits and there is evidence in Jane's letters that the number of callers did not fall off. None of the sons appeared at this stage to consider that their mother and sisters might prefer a more settled existence in a permanent home of their own; they envisaged that the three women would spend winters in rented accommodation in Bath and summers visiting relations, which is just what happened. In June 1805, they stayed at Steventon for a short while on their way to Godmersham, where they spent the rest of June and all of July. Mrs Austen accompanied Anna back to Steventon then, and Jane and Cassandra stayed on in Kent until September. September saw them all in Worthing, where they took lodgings until November, and by January they had returned to Steventon. From there, Jane and Cassandra travelled on to Manydown near Basingstoke to stay with their friends the Biggs and Mrs Austen returned to Bath to try to secure lodgings somewhere other than the poky environs of Trim Street. Cassandra and Jane eventually arrived back in Bath in March, after having spent most of 1805 living an unsatisfactory, nomadic life in other people's houses. Little wonder that Jane wrote little or nothing during this unsettled time, while she and her mother and sister were handed around the family. 'I think we are just the kind of people and party to be treated about among our relations;' she noted wryly in the spring before their travels began, 'we cannot be supposed to be very rich.'[7]

Their reliance on the men in the family for money and mobility was unavoidable, but at least they *could* be supported. Poor Mary Benn was not so fortunate. Her brother, the rector at Farringdon, had a large and ever increasing family – twelve by the time his sister died – which swallowed every penny of his income. Her Chawton neighbours, however, every bit as charitable as Miss Bates' kind friends in Highbury, were determined not to see her starve. Between them, the Papillons, Clements, Digweeds and Austens made sure that Miss Benn was provided with a good meal and company five days out of every seven. It is to be hoped that their benevolence went some way towards protecting her from the stone-throwing and name-calling endured by so many women in her situation. The Austen ladies did what they could, inviting her for dinner, replacing her old worn out fur wrap with a new shawl and entertaining her with readings from *Pride and Prejudice* two nights running: 'She was amused, poor soul!'[8] Poor soul! – Miss Benn at forty-two was only five years older than Jane Austen, but the younger woman was alive to the difference between a tolerable dependence and grinding poverty. There was not much that could be done when Miss Benn was turned out of her cottage so that the landlord's son could move in, and though her accommodation had been wretchedly damp and draughty, at least she had lived among generous friends. The lodgings she moved into after that were not as close to the Austens' cottage as formerly, since Jane surmised that Miss Benn would have to stay the night if invited to dinner. Only four more years of penury lay ahead of this unfortunate spinster; she died in near-destitute circumstances in 1815, at the age of forty-six.

Gentlewomen with reduced means depended for their comfort on the financial help provided by the extended family, which usually meant male relatives. In the absence of men, other solutions had to be found. Scraping a living on £100 a year, which was the minimum amount needed to keep one servant, and largely reliant on the charity of their neighbours, Miss Bates and her mother can just about get by, but their niece will have to make her own way in the world, as a governess. Jane Fairfax's fate seems inescapable; her entire education has been directed towards this end. Mrs Elton might crow about wax candles in Mrs Bragge's schoolroom, but Jane Fairfax's unenviable position as a governess would not be materially improved by such a luxury. She would be expected to work from seven in the morning to seven at night, seven days a week, with no real companionship or appreciation of her intellect. Mrs Elton's claims that Jane's musical talents alone would allow her to mix freely with the family and state her own terms are born of ignorance. A governess earned scant reward for her services; the going rate was between £12 and £30 a year, more if she could speak French fluently and play the harp. Emma has a clearer understanding of Jane Fairfax's destiny; that she is doomed to a life of humiliation, even though her accomplishments far outshine Emma's own: 'when she considered what all this elegance was destined to, what she was going to sink from, how she was going to live, it seemed impossible to feel anything but compassion and respect.'[9] Jane Fairfax as a governess would think herself fortunate to be the recipient of anyone's sympathy or respect. Miss Weeton, a governess for many years in the real world, experienced a very different set of responses to her lowly position and decided at the age of thirty-seven that she would rather marry than continue to suffer the trials of spinsterhood:

> . . . the finger of contempt, the smile of ridicule . . . An old maid is a stock for everyone to laugh at. Every article of dress, every word, every movement is satirized. Boys play tricks on them and are applauded. Girls sneer at them and are unreproved.[10]

Spinsters not educated to become governesses were expected to make themselves useful by taking on their married sisters' household duties during periods of indisposition or of lying-in and nursing. Many were keen to step into those sisters' shoes permanently if they died, but marriages between sisters-in-law and brothers-in-law were contrary to the Table of Kindred in *The Book of Common Prayer* and were often seen as verging on the incestuous. They were frowned on, but not illegal until the law changed in 1835. If challenged before this date, however, an annulment followed and all of the resultant children were declared illegitimate. This was a most unfair system, which operated against the interests of the whole family. The dead wife's sister was well known to the existing children and she probably lived of necessity and practicality under the same roof as the bereaved husband. This in itself created difficulties, since such an arrangement would have been considered improper without a chaperon, and how many families could afford to pay for a constant female companion? When Charles Austen married his dead wife's sister in 1820, Mrs Austen gave her qualified approval – while recognizing Harriet's usefulness to the children, she was not entirely taken with her sullen demeanour – but she was relieved that they had moved to live among strangers in Cornwall. She wrote to her granddaughter Anna in August:

> I am *now* very glad his residence is at such a distance, by and bye wonder and censure will subside and in a year or two he may be willing to change his station for one nearer his family and friends.[11]

Married women without private fortunes or adequate jointures written into their marriage settlements formed another needy group on the death of their husbands. In *Sense and Sensibility*, Jane Austen describes the contrasting positions of three widows: the wealthy Mrs Ferrars with a large fortune and property; Mrs Jennings with a generous jointure to live on, enough for her to keep a house in a smart area of London, and Mrs Dashwood, possessing no property and only £500 a year to share with her three daughters. The law of primogeniture disadvantaged many spinsters and widows – Mrs Dashwood loses Norland to her stepson, Mrs Bennet will lose Longbourne to Mr Collins – but not all estates were subject to this rule. Lady Catherine de Bourgh remained *in situ* at Rosings on Sir Lewis' demise and makes it clear that her daughter will eventually inherit the property. Single women at Jane Austen's level of society were not usually so fortunate, in that many of them did not have fathers with private houses to start with. On Mrs Lloyd's death in 1805, the rented house at Ibthorpe had to be relinquished, leaving the unmarried eldest daughter and a penurious old friend homeless. The Austen ladies offered Martha a home with them, but Mrs Stent struggled to find anyone who would take her in. 'Poor Mrs Stent!' Jane wrote to Cassandra with perceptive empathy, 'it has been her lot to be always in the way; but we must be merciful, for perhaps in time we may come to be Mrs Stents ourselves, unequal to anything & unwelcome to everybody'.[12]

Clergymen's widows and families were particularly vulnerable, as Jane Austen knew from her own experiences following her father's death in 1805. Mary and Caroline Austen faced the same fate on James' death at the end of 1819, when they were ousted from Steventon Rectory by the next incumbent, Henry Austen. Fourteen-year-old Caroline's description of Henry's tactless eagerness in taking over the parsonage recalls with unconscious irony Jane's annoyance at Mary and James' usurpation eighteen years before:

> He was always very affectionate in manner to us, and paid my mother every due attention, but his own spirits he could *not* repress, and it is not pleasant to *witness* the elation of your successor in gaining what *you* have lost; . . .[13]

Over the subsequent years, Mary and her daughter lived in various rented properties in the Newbury area, having lost their much loved home and the financial wherewithal to maintain their previous status. Mrs Austen and Cassandra's economic circumstances were adversely affected by James' death too, and they were grateful for the £100 yearly allowance which Mrs Leigh-Perrot eventually granted Mrs Austen in 1820, out of her considerable wealth. She must have been aware of her niece and sister-in-law's plight before this date, but what finally pricked her conscience and let the moths out of her purse is unclear. Mrs Austen had lost the £50 per annum James paid her, and since neither Henry, as a result of his bank's collapse, nor Frank and Charles, due to the rapid increase in their families, had been contributing anything towards her upkeep for the previous four years, she was struggling to make ends meet. Edward allowed her to stay in the Chawton house rent free and granted her £200 a year, but apart from that, she and her remaining daughter had little to live on. The small amounts which dribble into and out of the Austen ladies' accounts bear no comparison to the lump sums of £1,000 and £2,000 regularly invested in stock by Mrs Leigh-Perrot throughout the 1820s.[14]

Even well-off single women had their problems, of accommodation and mobility. Mary Crawford's fortune of £20,000 does not entitle her to live where she pleases; for the sake of respectability, she must find a home either with her sister and brother-in-law at Mansfield Parsonage, or with Henry at Everingham. She cannot travel alone, but must depend on the whim of her brother. Emma Woodhouse, with £30,000 and as much local consequence as she could wish, has never seen the sea, or even visited Box Hill, a mere seven miles away. The lack of status was another drawback: married women took precedence, no matter how questionable their character or intelligence. Lydia Wickham assumes a higher status than her two eldest sisters, even though their intelligence and maturity are vastly superior to hers; Mrs Elton precedes Emma into Highbury's dining and drawing rooms. It was a situation that Jane Austen, as a single woman, experienced time and again.

The common fate of the unmarried female taught many young women that it was best not to be too choosy about whom they would accept as husbands. Elizabeth Elliot, less than a year off her thirtieth birthday and determined to marry no one beneath the status of baronet, is likely to remain single, doomed to the disappointment of never seeing her marriage entered in her father's book of books, the *Baronetage of England*. In *The Watsons*, a less fastidious eldest daughter voices her fears about ending up an old maid, even though she is not particularly keen to marry:

> "I could do very well single for my own part – A little company, and a pleasant ball now and then, would be enough for me, if one could be young forever, but my father cannot provide for us, and it is very bad to grow old and be poor and laughed at. —"

The only remedy is marriage and she knows there is no point in setting her sights too high: '"I should not like marrying a disagreable man . . . but I do not think there *are* very many disagreable men; – I think I could like any good humoured man with a comfortable income."'[15] In a world where genteel young women with negligible fortunes must marry or face social denigration and humiliating reliance on their male relations, the choice between marrying or staying single could be relatively uncomplicated, as Jane Austen recognized. 'Single Women have a dreadful propensity for being poor —' she informed Fanny Knight, 'which is one very strong argument in favour of Matrimony.'[16] For those less discerning than Jane Austen or her heroines, marriage appeared a matter of necessity or expectation, rather than inclination – 'for, you know, we are always *to be* married till we *are*' was Miss Iremonger's not altogether serious observation to Miss Heber.[17] With a life of certain penury ahead of her, Lucy Steele's determination to hang on to Edward Ferrars – at least until she finds a man with more money – is understandable, if calculating. He is her best prospect for the future, as Mr Collins is Charlotte Lucas'. Marriage, for young women with no fortune, 'however uncertain of giving happiness, must be their pleasantest preservative from want.'[18] In some cases, other female members of the family could also be rescued from a necessitous existence by a prudent marriage. Isabella Thorpe, as the eldest and prettiest of the daughters, must, like Jane Bennet, marry well to improve the prospects of her sisters and ensure her mother a comfortable old age.

Plain girls with negligible fortunes existed in every corner of the kingdom and Charlotte Lucas' strategy for getting a husband was just one of many. Mary Bennet has to work harder than her prettier sisters at gaining accomplishments and eventually, according to Austen family tradition, gains one of Uncle Philips' clerks.[19] Plain girls could not afford the romantic ambitions of attractive girls in similar financial straits. An unexceptional woman with money, on the other hand, could expect to find a husband somehow – Mrs Grant with £5,000 is comfortably married, however affronted Lady Bertram might be at her 'being so well settled in life without being handsome'. Miss Campbell with £12,000 is obviously inferior to Jane Fairfax, in both beauty and accomplishments, but this does her no disservice with the rich and personable Mr. Dixon, who finds her attractive because she *is* ordinary. A lively, dark-eyed Elizabeth Bennet can aspire to a tall, handsome, rich Mr. Darcy and her beautiful elder sister gains a husband with £4,000 a year. Women with beauty *and* money could aim for baronets, or the younger sons of earls.

Beauty, enhanced by a fortune, made a difference to women's opportunity to make a good match, and marrying well is Mary Crawford's objective. She expects to marry to advantage, and does not object when her sister fixes on Tom Bertram as the man. The eldest son of a baronet is not considered too good for her, as she has beauty and accomplishments thrown in. Miss Crawford may choose her degree of wealth. Her fortune, invested at 5%, would provide a husband with £1,000 a year income. Her plans unravel when she becomes attracted to Edmund, but she cannot quite overcome her distaste of his chosen career or relinquish her ambition to have a house in London. At the end of the novel, she is still aware that she can command a husband with a title, but no one seems quite good enough. Maria Ward, the future Lady Bertram, with only £7,000, had captivated a baronet with her beauty. Her two daughters, with 'beauty and brilliant acquirements' are both on the lookout for rich husbands. The eldest Miss Ward, however, was not prepared to risk losing her looks while waiting for another Sir Thomas Bertram to turn up and 'found herself obliged to be attached to the Rev. Mr Norris . . . with scarcely any private fortune', six years after her younger sister's more advantageous match. As Jane Austen realistically points out, 'there certainly are not so many men of large fortune in the world, as there are pretty women to deserve them'.[20]

Women intent on avoiding the horrors of spinsterhood, plain and handsome alike, did their best to attract husbands without appearing to do so. Polite society dictated that it should be the man who did the chasing and choosing, the woman was to sit and wait and not reveal her preference until assured of a return. At the same time, there was universal suspicion that women were always out to trick men, any men, into matrimony. 'I am prevented from setting my black cap at Mr Maitland by his having a wife & ten Children. —' Jane commented tartly on society's unshakeable conviction that at twenty-five, she must be desperate to hunt down a husband. Female accomplishments, commonly the ability to play an instrument, draw, speak French, sew, dress to advantage and move elegantly, were indispensable in the marriage market and formed the limited constituents of what women were taught. The false pride aroused by such superficial acquirements was identified and deflated by Jane Austen in her fictional writing. Margaret and Matilda Lesley, early versions of Maria and Julia Bertram, possess boundless confidence in their abilities to attract men:

> We read, we work, we walk, and when fatigued with these employments, relieve our spirits either by a lively song, a graceful dance, or by some smart bon mot, and witty repartee. We are handsome . . . very handsome and the greatest of our perfections is that we are entirely insensible of them ourselves.[21]

Jane Austen at sixteen, the age at which she wrote *Lesley Castle*, recognized the contradictions inherent in the conspicuous exhibition of 'perfections' and the exercise of complete humility and modesty advocated in conduct literature. At thirty-eight, she built on that awareness in her creation of the Bertram sisters, whose 'vanity was in such good order that they seemed to be quite free from it . . . while the praises attending such behaviour . . .

served to strengthen them in believing they had no faults.'[22] In their Aunt Norris' opinion, the sole purpose of the kind of training they have received is to gain a good establishment: '"Give a girl an education, and introduce her properly into the world, and ten to one but she has the means of settling well, without farther expense to any body."'[23] Education is a main theme running through all of Jane Austen's fiction, but her use of the term comprehends personal growth through judicious reading, observation and experience, with the aim of reaching a better understanding of oneself and others. In *Persuasion*, the Musgrove girls return home from their expensive school in Exeter with plenty of self-esteem and musical talent, but while Anne Elliot approves their easy manners, she prefers her own 'elegance of mind'; in other words, her own natural taste and intelligence. None of the heroines has been 'brought up to the trade of *coming out*'.[24] Fanny Price resists exhibiting herself as a marriageable commodity by refusing drawing and music lessons, preferring instead to educate herself, under Edmund's guidance, by extensive reading. Emma Woodhouse and Lizzie Bennet fail to apply themselves seriously to their piano exercises and Catherine Morland, having little aptitude, gives up playing as soon as possible and is hopeless at sketching. Elinor Dashwood is proficient in drawing, Marianne in playing the piano, but these pursuits are followed for the pleasure they give to the practitioner and the sisters' catalogue of accomplishments ends there. Mary Crawford, on the other hand, knows exactly how to charm Edmund Bertram by displaying her shapely arms and ankles as she plays the harp. *The Mirror of Graces* certainly recognized the powerful combination of seductive curves and contours and recommended young women to master the harp above all instruments:

> the shape of the instrument is calculated, in every respect, to show a fine figure to advantage . . . the turn and polish of a beautiful hand and arm, the richly-slippered and well-made foot on the pedal stops, the gentle motion of a lovely neck, and, above all, the sweetly-tempered expression of an intelligent countenance, when the fair performer is seated unaffectedly, yet gracefully, at the harp.[25]

Conversations at Netherfield and Rosings highlight the demand for young women to perform, to demonstrate their talents in order to attract a husband. Darcy's criticism of the superficial female accomplishments admired by Mr Bingley – '"They all paint tables, cover skreens and net purses"' – carries some weight, but his high expectations of female acquirements are unrealistic. A woman must be a prodigy to be proficient in all of the areas Darcy specifies, as Elizabeth points out, but how many women wilted with inferiority when faced with such demands? He thinks that none but the most perfect woman will tempt him into matrimony, but he is 'caught' by Elizabeth's fine eyes and lively intelligence, even though her figure is not 'symmetrical'. His list of must-haves comprises physical as well as mental requirements and is impossibly prescriptive, but he quickly comes to realize that conventional accomplishments have nothing to do with Elizabeth's attraction – she does not play the piano brilliantly and confesses readily to possessing no aptitude for drawing.

Jane Austen's amoral heroine, Lady Susan, questions the advantages of a more than superficial education for her daughter and concludes that it is a waste of time for young women to acquire extensive knowledge in languages, arts and sciences: 'to be mistress of French, Italian, German, music, singing, drawing, etc., will gain a woman some applause, but will not add one lover to her list.'[26] Only 'grace and manner' are necessary for attracting men, as she has discovered for herself. That education could form a well-rounded character or exist as an end in itself would not occur to her, nor to many of her persuasion. Perhaps Lady Susan had in mind for her daughter the kind of instruction that the Bridges sisters of Goodnestone received at the 'Ladies' Eton' in Bloomsbury, which comprised little more than French, music and dancing and how to get into and out of a carriage decorously.[27] Female accomplishments, as opposed to education in the wider sense, were acquired for the express purpose of catching husbands, as the two Miss Beauforts in *Sanditon* are consciously aware:

> they had tolerable complexions, showy figures, an upright decided carriage and an assured look; — they were very accomplished and very ignorant, their time being divided between such pursuits as might attract admiration, and those labours and expedients of dexterous ingenuity, by which they could dress in a style much beyond what they *ought* to have afforded; they were some of the first in every change of fashion – and the object of all, was to captivate some man of much better fortune than their own.[28]

One spoof correspondent to a popular women's magazine, 'Deborah Oldstyle', deplored the neglect of domestic skills in favour of teaching what she considered useless accomplishments:

> Every body's daughter must now learn French, and music, and drawing, and I don't know what beside, till their poor heads are filled with such a medley of knowledge as is, in my opinion, just sufficient to make them ashamed of their relations, above their stations, and unfit for being either prudent wives or good mothers . . . Young ladies now are not taught to pickle cucumbers, or make a baby's cap, or a gentleman's shirt.'[29]

Although not sensibly expressed, a serious point is made – what was female education for? It was not, said Mary Wollstonecraft, merely to attract eligible men, to encourage talents which would keep prospective husbands amused, or to train women for domestic drudgery:

> Why are women to be thus bred up with a desire of conquest? . . . Must they be taught always to be pleasing? And when levelling their small artillery at the heart of man, is it necessary to tell them that a little sense is sufficient to render their attention *incredibly soothing*?[30]

Her final comment refers to the notion promoted in conduct literature that women should be little more than brow-soothers rather than independent thinkers. If women possessed any intelligence, John Gregory recommended that it should be concealed for their own good:

> Be even cautious in displaying your good sense. It will be thought you assume a superiority over the rest of the company. — But if you happen to have any learning, keep it a profound secret, especially from the men, who generally look with a jealous and malignant eye on a woman of great parts, and a cultivated understanding . . . The art of pleasing in conversation consists in making the company pleased with themselves.[31]

Drawing on the advice given by Gregory, Fordyce and a host of other writers, that women should hide from eligible men whatever learning they were fortunate enough to acquire from their haphazard education, Jane Austen mischievously took the argument to its logical conclusion:

> Where people wish to attach, they should always be ignorant. To come with

> a well-informed mind, is to come with an inability of administering to the vanity of others, which a sensible person would always wish to avoid. A woman especially, if she have the misfortune of knowing any thing, should conceal it as well as she can . . . I will only add in justice to men, that though to the larger and more trifling part of the sex, imbecility in females is a great enhancement of their personal charms, there is a portion of them too reasonable and too well informed themselves to desire any thing more in woman than ignorance.[32]

James Fordyce predictably deplored any kind of academic education for women, but he saved his most pointed criticism for the kind of learning which went on at the majority of boarding schools: '. . . they learn chiefly to dress, to dance, to speak bad French, to prattle much nonsense, to practise I know not how many pert conceited airs, and in consequence of all to conclude themselves Accomplished Women.'[33] Jane Austen would not have disagreed on this particular point. Following a visit to a young acquaintance in a London boarding school, she wrote to Cassandra:

> She looks very well & her hair is done up with an elegance to do credit to any Education . . . & the appearance of the room, so totally un-school-like, amused me very much. It was full of all the modern Elegancies – & if it had not been for some naked Cupids over the Mantlepeice, which must be a fine study for Girls, one should never have Smelt Instruction.[34]

Fordyce, however, had little to put in its place beyond an eighteenth-century version of domestic science, and this is where he and Jane Austen part company: '. . . no woman in the world ought to think it beneath her to be an oeconomist', he asserted, the study of which comprised an understanding of food prices, household maintenance, the management of servants, cleanliness, neatness and how to look after the furniture. Lady Catherine de Bourgh interests herself with such domestic minutiae in order to interfere in the running of Hunsford Parsonage, just as Jane foresaw her brother James' wife finding amusement in superintending the newly married Rices' household management at Deane Parsonage and scolding them into frugality.[35] '. . . these and such like articles will, if I mistake not, furnish ample scope for the exercise of your faculties, in the pursuit of what I have termed Domestic Accomplishments', Fordyce concludes, magnanimously throwing in needlework and drawing as leisure activities.[36]

Charlotte Lutterell's mania for cooking in *Lesley Castle* is an early sign of Jane Austen's opinion of such narrow precepts. For the insensitive Charlotte, cutting thin slices of beef was the element of her education that she took the most trouble to master. That Mr Collins has read and inwardly digested Fordyce's pronouncements is made clear, in his expectation that the Bennet girls have been taught how to cook and in his praise of Elizabeth's 'modesty' and 'economy', qualities which are nowhere near as evident as her independence of mind and candour – no virtues in Fordyce's book. As social beings, women, of course, should read, but only those books which would 'improve' the mind, which ruled out any novels not written by Samuel Richardson and any journals other than the *Spectator*. Intellectual studies would certainly damage the health and even more disastrously, 'hinder those family duties for which the sex are chiefly intended . . . in such cases, they would relinquish their just sphere, for one much less amiable, and much less beneficial' – beneficial to whom he does not need to explain, but explain he does: 'Your business chiefly is to read Men, in order to make yourselves agreeable and useful.'[37]

Conduct books laid down rules for every aspect of female existence, but they were not necessarily obeyed. Lydia Bennet's loud yawn which interrupts Mr Collins' reading of Fordyce's *Sermons* is refreshingly irreverent and was, it is hoped, a common reaction among her real-life contemporaries. Elizabeth Bennet breaks all the rules by walking three miles alone through muddy lanes and fields to reach her sister at Netherfield, and, like Catherine Morland, she says what she thinks without reserve. This unconventional behaviour earned the censure of Mary Russell Mitford, who, like the fictional Miss Bingley, considered Elizabeth pert and worldly, not fit to be the wife of Mr Darcy. Fanny Price's morality and humility come from her poor-relation circumstances and Edmund's choice of reading matter, but she also experiences jealousy and female rivalry. Catherine Morland reads and learns by heart various useless extracts from conduct literature, none of which can be applied to real life any more than the tales of gothic horror she absorbs. Her mother's recourse to a moral essay on female dissatisfaction, as a cure for Catherine's restlessness on her return from Northanger Abbey, is rendered redundant by the arrival of Henry Tilney. Anne Elliot and Elinor Dashwood combine rationality with romantic feelings, which is more than any conduct book would teach them to do. Jane Austen herself mocked Fordyce and Hannah More by making them appear ridiculous in her fiction and letters.

What kind of education would sustain those women who were destined never to marry? Mary Wollstonecraft posed a similar question in her critique of a system which encouraged women to be accomplished, but accomplish nothing towards their own uncertain futures:

> How women are to exist in that state where there is to be neither marrying nor giving in marriage, we are not told. For though moralists have agreed that the tenor of life seems to prove that *man* is prepared by various circumstances for a future state, they constantly concur in advising *woman* only to provide for the present. Gentleness, docility, and a spaniel-like affection are, on this ground, consistently recommended as the cardinal virtues of the sex; and, disregarding the arbitrary economy of nature, one writer has declared that it is masculine for a woman to be melancholy. She was created to be the toy of man, his rattle, and it must jingle in his ears whenever, dismissing reason, he chooses to be amused.[38]

Lady Mary Wortley Montagu, a noted 'blue-stocking' in the middle years of the eighteenth century, had expressed annoyance at the limitation on what women were taught:

> We are educated in the grossest ignorance, and no art omitted to stifle our natural reason. If some few get above their nurse's instructions, our knowledge must rest concealed and be as useless to the world as gold in a mine.[39]

Fifty years later, the relatively well educated, but conservative evangelical writer, Hannah More, was arguing the other way, advocating strictures in the sphere of female education. Books were to be read, not for enjoyment or to furnish interesting material for discussion, but to make a woman 'useful to others' in 'the station she was born to fill', as a married woman or as a spinster. Interestingly, she compared the narrowness of education for women to the Chinese custom of foot binding, even while counselling resignation and submission to the system as it stood.[40] She claimed not to see any necessity for concealing intelligence, but stated that modest women would not display it. Despite her own intellectual capabilities, she rehearsed all of the tired old arguments regarding man's superior mental powers and woman's possession of 'a lesser domestic territory' where she could exert some influence, no matter how trivial. Catharine Macaulay was one of the few outspoken writers who directly opposed More's doctrine of refined apathy: '. . . when the sex have been taught wisdom by education, they will be glad to give up indirect influence for rational privileges . . .'[41]

If men proved impervious to carefully cultivated accomplishments and ran a mile at the first sign of intelligence, then straightforward sex appeal might do the trick. Enough men in Jane Austen's fiction comment unreservedly on women's faces and figures to indicate that such appraisals were not uncommon. Sir Walter Elliot watches eighty-seven women walk past him in a Bath street, only to find none of them worth looking at. How many women did Mr Darcy observe in order to formulate his idea of the perfect figure? He certainly admires Elizabeth's body as she walks around the room at Netherfield, and notices that although her figure is not 'symmetrical', she is attractively slim and moves easily. He does not hesitate to praise Elizabeth's fine eyes to Miss Bingley. Sir Thomas Bertram on his return from Antigua notices that Fanny has grown into a woman and shares his thoughts on her physical development with Edmund, causing Fanny acute embarrassment when Edmund repeats her uncle's remarks to her. General Tilney flatters Catherine on her elegance and energy in walking and dancing. This overt focus on the female body turned men into voyeurs, on the lookout for the Georgian equivalent of eye-candy – women who curved in and out in all the right places, with the ankles of a thoroughbred. Their behaviour encouraged women to see each other as rivals for men's attention – Miss Bingley achieves her purpose in persuading Darcy to look at her by walking around the room with Elizabeth – and they criticized each other's physical attractions, or lack of them, as a matter of course. Caroline Bingley finds fault with Elizabeth's complexion, eyes, nose, skin, teeth and general deportment and Jane Austen herself is often highly critical of defects in appearance, large noses in particular, in her letters.

'Let not the other sex scrutinize too closely, nor demand that universal and correct symmetry in their wives and daughters which was never yet found but in the elaborately chiseled models of the sculptor's study',[42] demanded the writer of *The Mirror of Graces*, while focusing almost entirely on how women were to make themselves as near-perfect as possible for men. The beauty of the female body, although transient, would do the work of attracting the male before the qualities of the mind were realized:

> We must impress upon the yet ingenuous maid, that while beauty attracts, its influence is transient, unless it presents itself as the harbinger of that good-sense and principal which can alone secure the affection of a husband . . . woman was made to be the helpmate of man: that, by rendering herself pleasing in his sight, she is the assuager of his pains, the solacer of his woe, the sharer of his joys, . . . By making the fairness of the body the sign of the mind's purity, man is imperceptibly attracted to the object designed for him by heaven as the partner of his life, the future mother of his children, and the angel which is to accompany him into eternity.[43]

The writer, characteristically, attempts to have it both ways: after a hundred pages and more on dress and deportment, women are suddenly exhorted to regard their bodies as of secondary importance to the cultivation of their minds. Purity of thought 'links her with angels', and it is a woman's responsibility to respect and develop her inner qualities, not the writer's, whose only intention is to provide 'a little treatise on the dress of these admirable qualities, I do not suppose it demanded of me to enter so minutely into the subject of mind, as I otherwise should have esteemed it my duty'.[44] The writer's disclaimer in place, the subject of elegant deportment is once again taken up and expounded for another eighty or so pages.

The female body was to be exhibited for man's appreciation, but no woman must overstep the boundaries of modest behaviour, especially in the company of the John Willoughbys and Captain Tilneys of this world. Dire warnings were issued in the various women's magazines, alerting their readers to the depredations of upper-class rakes and the inevitable consequences of sex before marriage. The shame brought down upon the family by such a course of action was dwelt on with sentimental relish and the readers regaled with stories of suicide and ruined prospects:

> I would caution my fair readers, not to make free with men much superior to them in birth and fortune, lest it should happen, that, being seen so frequently in

> company with such, you at length forfeit your reputation, and be at last tempted to engage in a course of life which cannot but destroy every comfort a social being might otherwise enjoy . . .
>
> . . . one imprudent step will cost us a life of misery, and force us to drink of the cup of gall, till Death dashes it from our lips. It will blacken the prospect which but just now appeared so lively and gay, and shut out every ray of happiness from our dwelling. It will present friends whom we have grieved, hearts which our imprudence has broken; and the shades of our departed fathers and mothers looking down piteously upon us, and dropping "tears such as angels weep!"[45]

Most men wanted attractive wives, but they did not necessarily demand physical perfection or outstanding accomplishments. One Rowlandson cartoon of 1789 illustrates a bored husband, yawning in his chair, while his wife attempts to entertain him with harp, piano and lute.[46] By the end of the eighteenth century, men's views on women had undergone a subtle change, in that they were more likely to value well-informed, motivated wives, educated enough to be friends and companions, in preference to docile, downtrodden, domestic drudges or frivolous, empty-headed hypochondriacs. All of Jane Austen's heroes look for, and find, intelligent, companionable wives, yet their creator, just as clever and amusing as her heroines, never married.

12

An Old Maid At Last

'MATRIMONY, in the present age, is looked upon as a most insupportable yoke: – Wives and husbands are accounted the greatest clogs and burdens to those who give up the reins to their unbridled appetites',[1] declared the author of *Aristotle's Master-Piece* in 1800, and resistance to marriage there certainly was among the more cautious of both sexes. Every comfortably circumstanced bachelor dreaded the huge drain on his income that a wife and numerous children would occasion, and every financially secure spinster asked herself if becoming a childbearing machine and slave to a husband's whims was worth the gain in social status. Between 1793 and 1812, the number of marriages was low on average, with troughs in 1795 and 1800, compared with marriages in previous decades.[2] Many conduct-book writers focused on what they perceived to be a selfish female disinclination for the married state, without taking male reluctance into consideration, or the fact that there were just not enough men to provide husbands for the women who did hope to marry. The final chapter in one treatise, optimistically entitled *The Single Married, And The Married Happy*, concludes:

> The selfish state of Celibacy, or "*Single Blessedness*", will soon sink into disrepute; each single Lady will wish to become a Wife; and when exalted to that dignified station, will strive to adopt all the rules here laid down as the guide for her conduct.[3]

'Single blessedness' was just a polite term for the more derogatory 'old maid', a term commonly used at the time by men and women alike. There were worse epithets. 'Ape Leader' was one of them, listed in a popular slang dictionary and defined as: 'An old maid: their punishment after death for neglecting to increase and multiply, will be, it is said, leading apes in hell.'[4] William Hayley, author of the *Essay on Old Maids*, adopted a slightly more palliative tone. He came up with his own definition: '... an unmarried woman, who has compleated her fortieth year', but revealed that the women he had consulted looked at the matter from their own age perspective: unmarried women in their twenties considered all of their thirty-year-old unmarried friends 'absolute Old Maids'; those in their thirties thought forty-five should be the defining age and those in their fifties 'advance the aera I speak of to the age of sixty at least'.[5] In other words, no single woman wished to be thought an old maid, even though she might consider categorizing others as such. Jane Austen has Harriet Smith apply the term to Miss Bates, and sixteen-year-old Lydia Bennet derides her sister Jane as 'quite an old maid' at twenty-three.[6] Twenty-seven was the age which marked the end of a woman's romantic hopes, according to Marianne Dashwood. In her view, such a woman, if her single life were uncomfortable, would only marry for convenience and act as a kind of unpaid nurse for an older husband. At twenty-seven, Charlotte Lucas is considered a confirmed spinster by her despairing brothers, and Anne Elliot at the same age is seen by her father to be a hopelessly faded creature, who will never recover her bloom sufficiently to attract a husband.

Despite Hayley's protestations of admiration for the way in which single women dealt with their situation and his claim that he was a 'friend to the sisterhood', it was beyond his comprehension that some might have chosen to remain single:

> ... the mortifications of their narrow fortune must be considerably embittered by their disappointment in the great object of female hope. Without the minutest breach of delicacy, we may justly suppose, that it is the natural wish and expectation of every amiable girl, to settle happily in marriage ...[7]

He professed a profound sympathy for these supposedly thwarted females, especially when they were exposed to 'indelicate ridicule' by ill-bred men, who found it amusing to comment on their ageing faces and repeatedly wonder why they did not find themselves husbands, 'and very kindly hint to her, with equal delicacy of sentiment and language, that if she does not take great care, she will slip out of the world without answering the end of her creation'.[8] His understanding did not extend to those women who had created their own happiness, independent of husbands or children. Any woman who claimed to find her 'single blessedness' comfortable and desirable was, he asserted, 'acrimonious' and guilty of pronouncing 'the severest satires against her own heart'.[9] Yet a number of spinsters did consider their narrow escape from less-than-perfect marriages with gratitude: 'really there is so much Care in a Married State & fiddle faddle in most Men's Tempers that I Esteem myself vastly happier in having nothing to do with 'em . . .',[10] asserted one straight-talking single lady. Another foresaw that she would get no sense out of a husband whose entire existence centred on sporting activities:

> 'Tis an animal quite incapable of leading a rational life . . . It must always be running after a fox, a hare, a blue ribbon, a place or some such thing, or given up to play. I do think nature has given us women the best lot in this queer jumble of life.[11]

Elizabeth Iremonger expressed her views in less critical, but equally unequivocal terms, to her friend Mary Heber: 'Quiet & Retirement, Rural Simplicity & neatness . . . Books to my Taste, & a Friend to my Heart – these are requisite ingredients to my System of Happiness, & possessing these, I have not a Wish for more.'[12] The Iremongers of Wherwell Priory and the Hebers of Weston Hall were relatively affluent and their daughters did not need to marry. They travelled to London, stayed with friends and relations in country houses and cultivated strong female friendships, maintained through frequent correspondence and the occasional meeting. There is enough evidence in letters and personal journals of the time to suggest that a significant number of women in a secure financial position weighed their chances of happiness in marriage and chose to stay single. One such woman of twenty-seven recorded in her diary:

> I cannot wish to conceal from myself a gradual alteration taking place in my character, a respect and love for the duties of a single life, a dread of the selfishness, the littleness, the increase of worldly cares which accompanie marriage.[13]

When she reached twenty-nine, however, her brothers stepped in and found a husband for her, no doubt fearing that she would become a burden on their finances. The Revd John Gregory viewed the matter from a more enlightened perspective, warning his two daughters that 'nothing renders a woman more despicable, than her thinking it essential to happiness to be married. Besides the gross indelicacy of the sentiment, it is a false one, as thousands of women have experienced.'[14] He could afford to be liberal-minded; there was no need for the Gregory daughters to marry at all, since their father had the money to support them and his death would leave them well provided for. He prudently avoided the issue of those single women who had no financial safety net. In families where there was money, the pressure on single girls to find husbands lessened considerably. Eliza Chute's sister, Augusta Smith, told her daughter in no uncertain terms that she would be better off financially if she were to remain single, rather than marry a man with only a moderate income:

> . . . if you can really love him, & have not any ambitious or covetous thoughts, you may be happy upon that moderate income, but it will require prudence. If you prefer riches, you will have more of them in your single state.[15]

Mary Russell Mitford had no illusions regarding her marriage prospects, they were as nebulous as the likelihood of being asked to dance at any of the balls she attended. She possessed no fortune, was plain, fat and disconcertingly intelligent, apart from which, her parents relied on her income from writing to finance her father's debts and gambling habits. As young as twenty, she claimed to have no desire to marry:

> I know myself well enough to be sure that if any man were so foolish as to wish such a thing, and I were foolish enough to answer "yes," yet a timely fit of wisdom (caprice some might call it) would come upon me, and I should run away from the church door . . .[16]

Her equally unattractive mother had eloped with the fortune-hunting compulsive gambler, Dr Mitford. However, with no fortune and more sense, Mary was resigned to the fact that she would never marry. She made defensive jokes against herself in her letters to Sir William Elford and judging from the following description of her lumpish awkwardness, it is not surprising that her mother had been so caustic in her appraisal of Jane Austen's butterfly lightness at the Basingstoke balls:

> What, indeed, should I do at a dance with my dumpling of a person tumbling

> about like a cricket-ball on uneven ground, or a bowl rolling among nine-pins – casting off with the grace of a frisky Yorkshire cow, or going down the middle with the majesty of an overloaded hay-waggon pasing down a narrow lane?[17]

It was all very well for the writer of *The Mirror of Graces* to encourage beautiful young women to flaunt their physical assets – those of Miss Mitford's ilk were more at ease in the background, shunning the admiration which was not likely to be paid, while they gossiped comfortably with each other.

Two ladies who evaded the marriage market in a very public way were Sarah Ponsonby and Lady Eleanor Butler, who lived together for fifty years at Plas Newydd between 1778 and 1828, attracting both male and female interest and admiration. Exasperated by their relations' determination to match them with 'suitable' men, they ran off to Wales to live an idyllic life together, gardening, reading, drawing, writing letters and making excursions into the neighbourhood without a male escort. They became local celebrities, a tourist attraction for many famous visitors, including Walter Scott, William Wordsworth, the Dukes of York and Wellington, Hester Thrale and Madame de Genlis; in fact, they appeared in the 1810 edition of *A Guide To All The Watering And Sea-Bathing Places*:

> "The fairy palace of the vale," the residence of the Right Hon. Lady E. Butler, and Miss Ponsonby, whom an attachment as romantic as the situation they chose, but as beautiful to the affections, induced to quit the gay world, and retire to this sequestered spot, though the whole domain comprises little more than two acres, is picturesque in the extreme, and has already rendered Llangollen a kind of clasic ground . . .[18]

In August 1799, James Plumptre, having made the journey from his Cambridge college and typical of the many people who came to see the ladies, sent a note to their cottage from the Hand Inn in Llangollen. He received a gracious invitation to tea, 'which I immediately accepted, and met there Lady Stanley and her daughter & Mr Chapellow, formerly of Trinity College Cambridge. The Evening was passed in pleasing and literary conversation, and we all returned to the Inn at 10 o'clock.'[19] The wives of local landowners visited with their young daughters, who admired the pretty ornaments in the drawing room, petted the sleek Italian greyhound and were treated to the peaches which grew against the garden wall. One little girl remembered being told:

> They were so devoted to each other that they made a vow, and kept it, that they would never marry or be separated, but would always live together in their cottage and never leave it or sleep out for even one night.[20]

The ladies proved cultivated, charming hosts and their friendship was celebrated as romantically ideal. They spoke of each other in highly sentimental terms – 'my beloved', 'the darling of my heart', 'the joy of my life' – and their relationship thrived, in sickness and in health. A newspaper article in 1790, which hinted at a more questionable kind of alliance, was universally vilified. Miss Iremonger wrote to Miss Heber as soon as she had read it:

> I hope you have been incensed & concerned at the scurrilous illiberality of several Paragraphs lately in the Public Papers with regard to Miss Butler & Miss Ponsonby, attacking them most cruelly in the very heart of their Happiness. I heartily wish they could be insensible to it, as it must originate in the envy of *Esprits bornes*, who cannot understand the pure & innocent elegance of their lives; but in proportion to their own excellence & delicacy they are more alive to the pain of being hurt, & I am sorry to find they experience this most sensibly. To have Modest Retiring Worth bro't forth into Notice, merely to suffer infamous Abuse, is very shocking.[21]

The article itself, which appeared first in the *St James's Chronicle*, was subsequently reproduced in almost identical form in the *General Evening Post* and the *London Chronicle*, in July 1790. The two ladies were accused of having 'a strange antipathy to the male sex, whom they take every opportunity of avoiding . . .' which was patently untrue, since most of their hospitably received visitors were men. Miss Butler, the article continued,

> is tall and masculine. She wears always a riding-habit. Hangs up her hat with the air of a sportsman in the hall; and appears in all respects a young man, if we except the petticoat, which she still retains. Miss Ponsonby, on the contrary, is polite and effeminate, fair and beautiful.[22]

No one who knew Miss Butler would have recognized this sensationalized description of her – she was short, plump and fifty-one.[23] Miss Ponsonby was thirty-five. Edmund Burke and his family had visited the ladies in 1788, and it was to him that they turned for advice on the possibility of a libel action. In his reply, he touched on the 'indignation felt by every worthy mind' and deplored 'the baseness of the age you live in, that you suffer from the violence of calumny for the virtues that entitle you to the esteem of all who know how to esteem honour, friendship, principle, and dignity of thinking . . .' while holding out little hope of a successful case against the offending newspapers.[24] If such a prominent politician held this elevated view of the ladies' relationship, then many other decent men and women must have seen it in the same light, yet the fear of 'masculine' women and the threat their aspirations posed to male dominance in the family and professions continually reared its head in fiction and in conduct literature.

Without taking the extreme step of running off together, many women came to realize that they could find more pleasure in each other's company than they could in marrying. It was not that they consciously chose the single life above marriage; as the years passed, they merely drifted gently into it. Jane and Cassandra, lifelong friends and confidantes, just continued the relationship they had always shared, 'wedded to each other', as their mother said. A great-niece later attempted to define the sisters' relationship: 'The similarity of their fates endeared the two sisters to each other and made other sympathy unnecessary to each. No one was equal to Jane in Cassandra's eyes. And Jane looked up to Cassandra as one far wiser and better than herself.'[25] If the sentiments expressed in *Mansfield Park* are accepted as Jane Austen's own, then the fraternal tie ranked above the conjugal, and the earliest attachments, if unbroken, proved stronger than any subsequent connection, 'wounded by no opposition of interest, cooled by no separate attachment, and feeling the influence of time and absence only in its increase'.[26]

Marriage as an end in itself was an evil to be avoided. A miserable life of incompatibility or continual childbearing and rearing, together with the inevitable loss of liveliness and independent thought, were not worth the status and protection achieved. Jane Austen's no-nonsense advice to Fanny Knight outlined some of the consequences attendant on the surrender of autonomy – 'Oh! what a loss it will be when you are married. You are too agreable in your single state . . . I shall hate you when your delicious play of Mind is all settled down into conjugal & maternal affections.'[27] Jane Austen's niece Anna, the would-be novelist, had conceived her first child only two months into her marriage to Ben Lefroy and no more is heard of her novel-writing activities in letters to Aunt Jane after July 1815. Instead, she had become an object of pity, a poor animal, whose mental agility was overwhelmed by the demands of an uncontrollable reproductive system. Jane's message to Fanny was clear – don't be in any hurry to lose your figure, health and spirit through marrying too young and avoid marrying without affection at all costs. As early as 1798, when Jane was just twenty-three, her praise of Harriot Bridges shows how aware she was of the seventeen-year-old's good sense. She was not heading for the altar at the speed her three elder sisters had, but enjoying her freedom to flirt, to look around her, to admire and be admired. Jane thought that Harriot was taking a far more rational approach to life than Fanny, Sophia and Elizabeth, who had been obliged to grow up too fast by marrying before they were twenty.[28]

Jane Austen recognized very early on that continual childbearing and nursing took its toll on women's bodies and minds, and worse. At twenty-two, she sent Cassandra the news of two deaths in childbirth in the Steventon locality and remarked that only those comfortable, attractive surroundings dependent on wealth would arouse her envy of any new mother, or make her want 'to lay in' herself.[29] The death of two of her sisters-in-law during her lifetime as a result of childbearing and the evidence before her of a third's burgeoning fecundity, did not enamour her to marriage. An acute sense of relief is often detected underneath her callous humour – 'So, Lady Bridges in the delicate language of Coulson Wallop is *in for it*!'[30] Fear of sex, of married love, that this kind of knowledge engendered was understandable – better to stay single than face loss of self, maybe loss of life.

Living at home in quiet confinement was preferable to the noisy, exhausting environment created by too many children: 'The house seemed to have all the comforts of little Children, dirt & litter. Mr Dyson as usual looked wild, & Mrs Dyson as usual looked big',[31] reported Jane, after a morning visit to Baughurst Rectory, near Manydown. At this point in

1801, Mrs Dyson was encumbered with six children and pregnant with the seventh. Five more were to follow in the next nine years. Having a house filled with numerous children, if there were not servants enough to cope with the daily demands, was ruinous to conjugal bliss. Jane Austen was twenty-five when she made these observations, before Harris Bigg-Wither proposed marriage, before Edward Bridges might have had the idea of making her his wife, before she met the nameless suitor on a seaside holiday to whom she might have said yes had he not died. Her novels teach the lesson that children can drive a wedge between married couples and conversely, that a childless pair like the Crofts could be true companions, unfettered by the ties of parenthood. Mr and Mrs Gardiner are also seen as happily married and well matched, but most of the time the author pictures them *sans* offspring. It is the docile Jane Bennet who is left behind at Longbourne to care for the Gardiners' children, while the more adventurous Lizzie scampers off across half of Derbyshire with her unencumbered uncle and aunt. Having seen the effects of too many children on the domestic environment and on their mothers, Jane Austen did not display any signs of envy or regret; on the contrary, she was rather dismissive: 'I must now pause to make some observation on Mrs Heathcote's having got a litle Boy; – I wish her well to wear it out – & shall proceed: — Frank writes me word that he *is* to be in London tomorrow; . . .'[32] Too many women produced too many children for the news of yet another birth to be anything other than commonplace. Elizabeth Heathcote must get on with it as best she could; meanwhile, the arrival of a brother, house-hunting in Bath and the prospect of a drive out in a phaeton promised pleasure of a different order.

Despite her reservations, it was not the case that Jane Austen had expected to become an old maid. She created imaginary husbands for herself in the early 1790s, filling in three of the marriage entries in her father's parish register with fictitious spouses, perhaps dreaming of the day she would relinquish Austen for a new name. If Mrs Mitford's 'husband-hunting butterfly' description of her at the Basingstoke balls is anything to go by, she flirted as resolutely as any young woman of the time and was admired in her twenties by Charles Powlett, John Willing Warren, Charles Fowle, Tom Lefroy, Edward Bridges and a Mr Heartley with an estate. She was not immune to the attractions of the opposite sex, being particularly susceptible to the beautiful dark eyes of Harry Digweed, Edward Taylor of Bifrons in Kent and Benjamin Portal of Laverstoke. Men liked her too. In 1797, the Revd Samuel Blackall thought that he might be in want of a wife when he was introduced to Jane Austen by Mrs Lefroy. There is no evidence that he actually proposed marriage, although he appeared to be interested even before he met her, as Jane's comments on a letter from Blackall to Mrs Lefroy show:

> She showed me a letter which she had received from her friend . . . towards the end of which was a sentence to this effect: 'I am sorry to hear of Mrs Austen's illness. It would give me particular pleasure to have the opportunity of improving my acquaintance with that family – with a hope of creating to myself a nearer interest. But at present I cannot indulge any expectation of it.' This is rational enough; there is less love and more sense in it than sometimes appeared before, and I am very well satisfied. It will all go on exceedingly well, and decline away in a very reasonable manner. There seems no likelihood of his coming into Hampshire this Christmas, and it is therefore most probable that our indifference will soon be mutual, unless his regard, which appeared to spring from knowing nothing of me at first, is best supported by never seeing me.[33]

Mrs Lefroy handed over the letter with no comment, 'Perhaps she thinks she has said too much already,' remarked Jane. Maybe Mrs Lefroy had tried to engineer a match between Jane and Blackall by inviting him to Ashe to meet her. Had Jane made her indifference clear to him, in order to persuade him out of his apparently irrational love for her? Perhaps he had recognized that his financial situation did not allow for the support of a wife. He was certainly waiting for a rich living to fall vacant in Somerset and until he had gained this prize, he may have decided that he was better off single. Whatever the reason, Mr. Blackall's hopes of a closer alliance with the Austen family were relinquished, to Jane's apparent relief. Tom Lefroy still occupied her thoughts, but Mrs Lefroy pointedly said nothing about his recent visit to Ashe until Mr Austen asked where he was and learned that he had already left for London on his way back to Ireland. As for Samuel Blackall, he married Miss Lewis from Clifton in January 1813, after at last gaining the lucrative West Country living, his hopes and plans for which Jane had perhaps heard, as they sat in the drawing room at Steventon Rectory many years previously. She amused herself by creating a character for his wife, which gives us some idea of why she might have discouraged him fifteen years before: 'I would wish Miss Lewis to be of a silent turn & rather ignorant, but naturally intelligent & wishing to learn; – fond of cold veal pies, green tea in the afternoon, & a green window blind at night' – the compatible wife that Jane Austen realized she would not have been for the 'piece of . . . noisy Perfection' that was Samuel Blackall.[34]

Eliza de Feuillide, dealing in superlatives as usual, had considered both of her cousins 'perfect Beauties' who 'of course gain "hearts by dozens"'[35] on a visit to Steventon when Jane was coming up to sixteen and Cassandra was eighteen. Both were indeed thought to be pretty girls in the neighbourhood, although there were no financial incentives to marry either of them. Jane had no money beyond the £50 Thomas Knight left her in his will in 1794, and no income at all except for her £20 allowance from her father. Plenty of young, unmarried clergymen were known to her, but livings were not easily come by and when they were, the annual income barely supported a wife and family. In her eighteenth year, she had danced at the Dolphin Inn at Southampton, unaware of what the future held for her. Fifteen years later, with one, possibly two rejected marriage proposals behind her, she was back in the same room, reflecting on her life at thirty-three and concluding that although she felt the 'shame' of being older, she was thankful that she was still happy.[36] Although she had not expected to dance, she was approached by a Frenchman with black eyes, whom she willingly obliged. Another five years down the line, she was writing in the same vein, finding comfort in the fact that she was now considered to be middle-aged: 'By the bye, as I must leave off being young, I find many Douceurs in being a sort of Chaperon for I am put on the Sofa near the Fire & can drink as much wine as I like.'[37] She obviously regretted the passing of her youth and tried to appreciate the compensations of growing older, but her wry tone strikes a sad note, especially in the light of the illness waiting to strike in two years' time.

The rather dull, but comfortable style of dress she adopted at home – her niece Caroline described it as 'the garb of middle age' – was joyfully abandoned when she visited Henry in London, for a jaunty white satin cap decorated with 'a little white flower perking out of the left ear' and a gown 'trimmed everywhere with white ribbon plaited on'.[38] Mr Wyndham Knatchbull still found her attractive at the age of thirty-five – Jane heard that he considered her 'A pleasing looking young woman'[39] – and so did Henry Austen's solicitor William Seymour, who seriously considered making a proposal of marriage. He was five years older than Jane and had probably known her since he began acting for Henry in 1801. He was certainly interested in her in April 1811, when he attended a musical party at Henry's house in Sloane Street, where Jane described herself as surrounded by men:

> and what with Mr Hampson, Mr Seymour, Mr W. Knatchbull, Mr Guillemarde, Mr Cure, a Capt Simpson, brother to *the* Capt Simpson, besides Mr Walter & Mr Egerton . . . I had quite as much upon my hands as I could do.[40]

For some reason, Mr Seymour failed to come to the point, despite having plenty of opportunity. From Hans Place in October 1815, Jane wrote of the embarrassing circumstance of dining alone with him after Henry had retired to bed ill. By the winter, he had transferred his affection to a widow, but again made no proposal of marriage.[41] At thirty-seven she joked about marrying the recently widowed poet George Crabbe, promising to comfort him as best she could, but threatening to be a neglectful step-mother to any children his dead wife might have left behind.[42] Henry's physician Mr Haden provided her with clever conversation in the month before her fortieth birthday and enjoyed her company enough to continue entertaining her with music and wit on several successive evenings. Her letters at this time demonstrate that her single state allowed that 'delicious play of Mind' she had not been forced to sacrifice to 'conjugal & maternal affections'.

It is a great pity that no letters from Cassandra to her sister survive, since we are left with a rather subdued sense of her character, despite Jane's frequent references to her amusing style of writing. Cassandra's experience of spinsterhood was certainly different to her sister's. She spent more time at Godmersham, sometimes as long as five months, tending Elizabeth through her many confinements and supervising the rest of Edward's family. She took responsibility for the running of the cottage at

Chawton and relieved her younger sister of as much domestic anxiety as she could. At least her lot was better than that of the spinster who 'poor thing, with a plain person, no fortune, and vast kindness, was the purse and slave of every sick person who could possibly claim kindred to her'.[43] The usual apology advanced for unmarried women, that they were useful members of the family, who kept house when required and sank their own concerns in those of the extended families of brothers and sisters, nephews and nieces, might have applied to Cassandra, but would not have cut much ice with Jane Austen. Of course she took an interest in her brothers and their families and her letters teem with news and questions regarding their daily lives, but her own affairs kept her mind more than occupied. She frequently despaired of the constant stream of visitors and the need to feed and entertain them, especially when she wanted some uninterrupted time for writing. When her nephew James-Edward stayed at the Cottage for a week in Cassandra's absence, Jane greatly enjoyed his company, but was glad to see Friday:

> It had been a busy week, & I wanted a few days quiet, & exemption from the Thought & contrivances which any sort of company gives . . . Composition seems to me Impossible, with a head full of Joints of Mutton & doses of rhubarb.[44]

Sewing shirts for her brothers she undertook cheerfully, perhaps because that at least allowed her a quiet time for creative reflection. She would never have followed Charlotte Lutterell's example, staying single for the sole purpose of 'superintending and directing the dinner . . .'[45] She was only too ready to admit to complete indifference where household arrangements were concerned – 'You know how interesting the purchase of a sponge-cake is to me', she wrote with mock gravity to her sister.[46] At home in Chawton Cottage, Jane was responsible only for organizing breakfast, holding the keys to the tea, coffee and sugar chests and supervising the wine store. She had time to think while tinkling the piano keys, to take long walks in the countryside, to sit back and observe others, to write. In middle age, her powers of surveillance were still acute, if not even sharper than in her youth, and she lost none of her delight in lively company and conversation. At a concert in Kent, she found the renowned Miss Hammond strikingly handsome, but preferred 'her little, smiling, flirting Sister Julia'.[47] Behind

Jane Austen's quiet civility lurked an intolerance of the kind of insipid chat supplied by the morning visitors at Godmersham. She could only relieve her frustration at the mind-numbing discourse she was forced too often to endure, by penning flippant sketches to her sister. Of one party of ladies, she comments: 'Yes, they called, – but I do not think I can say anything more about them. They came & they sat & they went.'[48] This gains a retrospective irony in the light of Fanny's later criticism of her aunt's Steventon and Chawton acquaintances, that they were nothing more than mediocre, and her smug assertion that Jane was introduced to superior company in Kent. Elinor and Marianne Dashwood's experiences at Barton Park spring to mind, their utter boredom when subjected to discussions about children, in which they had no interest and could take no part. One particular gathering which wasted Jane's precious time provoked her to complain that it was a stupid affair altogether. Fanny had done what she could to draw people out, but the guests just sat and looked at each other and nobody had said anything of any note. The only interest Jane could derive from Miss Laura Chapman arose from her double-flounced gown and her romantic first name, while Mr W.'s cool manner and silence hardly helped the flow of conversation. It reached the stage where no-one could redeem the situation: Mr Mascall *did* talk, but too much, causing Jane to pronounce him conceited and vulgar.[49]

How did so-called refined society see Jane Austen at this stage of her life? Frank Austen confessed that she could appear reserved in unfamiliar company, preferring to save her warmth and liveliness for those close to her, but perhaps he had missed the point, or was reluctant to admit that his sister did not tolerate fools gladly. Like Marianne Dashwood, she was not prepared to waste words on those who did not deserve her attention. Sensitive as she was to complacency, lack of rational conversation guaranteed her silence, but surrounded by those who took the trouble to be entertaining, strangers or not, she could be animated and amusing. Anne Elliot's definition of good company is the author's own: 'clever, well-informed people, who have a great deal of conversation.'[50] A less-than-sympathetic description of the novelist that Mary Russell Mitford passed on to Sir William Elford in 1815, illustrates how uncomfortable Jane Austen's social reticence could be for those who failed to shine:

> I have discovered that our great favourite, Miss Austen, is my countrywoman; that mamma knew all her family intimately; and that she herself is an old maid (I beg her pardon – I mean a young lady) . . . and a friend of mine, who visits her now, says that she has stiffened into the most perpendicular, precise, taciturn piece of "single blessedness" that ever existed, and that, till *Pride and Prejudice* showed what a precious gem was hidden in that unbending case, she was no more regarded in society than a poker or a firescreen, or any other thin upright piece of wood or iron that fills its corner in peace and quietness. The case is very different now: she is still a poker – but a poker of whom every one is afraid. It must be confessed that this silent observation from such an observer is rather formidable.[51]

In the light of these remarks and knowing that Jane Austen's observational powers would have detected society's wariness of her, her description of Miss Bates, who 'had no intellectual superiority to . . . frighten those who might hate her, into outward respect',[52] carries added significance. Jane at least had the satisfaction of suspecting that her own mental acuity could command a show of deference, even if fear and dislike lay beneath the veneer. Her strong sense of self-preservation in such stifling company surfaces in mock-serious caricature, in her fiction and in her letters. She had to laugh, or she would have cried.

Single life had undoubted consolations for Jane Austen. She had no illusions about the impossibility of writing novels while bringing up children and she must have seen that her niece Anna, once pregnant, would be forced to forget her literary ambitions. Her ability to create fictional characters that she could send out into the world more than compensated for the lack of babies. *Pride and Prejudice* was her 'own darling child',[53] and every one of her novels aroused in her a fierce generative pride. Of *Sense and Sensibility* she declared in a letter to Cassandra, 'I can no more forget it, than a mother can forget her sucking child.'[54] One of her great-nieces recognised her aunt's quiet gratitude for her own single state, implied in her comments on the married women she knew:

> she always said that her books were her children, and supplied her sufficient interest for happiness; and some of her letters, triumphing over the married women of her acquaintance, and rejoicing in her own freedom from care were most amusing.[55]

In the fictional worlds Jane Austen created for her heroines, the right husband is always located and gained, and there is no doubt that she knew of women in the real world who did find happiness in marriage, but faced with the choice of marrying without affection and producing innumerable children, or remaining single and relatively free of domestic cares, the novelist herself opted for the latter course. What Miss Elizabeth Iremonger called her 'Tabby Determinations' accord well with Jane Austen's principles: 'With *no right* to be difficult therefore, I profess myself *extremely* difficult, & am clearly of opinion that to be *without* a Companion is far preferable to the being tied to a *disagreable* one.'[56] Harris Bigg-Wither and his fifteen hundred Hampshire acres were, thankfully, no competition for the characters waiting to spring fully formed from the novelist's head into six works of genius. However sympathetic she might be to the many Charlotte Lucases who married men they neither loved nor respected to gain a house and a change in status, Jane Austen knew that for her, the prospect of becoming an old maid at last was her best chance of self-fulfilment.

Notes

ABBREVIATIONS

GENERAL

AP	Austen-Leigh, R. A. (1942), *Austen Papers 1704–1856.* London: Spottiswoode, Ballantyne & Co.
FCL Family History	Lefroy, Fanny-Caroline, Family History 1880–5 (HRO 23M93/85/2).
JA Letters	Le Faye, Deirdre (1995), *Jane Austen's Letters.* Oxford: Oxford University Press.
Memoir	Austen-Leigh, J. E. (1871), *A Memoir of Jane Austen.* London: Richard Bentley and Son.

WORKS BY JANE AUSTEN

S&S	*Sense and Sensibility*
P&P	*Pride and Prejudice*
MP	*Mansfield Park*
E	*Emma*
NA	*Northanger Abbey*
P	*Persuasion*

Lady Susan
The Watsons
Sanditon
Catharine, or The Bower
Frederic and Elfrida
Jack and Alice
Lesley Castle
The Three Sisters

INSTITUTIONS

BL	British Library
HRO	Hampshire Record Office
LPL	Lambeth Palace Library
CLA	Shakespeare Centre Library and Archive

Notes to Chapter 1: The Advantage of Choice

1 Colman, George and Garrick, David (1776), *The Clandestine Marriage*. London: T. Becket, I, ii.
2 Lye, Francis (1828), *The Single Married, and the Married Happy*. Cheltenham: Francis Lye, p. 5.
3 Le Faye, D. (2004), *Jane Austen: A Family Record* (2nd edn). Cambridge: CUP, p. 46.
4 Anon. (1809), *The New Guide to Matrimony*. London: T. Hughes, p. 19.
5 Lye, *op. cit.*, p. 19.
6 *JA Letters*, 62, p. 157.
7 *E*, Vol. I, Ch. 2, p. 18.
8 *JA Letters*, 61, pp. 153–4.
9 Anon. (1809), *The New Guide to Matrimony*. London: T. Hughes, pp. 22–3.
10 *JA Letters*, 1 and 2, pp. 1–4.
11 Chapman, R. W. (1948), *Jane Austen Facts and Problems*. Oxford: The University Press, p. 58.
12 *Memoir*, p. 186.
13 *S&S*, Vol. III, Ch. 14, p. 350.
14 Anon. (1809), *The New Guide to Matrimony*. London: T. Hughes, p. ix.
15 Wollstonecraft, Mary (1787), *Thoughts on the Education of Daughters*. London: J. Johnson, p. 81.
16 *MP*, Vol. I, Ch. 4, p. 41.
17 *MP*, Vol. II, Ch. 6, p. 214.
18 *JA Letters*, 50, p. 121.
19 Anon. (1816), *The Whole Duty of Woman or A Guide to the Female Sex*. Glasgow: W. M. Borthwick, pp. 56–7.
20 Anon. (1809), *The New Guide to Matrimony*. London: T. Hughes, pp. vii–viii.
21 *Frederic and Elfrida*, p. 43.
22 *Jack and Alice*, p. 57.
23 *The Lady's Magazine*, March 1811, Vol. XLII. London: G. Robinson.

24 Bamford, Francis (ed.) (1936), *Dear Miss Heber, An Eighteenth Century Correspondence*. London: Constable, pp. 113–14.

25 Stone, Lawrence (1979), *The Family, Sex and Marriage In England 1500–1800*. London: Weidenfeld and Nicholson, p. 318.

26 *E*, Vol. II Ch. 4, p. 171.

27 *The Rambler*, Vol. II, No. 97, 1751. London: E. Earle, p. 274.

28 *JA Letters*, 37, p. 88.

29 *Ibid.*, 62, p. 156.

30 *Ibid.*, 30, p. 69.

31 Foreman, Amanda (1998), *Georgiana, Duchess of Devonshire*. London: HarperCollins, p. 74.

32 Cavendish, Georgiana, Duchess of Devonshire (1779), *The Sylph*, (Letter 10: To Miss Grenville). London: T. Lowndes.

33 Fairfax-Lucy, A. (1985), *Mistress of Charlecote: The Memoirs of Mary Elizabeth Lucy*. London: Victor Gollancz, p. 28.

34 Stanhope, Eugenia (1798), *The Deportment of a Married Life*. London: Mr Hodges, p. 53.

35 *The Watsons*, p. 113.

36 Le Faye, D. (2002), *Jane Austen's 'Outlandish Cousin': The Life and Letters of Eliza de Feuillide*. London: British Library, p. 55.

37 As published in *AP*, p. 228, with transcript corrected by Deirdre Le Faye.

Notes to Chapter 2: The Power of Refusal

1 Stone, Lawrence (1979), *The Family, Sex and Marriage In England 1500–1800*. London: Weidenfeld and Nicholson, Plate 14. This cartoon from 1785 shows an adoring man kneeling at a woman's side, but his intentions are not specified.

2 Davidoff, Leonora and Hall, Catherine (1987), *Family Fortunes*. London: Hutchinson, p. 326.

3 Eliza Chute's Diary (HRO 23M93/70/1/3).

4 Knatchbull-Hugessen, Sir Hughe (1960), *Kentish Family*. London: Methuen, p. 166.

5 *P*, Vol. II, Ch. 11, p. 222.

6 *MP*, Vol. III, Ch. 17, p. 437.

7 *S&S*, Vol. III, Ch. 13, p. 336.

8 *E*, Vol. III, Ch. 13, p. 404.

9 *E*, Vol. I, Ch. 15, p. 123.

10 Gregory, J., in Wollstonecraft, Mary (1792/1997), *A Vindication of the Rights of Woman*. Edited by Ashley Tauchert. London: Everyman, p. 283.
11 Herbert, Dorothea (1930), *Retrospections of Dorothea Herbert*. London: Gerald Howe, Vol. I, p. 126.
12 *Ibid.*, Vol. I, p. 139.
13 Kenyon, Olga (1992), *800 Years of Women's Letters*. Stroud: Sutton, pp. 93–4.
14 *E*, Vol. I, Ch. 7, p. 51.
15 *E*, Vol. I, Ch. 8, p. 59.
16 Le Faye, D. (2002), *Jane Austen's 'Outlandish Cousin': The Life and Letters of Eliza de Feuillide*. London: British Library, p. 53.
17 *Ibid.*, p. 79.
18 *Ibid.*, p. 116.
19 *Ibid.*, p. 129.
20 *Ibid.*, p. 132.
21 *Ibid.*, p. 139.
22 *Ibid.*, p. 142.
23 *Ibid.*, p. 154.
24 Lye, Francis (1828), *The Single Married, and the Married Happy*. Cheltenham: Francis Lye, p. 9.
25 Woodforde, James (1978), *The Diary Of A Country Parson 1758–1802*. Edited by John Beresford. Oxford: OUP, pp. 113–14.
26 Gisborne, Thomas (1810), *An Enquiry Into The Duties of the Female Sex* (9th edn). London: T. Cadell, pp. 258–9.
27 Le Faye, Deirdre (2000a), *Fanny Knight's Diaries*. Chawton: The Jane Austen Society, pp. 18 and 20.
28 *JA Letters*, 75, p. 193.
29 FCL Family History.
30 *JA Letters*, 90, pp. 231–2.
31 Le Faye, Deidre (2000a), *Fanny Knight's Diaries*. Chawton: The Jane Austen Society, p. 21.
32 *JA Letters*, 109, p. 279.
33 *E*, Vol. III, Ch. 13, p. 400.
34 *JA Letters*, 114, p. 286.
35 *Ibid.*, 151, pp. 329 and 331.
36 Caroline Austen's letter to Amy Austen 1870, in Le Faye, D. (2004), *Jane Austen: A Family Record* (2nd edn). Cambridge: CUP, pp. 137 and 138.
37 *JA Letters*, 47, p. 112.
38 *Ibid.*, 55, p. 136.

39 *Ibid.*, 57, p. 145.
40 Wollstonecraft, Mary (1787), *Thoughts on the Education of Daughters*. London: J. Johnson, pp. 85–86.
41 *JA Letters*, 89, p. 226.
42 *MP*, Vol. III, Ch. 17, pp. 436 and 437.
43 *P*, Vol. I, Ch. 11, pp. 92 and 93.

Notes to Chapter 3: An Acquaintance Formed in a Public Place

1 *JA Letters*, 56, p. 140.
2 *NA*, Vol. I, Ch. 1, p. 18.
3 *JA Letters*, 2, p. 3.
4 *P&P*, Vol. I, Ch. 3, p. 11.
5 *JA Letters*, 24, p. 53.
6 Darton, F. J. Harvey (ed.) (1910), *The Life and Times of Mrs Sherwood*. London: Wells, Gardner, Darton, p. 164.
7 *JA Letters*, 62, p. 157.
8 Gisborne, Thomas (1810), *An Enquiry Into The Duties of the Female Sex* (9th edn). London: T. Cadell, p. 192.
9 Fordyce, James (1786), *Sermons to Young Women* (10th edn). London: T. Cadell, p. 237.
10 Grosvenor Myer, Valerie (1997), *Obstinate Heart*. London: Michael O'Mara Books, p. 78.
11 Anon. (1811), *The Mirror of Graces or The English Lady's Costume*. London: B. Crosby, pp. 170 and 171.
12 *Ibid.*, p. 187.
13 *Ibid.*, pp. 188–9.
14 *JA Letters*, 62, p. 157 and 36, p. 86.
15 Anon. (1811), *The Mirror of Graces or The English Lady's Costume*. London: B. Crosby, p. 19.
16 *Ibid.*, pp. 130–2.
17 Grose, Francis (1783), *Guide to Health, Beauty, Riches and Honour*. London: S. Hooper, pp. 16, 17, 20.
18 *The Lady's Monthly Museum*, Vol. 1, October 1798. London: Vernor and Hood, pp. 289–91.
19 Johnson, R. Brimley (ed.) (1925), *The Letters of Mary Russell Mitford*. London: The Bodley Head, pp. 47–8.

20 Darton, *op. cit.*, p. 169.
21 Anon. (1810), *A Guide to all the Watering and Sea-Bathing Places*. London: Richard Phillips, p. 173.
22 *Ibid.*, p. 150.
23 Anon. (1825), *Sketches of Young People; or, A Visit to Brighton* (2nd edn). London: Harvey and Darton, p. 47.
24 Anon. (1810), *A Guide to all the Watering and Sea-Bathing Places*. London: Richard Phillips, p. 85.
25 Murray, Venetia (1998), *High Society: A Social History of the Regency Period, 1788–1830*. London: Viking, p. 259.
26 Anon. (1810), *A Guide to all the Watering and Sea-Bathing Places*. London: Richard Phillips, pp. 90–91.
27 *Ibid.*, pp. 451 and 455.
28 Climenson, Emily J. (ed.) (1899), *Passages from the Diaries of Mrs. Philip Lybbe Powys of Hardwick House, Oxon, AD 1756 to 1808*. London: Longmans, Green, and Co., p. 265.
29 *JA Letters*, 114, p. 286.
30 *P*, Vol. II, Ch. 11, p. 217.
31 Le Faye, D. (2004), *Jane Austen: A Family Record* (2nd edn). Cambridge: CUP, p. 267.
32 *E*, Vol. III, Ch. 12, p. 392.
33 *E*, Vol. III, Ch. 16, p. 430.
34 Letter from Eliza Chute to Emma Smith, 7–9/10/1828 (HRO 23M93/87/3/108).
35 FCL Family History.
36 *P*, Vol. II, Ch. 9, p. 195.
37 *NA*, Vol. II, Ch. 16, pp. 232–3.

Notes to Chapter 4: White Satin and Lace Veils

1 HRO 71M82/PR3.
2 Woodforde, James (1978), *The Diary Of A Country Parson 1758–1802*. Edited by John Beresford. Oxford: OUP, pp. 257 and 295.
3 *JA Letters*, 21, p. 45 and Letter 36, p. 85.
4 *Ibid.*, 43, p. 99.
5 Johnson, R. Brimley (ed.) (1925), *The Letters of Mary Russell Mitford*. London: The Bodley Head, p. 57.
6 Monsarrat, Ann (1973), *And the Bride Wore . . . The Story of the White Wedding*. London: Gentry Books, p. 96.

7 *JA Letters*, 128, p. 300; and 88, p. 222.
8 Fawcett, Trevor (2002), *Bath Commercialis'd: Shops, Trades And Market At The 18th-Century Spa*. Bath: Ruton, Introduction.
9 *Bath Chronicle*, 6 February 1798. Bath: Richard Cruttwell.
10 Fawcett, *op. cit.*, pp. 68 and 41.
11 *E*, Vol. II, Ch. 18, p. 289.
12 Bamford, Francis (ed.) (1936), *Dear Miss Heber, An Eighteenth Century Correspondence*. London: Constable, pp. 14 and 15.
13 *Ackermann's Repository of Arts*, Vol. I, No. 3, 1809, p. 187. London: R. Ackermann.
14 Le Faye, D. (2002), *Jane Austen's 'Outlandish Cousin': The Life and Letters of Eliza de Feuillide*. London: British Library, p. 137.
15 Foreman, Amanda (1998), *Georgiana, Duchess of Devonshire*. London: HarperCollins, p. 20.
16 Brabourne, Lord (1884), *Letters of Jane Austen*. London: Richard Bentley, p. 354.
17 *JA Letters*, 103, 107, pp. 266 and 276.
18 Cowley, Mrs (1782), *The Belle's Stratagem*. London: Thomas Cadell, p. 17.
19 Herbert, Dorothea (1930), *Retrospections of Dorothea Herbert*. London: Gerald Howe, Vol. I, p. 121.
20 Johnson, *op. cit.*, p. 136.
21 *E*, Vol. III, Ch. 19, p. 453.
22 Cunnington, Phillis and Lucas, Catherine (1972), *Costume for Births, Marriages and Deaths*. London: Adam and Charles Black, p. 103.
23 *JA Letters*, 65, p. 168.
24 FCL Family History.
25 Herbert, *op. cit.*, Vol. I, pp. 118 and 119–20.
26 Austen, Caroline (1986), *Reminiscences of Caroline Austen*. Chawton: The Jane Austen Society, p. 40.
27 Monsarrat, *op. cit.*, p. 124.
28 Cunnington and Lucas, *op. cit.*, p. 81.
29 Thackeray, W. M. (1968), *Vanity Fair*. London: Penguin Classics, p. 259.
30 Herbert, *op. cit.*, Vol. I, p. 121.
31 Freemantle, A., ed., *The Wynne Diaries*, in Cunnington and Lucas, *op. cit.*, p. 62.
32 Scott, the Hon. Caroline Lucy (1828), *A Marriage in High Life*. London: Henry Colburn, p. 8.
33 *JA Letters*, 97, p. 255.
34 Monsarrat, *op. cit.*, p. 120.
35 Herbert, *op. cit.*, Vol. I, p. 122.

36 Cunnington and Lucas, *op. cit.*, p. 109.
37 Thackeray, *op. cit.*, p. 257.
38 Monsarrat, *op. cit.*, pp. 81 and 96.
39 Scarisbrick, Diana (2007), *Rings, Jewelry of Power, Love and Loyalty*. London: Thames and Hudson, pp. 104 and 102.
40 *JA Letters*, 7, p. 12.
41 *Ibid.*, 22, pp. 47–8.
42 Le Faye, D. (2002), *Jane Austen's 'Outlandish Cousin': The Life and Letters of Eliza de Feuillide*. London: British Library, p. 108.
43 Bishop, P. et al. (2002), *Pickpocketing The Rich: Portrait Painting in Bath 1720–1800*. Bath: The Holburne Museum of Art, p. 14.
44 *The Albion Collection of Fine Portrait Miniatures* (2004). London: Bonhams, Plate 127.
45 Sumner, Ann and Walker, Richard (1999), *Secret Passion to Noble Fashion: The World of the Portrait Miniature*. Bath: Holburne Museum of Art, Plate 11, p. 27.
46 *The Three Sisters*, pp. 90 and 93.

Notes to Chapter 5: Where N Takes M, For Better, For Worse

1 Le Faye, D. (2002), *Jane Austen's 'Outlandish Cousin': The Life and Letters of Eliza de Feuillide*. London: British Library, pp. 117–18.
2 Stoneleigh Papers (SCLA DR/18/31/861).
3 *JA Letters*, 107, p. 275.
4 LPL (F VII/3/10).
5 Scarisbrick, Diana (2007), *Rings, Jewelry of Power, Love and Loyalty*. London: Thames and Hudson, pp. 86 and 100.
6 Bamford, Francis (ed.) (1936), *Dear Miss Heber, An Eighteenth Century Correspondence*. London: Constable, p. 109.
7 Woodforde, James (1978), *The Diary Of A Country Parson 1758–1802*. Edited by John Beresford. Oxford: OUP, p. 410.
8 *Ibid.*, p. 326.
9 LPL (F VII/3/10).
10 Bamford, *op. cit.*, p. 234.
11 Monsarrat, *op. cit.*, p. 96.
12 Gillis, John R. (1985), *For Better, For Worse – British Marriages, 1600 to the Present*. Oxford: OUP, p. 137.
13 Monsarrat, *op. cit.*, pp. 82–3.

14 Herbert, Dorothea (1930), *Retrospections of Dorothea Herbert.* London: Gerald Howe, Vol. I, p. 127.
15 Bamford, *op. cit.*, pp. 15–6.
16 Scott, the Hon. Caroline Lucy (1828), *A Marriage in High Life.* London: Henry Colburn, p. 3.
17 Climenson, Emily J. (ed.) (1899), *Passages from the Diaries of Mrs. Philip Lybbe Powys of Hardwick House, Oxon, AD 1756 to 1808.* London: Longmans, Green, and Co., p. 277.
18 Austen, Caroline (1986), *Reminiscences of Caroline Austen.* Chawton: The Jane Austen Society, pp. 39–40.
19 Eliza Chute's Diaries (HRO 23M93/70/1/3).
20 Austen, Caroline, *op. cit.* (1986), p. 39.
21 *MP*, Vol. III, Ch. 12, p. 386.
22 *JA Letters*, 38, p. 91.
23 Lefroy, Helen and Turner, Gavin (eds) (2007), *The Letters of Mrs Lefroy.* Chawton: The Jane Austen Society, pp. 39–40.
24 Austen, Caroline, *op. cit.* (1986), p. 40.
25 *Lesley Castle*, p. 6.
26 Herbert, *op. cit.*, Vol. I, p. 122.
27 Johnson, R. Brimley (ed.) (1925), *The Letters of Mary Russell Mitford.* London: The Bodley Head, p. 137.
28 Herbert, *op. cit.*, Vol. I, p. 122.
29 *JA Letters*, 57, p. 145.
30 Woodforde, *op. cit.*, p. 491.
31 Lane, Maggie (1995), *Jane Austen and Food.* London: Hambledon, p. 68.
32 Johnson, *op. cit.*, p. 137.
33 *JA Letters*, 118, p. 289.
34 *The Gentleman's Magazine*, May 1808, London: J. Nichols and Son, p. 458.
35 *Ibid.*, January 1806, p. 87.
36 *The Lady's Magazine*, April 1811, Vol. XLII. London: G. Robinson.
37 *JA Letters*, 60, p. 151.
38 *Memoir*, p. 74.
39 *Memoir*, p. 234; *JA Letters*, p. 409.
40 *JA Letters*, p. 524.

Notes to Chapter 6: Wedding Journeys

1 Bamford, Francis (ed.) (1936), *Dear Miss Heber, An Eighteenth Century Correspondence*. London: Constable, pp. 29 and 30.
2 *Ibid.*, p. 14.
3 Various Authors (1813), *Letters on Courtship and Marriage*. Trenton: Daniel Fenton and James J. Wilson. On p. 105. The Revd John Witherspoon uses the word 'honey-moon' to describe that period of time immediately after marriage.
4 Scott, the Hon. Caroline Lucy (1828), *A Marriage in High Life*. London: Henry Colburn, p. 81.
5 Monsarrat, Ann (1973), *And the Bride Wore . . . The Story of the White Wedding*. London: Gentry Books, pp. 82 and 95.
6 Anon. (1825), *Sketches of Young People; or, A Visit to Brighton* (2nd edn). London: Harvey and Darton, p. 64.
7 Marchand, Leslie A. (ed.) (1973–1994), *Byron's Letters and Journals, Vol. III*. London: John Murray, p. 260.
8 *JA Letters*, 34, p. 80.
9 Anon. (1810), *A Guide to all the Watering and Sea-Bathing Places*. London: Richard Phillips, p. 221.
10 Pedley, Avril (ed.) (2007), *A Georgian Marriage*. Wimborne Minster: The Dovecote Press, pp. 206–7.
11 Anon. (1810), *A Guide to all the Watering and Sea-Bathing Places*. London: Richard Phillips, p. 284.
12 Lefroy, Helen and Turner, Gavin (eds) (2007), *The Letters of Mrs Lefroy*. Chawton: The Jane Austen Society, p. 177.
13 Herbert, Dorothea (1930), *Retrospections of Dorothea Herbert*. London: Gerald Howe, Vol. I, p. 122.
14 Monsarrat, *op. cit.*, p. 97.
15 Pedley, *op. cit.*, p. 257.
16 Bamford, *op. cit.*, p. 29.
17 Monsarrat, *op. cit.*, p. 95.
18 E., Vol. II, Ch. 14, p. 260.
19 *JA Letters*, 77, p. 197.
20 Le Faye, D. (2004), *Jane Austen: A Family Record* (2nd edn). Cambridge: CUP, p. 100.
21 *JA Letters*, 13 and 30, pp. 24 and 70.
22 Letter from Mrs Charles Powlett to Miss P. Peters, 20/6/1799 (HRO 72M92/18/10).
23 *JA Letters*, 109, p. 281.
24 *Ibid.*, 25, p. 56.

Notes to Chapter 7: Scandal and Gossip

1 *Bon Ton Magazine*, Vol. II, No. 11, 1 March 1819. London: J. Johnston, pp. 313–14.
2 *MP*, Vol. III, Ch. 15, pp. 408–9.
3 Herbert, Dorothea (1930), *Retrospections of Dorothea Herbert*. London: Gerald Howe, Vol. I, pp. 129–30.
4 *JA Letters*, 53, p. 131.
5 *Ibid.*, p. 570.
6 Chapman, R. W. (1952), *Jane Austen's Letters to her Sister Cassandra and Others* (2nd edn.). London: OUP, Note 197.
7 Bamford, Francis (ed.) (1936), *Dear Miss Heber, An Eighteenth Century Correspondence*. London: Constable, p. 110.
8 *JA Letters*, 27, pp. 60–1.
9 *Ibid.*, 36, p. 85.
10 *Ibid.*, 30, p. 71.
11 *Ibid.*, 96, p. 253.
12 *Ibid.*, p. 463.
13 *Ibid.*, 153, p. 333.
14 *MP*, Vol. III, Ch. 15, p. 410.
15 *MP*, Vol. III, Ch. 17, pp. 431 and 435.
16 Macaulay, Catherine (1790), *Letters on Education*. Letter XXIII. London: C. Dilly. p. 210.
17 Trumbach, Randolph (1998), *Sex and the Gender Revolution, Vol. I*. Chicago: University of Chicago Press, p. 409.
18 *The Gentleman's Magazine*, March 1825. London: Nichols, Son and Bentley, p. 275.
19 *JA Letters*, 36, p. 85.
20 Darton, F. J. Harvey (ed.) (1910), *The Life and Times of Mrs Sherwood*. London: Wells, Gardner, Darton, pp. 155 and 156.
21 Gisborne, Thomas (1810), *An Enquiry Into The Duties of the Female Sex* (9th edn). London: T. Cadell, pp. 183–4.
22 Stone, Lawrence (1979), *The Family, Sex and Marriage In England 1500–1800*. London: Weidenfeld and Nicholson, p. 284.
23 Price, Cecil (ed.) (1973), *The Rivals, in The Dramatic Works of Richard Brinsley Sheridan, Vol. I*. Oxford: Clarendon Press, Vol. I, p. 135.
24 Hibbert, Christopher (ed.) (1968), *An American in Regency England: Louis Simond*. London: Robert Maxwell, pp. 85–6.
25 Pennant, Thomas (1790), *A Tour in Scotland and Voyage to the Hebrides*. London: Benjamin White, pp. 94–5.

26 *The Lady's Magazine*, Vol. XLII, May 1811. London: G. Robinson.
27 *Ibid.*, Vol. XLII, April 1811.
28 Bamford, *op. cit.*, p. 224.
29 *S&S*, Vol. III, Ch. 14, p. 350.
30 Le Faye, Deirdre (2006b), 'Jane Austen in Gloucestershire', *The Jane Austen Society Report*, pp. 23–4.
31 Le Faye, Deirdre (2006a), *A Chronology of Jane Austen and her Family*. CUP, p. 630.
32 Letter from Edward Knight (Austen) to Mary Austen (Lloyd), 18/5/1826 (HRO 23M93/62/2/8).
33 Woodforde, James (1978), *The Diary Of A Country Parson 1758–1802*. Edited by John Beresford. Oxford: OUP, p. 398.
34 Honan, Park (1996), *Jane Austen: Her Life*. New York: St Martin's Griffin, pp. 105–6.
35 Herbert, *op. cit.*,Vol. II, pp. 363–4.
36 *P&P*, Vol. III, Ch. 6, pp. 281–2.
37 Fordyce, James (1786), *Sermons to Young Women* (10th edn). London: T. Cadell, p. 17.
38 *The Public Advertiser*, 13 August 1791. London.
39 *Jack and Alice*, p. 50.
40 Bamford, *op. cit.*, pp. 35–6.
41 *JA Letters*, 26, 27 and 28, pp. 59, 61 and 64.
42 *Ibid.*, 5, p. 8.
43 *E*, Vol. III, Ch. 17, p. 438.
44 *P&P*, Vol. III, Ch. 13, p. 331.
45 *S&S*, Vol. II, Ch. 7, p. 173.
46 *S&S*, Vol. II, Ch. 8, p. 182.
47 Bamford, *op. cit.*, p. 92.
48 *P&P*, Vol. III, Ch. 15, p. 344.
49 *JA Letters*, 30, p. 70.
50 *Ibid.*, 151, p. 330.

Notes to Chapter 8: A Contract of Mutual Agreeableness

1 *P*, Vol. II, Ch. 6, p. 160.
2 *P*, Vol. I, Ch. 8, pp. 59–60.
3 *P&P*, Vol. III, Ch. 8, p. 295.
4 Hays, Mary (1793), *Letters and Essays, Moral, and Miscellaneous*. London: T. Knott, p. 22.

5 *S&S*, Vol. I, Ch. 3, p. 19.
6 Lye, Francis (1828), *The Single Married, and the Married Happy*. Cheltenham: Francis Lye, p. 22.
7 Gisborne, Thomas (1810), *An Enquiry Into The Duties of the Female Sex* (9th edn). London: T. Cadell, p. 256.
8 Titus 2.5.
9 Fordyce, James (1786), *Sermons to Young Women* (10th edn). London: T. Cadell, p. 110.
10 *Ibid.*, p. 208.
11 *Ibid.*, p. 213.
12 Wollstonecraft, Mary (1792/1997), *A Vindication of the Rights of Woman*. Edited by Ashley Tauchert. London: Everyman, p. 108.
13 Stanhope, Eugenia (1798), *The Deportment of a Married Life*. London: Mr Hodges, pp. 2 and 235.
14 *Ibid.*, p. 17.
15 Austen, Caroline (1991), *My Aunt Jane Austen*. Chawton: The Jane Austen Society, p. 6.
16 Tomalin, Claire (1997), *Jane Austen: A Life*. London: Viking, p. 38.
17 Austen, Caroline (1986), *Reminiscences of Caroline Austen*. Chawton: The Jane Austen Society, p. 25.
18 *JA Letters*, 54, p. 134.
19 FCL Family History.
20 *JA Letters*, 55, p. 137.
21 *Ibid.*, 10, p. 16.
22 *Ibid.*, 21, p. 46.
23 *Ibid.*, 13, p. 24.
24 *Ibid.*, 51, p. 122.
25 *Ibid.*, 60, p. 151.
26 *Ibid.*, 37, p. 88.
27 *Ibid.*, 36, p. 85.
28 *Ibid.*, 30, p. 71.
29 *Ibid.*, 50, p. 121.
30 *Ibid.*, 49, p. 116.
31 *Ibid.*, 89, p. 225.
32 FCL Family History.
33 *JA Letters*, 159, p. 340–1.
34 *P*, Vol. I, Ch. 6, p. 41.
35 Le Faye, D. (2002), *Jane Austen's 'Outlandish Cousin': The Life and Letters of Eliza de Feuillide*. London: British Library, pp. 152–3.

36 *JA Letters*, 43, p. 102.
37 Letter from Anna Lefroy to James-Edward Austen-Leigh, Dec. 1864 (HRO 23M93/97/4).
38 *JA Letters*, 14, p. 27.
39 Lord Byron, in Ponsonby, Arthur (ed.) (1923), *English Diaries From the XVIth to the XXth Century* (2nd edn). London: Methuen, p. 267.
40 *E*, Vol. I, Ch. 11, p. 89.
41 *E*, Vol. I, Ch. 17, p. 132.
42 Letter from Anna Lefroy to James-Edward Austen-Leigh, Dec. 1864 (HRO 23M93/97/4).
43 *JA Letters*, 4, p. 6.
44 Le Faye, D. (2004), *Jane Austen: A Family Record* (2nd edn). CUP, p. 140.
45 Gisborne, *op. cit.*, p. 366.
46 *JA Letters*, 29, p. 68.
47 *Ibid.*, 56, p. 141.
48 As published in *AP*, p. 249, with transcript corrected by Deirdre Le Faye.
49 *JA Letters*, 86, p. 216.
50 *Ibid.*, 92, p. 239.
51 *Ibid.*, 92, p. 238.
52 *Ibid.*, 92, p. 240.
53 FCL Family History.
54 Letter from Anna Lefroy to James Edward Austen Leigh, 26/10/1818 (HRO 23M93/86/3c-116).
55 Le Faye, D. (2004), *Jane Austen: A Family Record* (2nd edn). CUP, p. 264.
56 Le Faye, Deirdre (2006a), *A Chronology of Jane Austen and her Family*. CUP, p. 608.
57 *S&S*, Vol. III, Ch. 8, p. 343.
58 As published in *AP*, pp. 241 and 244, with transcripts corrected by Deirdre Le Faye.
59 As published in *AP*, pp. 291 and 292, with transcripts corrected by Deirdre Le Faye.
60 As published in *AP*, p. 191, with transcript corrected by Deirdre Le Faye.
61 As published in *AP*, p. 259, with transcript corrected by Deirdre Le Faye.
62 As published in *AP*, p. 292, with transcript corrected by Deirdre Le Faye.
63 *S&S*, Vol. III, Ch. 14, p. 352.

Notes to Chapter 9: Domestic Happiness Overthrown

1 Ponsonby, Arthur (ed.) (1923), *English Diaries From the XVIth to the XXth Century* (2nd edn). London: Methuen, p. 246.

2 Darton, F. J. Harvey (ed.) (1910), *The Life and Times of Mrs Sherwood*. London: Wells, Gardner, Darton, p. 158.
3 Weeton, Ellen (1969), *Miss Weeton's Journal of a Governess, Vol. II: 1811–1825*. Edited by E. Hall. Newton Abbot: David and Charles reprint, p. 134.
4 *Ibid.*, pp. 145–6.
5 Letter from Mary Gosling to Eliza Chute, 24/12/1795 (HRO 23M93/70/3/30).
6 *MP*, Vol. II, Ch. 4, p. 197.
7 Anon. (1816), *The Whole Duty of Woman or A Guide to the Female Sex*. Glasgow: W. M. Borthwick, pp. 52–3.
8 Stanhope, Eugenia (1798), *The Deportment of a Married Life*. London: Mr Hodges, p. 6.
9 Fordyce, James (1786), *Sermons to Young Women* (10th edn). London: T. Cadell, p. 141.
10 Anon. (1811), *The Mirror of Graces or The English Lady's Costume*. London: B. Crosby, pp. 70–1.
11 Johnson, R. Brimley (ed.) (1925), *The Letters of Mary Russell Mitford*. London: The Bodley Head, p. 68.
12 Various Authors (1813), *Letters on Courtship and Marriage*. Trenton: Daniel Fenton and James J. Wilson, p. 23.
13 Lye, Francis (1828), *The Single Married, and the Married Happy*. Cheltenham: Francis Lye, p. 18.
14 Gregory, J., in Wollstonecraft, Mary (1792/1997), *A Vindication of the Rights of Woman*. Edited by Ashley Tauchert. London: Everyman, p. 286.
15 *MP*, Vol. I, Ch. 5, p. 44.
16 Wollstonecraft, Mary (1787), *Thoughts on the Education of Daughters*. London: J. Johnson, p. 84.
17 *P&P*, Vol. III, Ch. 8, p. 296.
18 Various Authors (1813), *Letters on Courtship and Marriage*. Trenton: Daniel Fenton and James J. Wilson. p. 27.
19 Wollstonecraft, *op. cit.* (1787), p. 94.
20 *P&P*, Vol. III, Ch. 17, p. 356.
21 Fordyce, *op. cit.*, p. 106.
22 *P&P*, Vol. II, Ch. 19, p. 228.
23 *S&S*, Vol. I, Ch. 20, p. 109.
24 *E*, Vol. III, Ch. 11, p. 387.
25 *MP*, Vol. III, Ch. 6, p. 340.
26 Gisborne, Thomas (1810), *An Enquiry Into The Duties of the Female Sex* (9th edn). London: T. Cadell, p. 256.

27 *S&S*, Vol. I, Ch. 8, p. 39.
28 *S&S*, Vol. III, Ch. 9, p. 315.
29 *JA Letters*, 60, p. 150.
30 *Ibid.*, 106, p. 274.
31 Fordyce, *op. cit.*, p. 246.
32 *JA Letters*, 90, p. 231.
33 *Ibid.*, 94, p. 246.
34 *Ibid.*, 63, p. 159.
35 Stanhope, *op. cit.*, p. 19.
36 Letter from Eliza Chute to Eliza Gosling, 29/9/1800 (HRO 23M93/74/1/3).
37 *MP*, Vol. I, Ch. 12, p. 108.
38 *E*, Vol. II, Ch. 18, p. 291.
39 *E*, Vol. II, Ch. 1, p. 149.
40 Letter from S. Smith to Eliza Chute, 2/1/1794 (HRO 23M93/70/3).
41 Letter from S. Smith to Eliza Chute, 25/10/1793 (HRO 23M93/70/3/1).
42 Letter from S. Smith to Eliza Chute, 18/2/1794 (HRO 23M93/70/3/8).
43 Lye, *op. cit.*, p. 42.
44 *JA Letters*, 36, p. 85.
45 *Ibid.*, 50, p. 119.
46 *Ibid.*, 54, p. 134.
47 *Ibid.*, 54, p. 135.
48 Hasted, Edward, Canterbury Diocesan Record Office, Irby Collection U.11, v / 514, in *JA Letters*, p. 556.
49 Anon. (1816), *The Whole Duty of Woman or A Guide to the Female Sex*. Glasgow: W. M. Borthwick, p. 53.
50 Kenrick, William (1771), *Free Thought on Seduction, Adultery, and Divorce, By a Civilian*. London: J. Bell, pp. 124–6.
51 *Ibid.*, pp. 292–3.
52 Boswell, J. (1906), *Life of Samuel Johnson, LLD, Vol. II*. London: Everyman, p. 288.
53 Stanhope, *op. cit.*, pp. 37 and 40.
54 *Ibid.*, p. 114.
55 Hays, Mary (1798), *Appeal to the Men of Great Britain in Behalf of Women*. London: J. Johnson and J. Bell, pp. 48–50.
56 Stanhope, *op. cit.*, p. 5.
57 *NA*, Vol. I, Ch. 10, p. 74.

Notes to Chapter 10: The Simple Regimen of Separate Rooms

1 *The Loiterer*, Saturday, 15 August 1789. Oxford: P. Byrne, p. 172.
2 Letter from Tysoe Saul Hancock to Philadelphia Hancock, 23/9/1772 (BL AddMss 29, 236, ff 14R – 16V).
3 Bamford, Francis (ed.) (1936), *Dear Miss Heber, An Eighteenth Century Correspondence*. London: Constable, p. 205.
4 Le Faye, D. (2002), *Jane Austen's 'Outlandish Cousin': The Life and Letters of Eliza de Feuillide*. London: British Library, p. 118.
5 *Ibid.*, pp. 141 and 150.
6 *JA Letters*, 11, p. 20.
7 Le Faye, D. (2002), *Jane Austen's 'Outlandish Cousin': The Life and Letters of Eliza de Feuillide*. London: British Library, p. 118.
8 *JA Letters*, 145, p. 320.
9 Sales, Roger (1997), *Jane Austen and Representations of Regency England*. London: Routledge, pp. 50 and 9.
10 Stone, Lawrence (1979), *The Family, Sex and Marriage In England 1500–1800*. London: Weidenfeld and Nicholson, p. 542.
11 *JA Letters*, 56, p. 140.
12 *Ibid.*, 151, p. 330.
13 *Ibid.*, 153, p. 332.
14 *Ibid.*, 155, p. 336.
15 McLaren, Angus (1984), *Reproductive Rituals*. London: Methuen, p. 70.
16 Wollstonecraft, Mary (1792/1997), *A Vindication of the Rights of Woman*. Edited by Ashley Tauchert. London: Everyman, pp. 218–19.
17 Anon. (1800), *Aristotle's Master-Piece*. London: J. Urquihart, p. 24.
18 Grose, F., (1796), *Dictionary of the Vulgar Tongue* (3rd edn). London: Hooper and Co.
19 Weeton, Ellen (1969), *Miss Weeton's Journal of a Governess, Vol. I*. Edited by E. Hall. Newton Abbot: David and Charles reprint, p. 60.
20 Mears, M. (1797), *The Pupil of Nature: or Candid Advice to the Fair Sex*. London: Faulder, pp. 92–3.
21 *The Diary: or Woodfall's Register*, Monday, 11 April 1791. London: William Woodfall.
22 Cited in *The Gentleman's Magazine*, 'Obstetrical Delinquency', November 1810. London: J. Nichols and Son, p. 410.
23 *Aris's Birmingham Gazette*, 10 January 1791. Birmingham: Thomas Aris. Also in many other daily newspapers.

24 Porter, Roy (1982), *English Society in the Eighteenth Century*. London: Allen Lane, p. 41.
25 McLaren, *op. cit.*, p. 95.
26 Kenyon, Olga (1992), *800 Years of Women's Letters*. Stroud: Sutton, pp. 118–19.
27 *JA Letters*, 32, p. 76.
28 Miller, Joseph (1722), *Botanicum Officinale; or a Compendious Herbal*. London: E. Bell, p. 383.
29 Burns, John (1806), *Observations on Abortion, Containing An Account of the Manner in which it is accomplished, the Causes which produced it, and the Method of preventing or treating it*. London: Longman, Hurst, Rees and Orme, pp. 59–60, 64, 66.
30 Buchan, William (1817), *Domestic Medicine or, the Family Physician*. Dunbar: G. Millar, pp. 510 and 371.
31 *Ibid.*, 1817.
32 Buchan, William (1825), *The Cottage Physician, and Family Adviser; or Every Man His Own Doctor and Herbalist*. London: Sherwood and Co., p. 58.
33 Buchan, William (1817), *Domestic Medicine or, the Family Physician*. Dunbar: G. Millar, p. 365.
34 *AP*, p. 29.
35 *JA Letters*, 153, p. 332.
36 Letter from Lady Northampton to Eliza Chute, 7/3/1797 (HRO 23M93/70/3/41).
37 Letter from Eliza Chute to Eliza Gosling, 29/9/1800 (HRO 23M93/74/1/3).
38 McLaren, *op. cit.*, p. 63.
39 *JA Letters*, 10, p. 17.
40 Martin, Joanna (2004), *Wives and Daughters: Women and Children in the Georgian Country House*. London and New York: Hambledon and London, p. 78.
41 Tomalin, Claire (1996?), 'Amour and Avarice', *The Daily Telegraph*. London: The Telegraph plc.

Notes to Chapter 11: The Years of Danger

1 Stone, Lawrence (1979), *The Family, Sex and Marriage In England 1500–1800*. London: Weidenfeld and Nicholson, pp. 380–1.
2 *E*, Vol. I, Ch. 10, p. 83.
3 Hayley, William (1785), *Essay on Old Maids*. London: T. Cadell, p. 7.
4 Wollstonecraft, Mary (1792/1997), *A Vindication of the Rights of Woman*. Edited by Ashley Tauchert. London: Everyman, p. 74.

5 *S&S*, Vol. I, Ch. 2, p. 14.
6 As published in *AP*, p. 235, with transcript corrected by Deirdre Le Faye.
7 *JA Letters*, 43, p. 101.
8 *Ibid.*, 78, 79, pp. 200 and 201.
9 *E*, p. 157.
10 Stone, *op. cit.*, p. 386.
11 FCL Family History.
12 *JA Letters*, 44, p. 103.
13 Austen, Caroline (1986), *Reminiscences of Caroline Austen*. Chawton: The Jane Austen Society, p. 57.
14 Le Faye, Deidre, (2006a), *A Chronology of Jane Austen and her Family*. Cambridge: CUP, pp. 606–39.
15 *The Watsons*, pp. 109 and 110.
16 *JA Letters*, 153, p. 332.
17 Bamford, Francis (ed.) (1936), *Dear Miss Heber, An Eighteenth Century Correspondence*. London: Constable, p. 120.
18 *P&P*, p. 120.
19 *Memoir*, p. 119.
20 *MP*, Vol. I, Ch. 1, p. 5.
21 *Lesley Castle*, p. 4.
22 *MP*, p. 34.
23 *MP*, p. 8.
24 *MP*, Vol. II, Ch. 9, p. 246.
25 Anon. (1811), *The Mirror of Graces or The English Lady's Costume*. London: B. Crosby, pp. 194–5.
26 *Lady Susan*, p. 51.
27 Le Faye, D. (2004), *Jane Austen: A Family Record* (2nd edn). Cambridge: CUP, p. 70.
28 *Sanditon*, p. 206.
29 *The Lady's Monthly Museum*, Vol. 12, July 1820. London: Dean and Munday, pp. 6–7.
30 Wollstonecraft, *op. cit.* (1792), p. 107.
31 Gregory, J., in Wollstonecraft, *op. cit.* (1792), p. 279.
32 *NA*, p. 106.
33 Fordyce, James (1786), *Sermons to Young Women* (10th edn). London: T. Cadell, p. 25.
34 *JA Letters*, 84, p. 211.
35 *Ibid.*, 31, p. 74.

36 Fordyce, *op. cit.*, p. 227.
37 *Ibid.*, pp. 283 and 273.
38 Wollstonecraft, *op. cit.* (1792), p. 38.
39 In Gillie, C. (1985), *A Preface to Jane Austen*. London and New York: Longman, p. 99.
40 More, Hannah (1799), *Strictures on the Modern System of Female Education*. London: T. Cadell, pp. 1, 14 and 23.
41 Macaulay, Catherine (1790), *Letters on Education*. London: C. Dilly, p. 215.
42 Anon. (1811), *The Mirror of Graces or The English Lady's Costume*. London: B. Crosby, p. 131.
43 *Ibid.*, pp. 16–17.
44 *Ibid.*, p. 164.
45 *The Lady's Monthly Museum*, Vol. 1, October 1798. London: Vernor and Hood, pp. 306–7.
46 Stone, L., *op. cit.*, Plate 20.

Notes to Chapter 12: An Old Maid At Last

1 Anon. (1800), *Aristotle's Master-Piece*. London: J. Urquihart, p. 17.
2 Chalklin, C. W. (1974), *The Provincial Towns of Georgian England*. London: Edward Arnold, pp. 298–9.
3 Lye, Francis (1828), *The Single Married, and the Married Happy*. Cheltenham: Francis Lye, pp. 42–3.
4 Grose, Francis (1796), *Dictionary of the Vulgar Tongue* (3rd edn). London: Hooper and Co.
5 Hayley, William (1785), *Essay on Old Maids*. London: T. Cadell, pp. 2–3.
6 *P&P*, Vol. II, Ch. 16, p. 213.
7 Hayley, *op. cit.*, p. 8.
8 *Ibid.*, pp. 16–17.
9 *Ibid.*, pp. 12–13.
10 Vickery, Amanda (2003), *The Gentleman's Daughter*. New Haven and London: Yale University Press, p. 40.
11 Tillyard, S. (1995) Aristocrats. Caroline, Louisa and Sarah Lennox, 1740–1832, pp. 100–101, in Gatrell, V. (2006), *City of Laughter, Sex and Satire in Eighteenth Century London*. London: Atlantic Books, p. 387.
12 Bamford, Francis (ed.) (1936), *Dear Miss Heber, An Eighteenth Century Correspondence*. London: Constable, p. 100.

13 Davidoff, Leonora and Hall, Catherine (1987), *Family Fortunes*. London: Hutchinson, p. 325.

14 Waldron, Mary (1999), *Jane Austen and the Fiction of Her Time*. Cambridge: CUP, p. 46.

15 Letter from Augusta Smith to Augusta Smith, 12/12/1826 (HRO 23M93/87/3/38).

16 Johnson, R. Brimley (ed.) (1925), *The Letters of Mary Russell Mitford*. London: The Bodley Head, p. 19.

17 *Ibid.*, p. 132.

18 Anon. (1810), *A Guide to all the Watering and Sea-Bathing Places*. London: Richard Phillips, p. 485.

19 Ousby, Ian (ed.) (1992), *James Plumptre's Britain: The Journals of a Tourist in the 1790s*. London: Hutchinson, p. 162.

20 Fairfax-Lucy, A. (1985), *Mistress of Charlecote: The Memoirs of Mary Elizabeth Lucy*. London: Victor Gollancz, p. 20.

21 Bamford, *op. cit.*, pp. 80–81.

22 *St James's Chronicle*, 'Extraordinary Female Affection', 17–20 July 1790. London: Henry Baldwin.

23 Jones, Darryl (1995), 'Frekes, Monsters and the Ladies: Attitudes to Female Sexuality in the 1790s', *Literature and History*, 3rd series, 4. Manchester: Manchester University Press.

24 Cobban, A. and Smith, R. A. (eds) (1967) *The Correspondence of Edmund Burke*. Cambridge: CUP, pp. 131–2.

25 FCL Family History.

26 *MP*, Vol. II, Ch. 6, p. 217.

27 *JA Letters*, 151, p. 329.

28 *Ibid.*, 15, p. 31.

29 *Ibid.*, 13, p. 24.

30 *Ibid.*, 29, p. 68.

31 *Ibid.*, 35, p. 81.

32 *Ibid.*, 38, p. 90.

33 *Ibid.*, 11, p. 19.

34 *Ibid.*, 86, p. 216.

35 Le Faye, D. (2002), *Jane Austen's 'Outlandish Cousin': The Life and Letters of Eliza de Feuillide*. London: British Library, p. 103.

36 *JA Letters*, 62, p. 157.

37 *Ibid.*, 96, p. 251.

38 *Ibid.*, 87, p. 220.

39 *Ibid.*, 72, p. 186.

40 *Ibid.*, 71, p. 183.
41 Le Faye, Deirdre (2000b), 'Jane Austen's Laggard Suitor. Notes and Queries', *Oxford Journals*, Notes and Queries. Oxford: OUP, September, pp. 301–4.
42 *JA Letters*, 93, p. 243.
43 Darton, F. J. Harvey (ed.) (1910), *The Life and Times of Mrs Sherwood*. London: Wells, Gardner, Darton, p. 141.
44 *JA Letters*, 145, p. 321.
45 *Lesley Castle*, p. 17.
46 *JA Letters*, 52, p. 128.
47 *Ibid.*, 96, p. 252.
48 *Ibid.*, 96, p. 253.
49 *Ibid.*, 92, p. 237.
50 *P*, Vol. II, Ch. 4, p. 140.
51 Johnson, *op. cit.*, p. 127.
52 *E*, p. 22.
53 *JA Letters*, 79, p. 201.
54 *Ibid.*, 71, p. 182.
55 Caroline Hubback, in Chapman, R. W. (1948), *Jane Austen Facts and Problems*. Oxford: The University Press, p. 67.
56 Bamford, *op. cit.*, pp. 20 and 21.

Bibliography

ABBREVIATIONS

BL	British Library
HRO	Hampshire Record Office
LPL	Lambeth Palace Library
SCLA	Shakespeare Centre Library and Archive

UNPUBLISHED SOURCES

Eliza Chute's Diaries (HRO 23M93/70/1/3).
Lefroy, Fanny-Caroline, Family History 1880–5 (HRO 23M93/85/2).
Letter from Anna Lefroy to James-Edward Austen-Leigh, 26/10/1818 (HRO 23M93/86/3c-116).
Letter from Anna Lefroy to James-Edward Austen-Leigh, Dec. 1864 (HRO 23M93/97/4).
Letter from Augusta Smith to Emma Austen-Leigh, 12/12/1826 (HRO 23M93/87/3/38).
Letter from Edward Knight (Austen) to Mary Austen (Lloyd), 18/5/1826 (HRO 23M93/62/2/8).
Letter from Eliza Chute to Eliza Gosling, 29/9/1800 (HRO 23M93/74/1/3).
Letter from Eliza Chute to Emma Smith, 7–9/10/1828 (HRO 23M93/87/3/108).
Letter from Lady Northampton to Eliza Chute, 7/3/1797 (HRO 23M93/70/3/41).
Letter from Mary Gosling to Eliza Chute, 24/12/1795 (HRO 23M93/70/3/30).
Letter from Mrs Charles Powlett to Miss P. Peters, 20/6/1799 (HRO 72M92/18/10).
Letter from S. Smith to Eliza Chute, 18/2/1794 (HRO 23M93/70/3/8).
Letter from S. Smith to Eliza Chute, 2/1/1794 (HRO 23M93/70/3).

Letter from S. Smith to Eliza Chute, 25/10/1793 (HRO 23M93/70/3/1).
Letter from Tysoe Saul Hancock to Philadelphia Hancock, 23/9/1772 (BL AddMss 29, 236, ff 14R – 16V).
Stoneleigh Papers (SCLA DR/18/31/861).

MONOGRAPHS AND JOURNAL ARTICLES

Anon. (1810), *A Guide to all the Watering and Sea-Bathing Places*. London: Richard Phillips.
Anon. (1800), *Aristotle's Master-Piece*. London: J. Urquihart.
Anon. (1825), *Sketches of Young People; or, A Visit to Brighton* (2nd edn). London: Harvey and Darton.
Anon. (1811), *The Mirror of Graces or The English Lady's Costume*. London: B. Crosby.
Anon. (1809), *The New Guide to Matrimony*. London: T. Hughes.
Anon. (1816), *The Whole Duty of Woman or A Guide to the Female Sex*. Glasgow: W. M. Borthwick.
Austen, Caroline (1986), *Reminiscences of Caroline Austen*. Chawton: The Jane Austen Society.
——(1991), *My Aunt Jane Austen*. Chawton: The Jane Austen Society.
Austen, Jane (1974), *Lady Susan/The Watsons/Sanditon*. Edited by Margaret Drabble. London: Penguin Classics.
——(2003), *Emma*. Edited by Fiona Stafford. London: Penguin Classics.
——(2003), *Mansfield Park*. Edited by Kathryn Sutherland. London: Penguin Classics.
——(2003), *Northanger Abbey*. Edited by Marilyn Butler. London: Penguin Classics.
——(2003), *Persuasion*. Edited by Gillian Beer. London: Penguin Classics.
——(2003), *Pride and and Prejudice*. Edited by Vivien Jones. London: Penguin Classics.
——(2003), *Sense and and Sensibility*. Edited by Ros Ballaster. London: Penguin Classics.
——(2005), *Lesley Castle*. London: Hesperus Press.
Austen, Jane and Brontë, Charlotte (1986), *Catharine, or The Bower, The Juvenilia of Jane Austen and Charlotte Brontë*. Edited by Frances Beer. London: Penguin Classics.
——(1986), *Frederic and Elfrida, The Juvenilia of Jane Austen and Charlotte Brontë*. Edited by Frances Beer. London: Penguin Classics.
——(1986), *Jack and Alice, The Juvenilia of Jane Austen and Charlotte Brontë*. Edited by Frances Beer. London: Penguin Classics.

——(1986) *Love and Freindship, The Juvenilia of Jane Austen and Charlotte Brontë*. Edited by Frances Beer. London: Penguin Classics.

——(1986), *The Three Sisters, The Juvenilia of Jane Austen and Charlotte Brontë*. Edited by Frances Beer. London: Penguin Classics.

Austen-Leigh, J. E. (1871), *A Memoir of Jane Austen*. London: Richard Bentley and Son.

Austen-Leigh, R. A. (1942), *Austen Papers 1704–1856*. London: Spottiswoode, Ballantyne and Co.

Bamford, Francis (ed.) (1936), *Dear Miss Heber, An Eighteenth Century Correspondence*. London: Constable.

Bishop, P., Fawcett, T., Hayes, J., Posnett, D., Sloman, S. and Wright, A. (2002), *Pickpocketing The Rich: Portrait Painting in Bath 1720–1800*. Bath: The Holburne Museum of Art.

Boswell, J. (1906), *Life of Samuel Johnson, LLD, Vol. II*. London: Everyman.

Brabourne, Lord (1884), *Letters of Jane Austen*. London: Richard Bentley.

Buchan, William (1817), *Domestic Medicine or, the Family Physician*. Dunbar: G. Millar.

——(1825), *The Cottage Physician, and Family Adviser; or Every Man His Own Doctor and Herbalist*. London: Sherwood and Co.

Burns, John (1806), *Observations on Abortion, Containing An Account of the Manner in Which it is Accomplished, the Causes which Produced it, and the Method of Preventing or Treating it*. London: Longman, Hurst, Rees and Orme.

Chalklin, C. W. (1974), *The Provincial Towns of Georgian England*. London: Edward Arnold.

Cavendish, Georgiana, Duchess of Devonshire (1779), *The Sylph*. London: T. Lowndes.

Chapman, R. W. (1948), *Jane Austen Facts and Problems*. Oxford: The University Press.

——(1952), *Jane Austen's Letters to her Sister Cassandra and Others* (2nd edn.). London: Oxford University Press.

Climenson, Emily J. (ed.) (1899), *Passages from the Diaries of Mrs. Philip Lybbe Powys of Hardwick House, Oxon, AD 1756 to 1808*. London: Longmans, Green, and Co.

Colman, George and Garrick, David (1776), *The Clandestine Marriage*. London: T. Becket.

Cobban, A. and Smith, R. A. (eds) (1967) *The Correspondence of Edmund Burke*. Cambridge: Cambridge University Press.

Cowley, Mrs (1782), *The Belle's Stratagem*. London: T. Cadell.

Culpeper, Nicholas (1835), *The Complete Herbal*. London: Thomas Kelly.

Cunnington, Phillis and Lucas, Catherine (1972), *Costume for Births, Marriages and Deaths*. London: Adam and Charles Black.
Darton, F. J. Harvey (ed.) (1910), *The Life and Times of Mrs Sherwood*. London: Wells, Gardner, Darton.
Davidoff, Leonora and Hall, Catherine (1987), *Family Fortunes*. London: Hutchinson.
Fairfax-Lucy, A. (1985), *Mistress of Charlecote: The Memoirs of Mary Elizabeth Lucy*. London: Victor Gollancz.
Fawcett, Trevor (2002), *Bath Commercialis'd: Shops, Trades And Market At The 18th-Century Spa*. Bath: Ruton.
Fordyce, James (1786), *Sermons to Young Women* (10th edn). London: T. Cadell.
Foreman, Amanda (1998), *Georgiana, Duchess of Devonshire*. London: HarperCollins.
Gatrell, V. (2006), *City of Laughter, sex and satire in Eighteenth Century London*. London: Atlantic Books.
Gillie, C. (1985), *A Preface to Jane Austen*. London and New York: Longman.
Gillis, John R. (1985), *For Better, For Worse – British Marriages, 1600 to the Present*. New York and Oxford: Oxford University Press.
Gisborne, Thomas (1810), *An Enquiry Into The Duties of the Female Sex* (9th edn). London: T. Cadell.
Grose, Francis (1783), *Guide to Health, Beauty, Riches and Honour*. London: S. Hooper.
——(1796), *Dictionary of the Vulgar Tongue* (3rd edn). London: Hooper & Co.
Grosvenor Myer, Valerie (1997), *Obstinate Heart*. London: Michael O'Mara Books.
Hayley, William (1785), *Essay on Old Maids*. London: T. Cadell.
Hays, Mary (1798), *Appeal to the Men of Great Britain in Behalf of Women*. London: J. Johnson and J. Bell.
——(1793), *Letters and Essays, Moral, and Miscellaneous*. London: T. Knott.
Herbert, Dorothea (1930), *Retrospections of Dorothea Herbert, Vol. I: 1700–1789, Vol. II: 1789–1806*. London: Gerald Howe.
Hibbert, Christopher (ed.) (1968), *An American in Regency England: Louis Simond*. London: Robert Maxwell.
Honan, Park (1996), *Jane Austen: Her Life*. New York: St Martin's Griffin.
Johnson, R. Brimley (ed.) (1925), *The Letters of Mary Russell Mitford*. London: The Bodley Head.
Jones, Darryl (1995), 'Frekes, Monsters and the Ladies: Attitudes to Female Sexuality in the 1790s', *Literature and History*, 3rd series, 4. Manchester: Manchester University Press.
Kenrick, William (1771), *Free Thought on Seduction, Adultery, and Divorce, By a Civilian*. London: J. Bell.

Kenyon, Olga (1992), *800 Years of Women's Letters*. Stroud: Sutton.
Knatchbull-Hugessen, Sir Hughe (1960), *Kentish Family*. London: Methuen.
Lane, Maggie (1995), *Jane Austen and Food*. London: Hambledon.
Le Faye, Deirdre (1995), *Jane Austen's Letters*. Oxford: Oxford University Press.
——(2000a), *Fanny Knight's Diaries*. Chawton: The Jane Austen Society.
——(2000b), 'Jane Austen's Laggard Suitor. Notes and Queries', *Oxford Journals*, September. Oxford: Oxford University Press.
——(2002), *Jane Austen's 'Outlandish Cousin': The Life and Letters of Eliza de Feuillide*. London: British Library.
——(2004), *Jane Austen: A Family Record* (2nd edn). Cambridge: Cambridge University Press.
——(2006a), *A Chronology of Jane Austen and her Family*. Cambridge: Cambridge University Press.
——(2006b), 'Jane Austen in Gloucestershire', *The Jane Austen Society Report*.
Lefroy, Helen and Turner, Gavin (eds) (2007), *The Letters of Mrs Lefroy*. Chawton: The Jane Austen Society.
Lye, Francis (1828), *The Single Married, and the Married Happy*. Cheltenham: Francis Lye.
Macaulay, Catherine (1790), *Letters on Education*. London: C. Dilly.
Marchand, Leslie A. (ed.) (1973–1994), *Byron's Letters and Journals, Vol. III*. London: John Murray.
Martin, Joanna (2004), *Wives and Daughters: Women and Children in the Georgian Country House*. London: Hambledon and London.
McLaren, Angus (1984), *Reproductive Rituals*. London: Methuen.
Mears, M. (1797), *The Pupil of Nature: or candid advice to the Fair Sex*. London: Faulder.
Miller, Joseph (1722), *Botanicum Officinale; or a Compendious Herbal*. London: E. Bell.
Monsarrat, Ann (1973), *And the Bride Wore . . . The Story of the White Wedding*. London: Gentry Books.
More, Hannah (1799), *Strictures on the Modern System of Female Education*. London: T. Cadell.
Murray, Venetia (1998), *High Society: A Social History of the Regency Period, 1788–1830*. London: Viking.
Ousby, Ian (ed.) (1992), *James Plumptre's Britain: The Journals of a Tourist in the 1790s*. London: Hutchinson.
Pedley, Avril (ed.) (2007), *A Georgian Marriage*. Wimborne Minster: The Dovecote Press.
Pennant, Thomas (1790), *A Tour in Scotland and Voyage to the Hebrides*. London: Benjamin White.

Ponsonby, Arthur (ed.) (1923), *English Diaries From the XVIth to the XXth Century* (2nd edn). London: Methuen.
Porter, Roy (1982), *English Society in the Eighteenth Century*. London: Allen Lane.
Price, Cecil (ed.) (1973), *The Rivals, in The Dramatic Works of Richard Brinsley Sheridan, Vol. I*. Oxford: Clarendon Press.
Sales, Roger (1997), *Jane Austen and Representations of Regency England*. London: Routledge.
Scarisbrick, Diana (2007), *Rings, Jewelry of Power, Love and Loyalty*. London: Thames and Hudson.
Scott, the Hon. Caroline Lucy (1828), *A Marriage in High Life*. London: Henry Colburn.
Selwyn, David (1999), *Jane Austen and Leisure*. London: Hambledon.
Stanhope, Eugenia (1798), *The Deportment of a Married Life*. London: Mr Hodges.
Stone, Lawrence (1979), *The Family, Sex and Marriage In England 1500–1800*. London: Weidenfeld and Nicholson.
Sumner, Ann and Walker, Richard (1999), *Secret Passion to Noble Fashion: The World of the Portrait Miniature*. Bath: Holburne Museum of Art.
Thackeray, W. M. (1968), *Vanity Fair*. London: Penguin Classics.
The Albion Collection of Fine Portrait Miniatures (2004). London: Bonhams.
Tomalin, Claire (1996?), 'Amour and Avarice', *The Daily Telegraph*. London: *The Telegraph* plc.
——(1997), *Jane Austen: A Life*. London: Viking.
Trumbach, Randolph (1998), *Sex and the Gender Revolution, Vol. I*. Chicago: University of Chicago Press.
Various Authors (1813), *Letters on Courtship and Marriage*. Trenton: Daniel Fenton and James J. Wilson.
Vickery, Amanda (2003), *The Gentleman's Daughter*. New Haven and London: Yale University Press.
Waldron, Mary (1999), *Jane Austen and the Fiction of Her Time*. Cambridge: Cambridge University Press.
Weeton, Ellen (1969), *Miss Weeton's Journal of a Governess, Vol. I; Vol. II: 1811–1825*. Edited by E. Hall. Newton Abbot: David and Charles reprint.
Wollstonecraft, Mary (1787), *Thoughts on the Education of Daughters*. London: J. Johnson.
——(1792/1997), *A Vindication of the Rights of Woman*. Edited by Ashley Tauchert. London: Everyman.
Woodforde, James (1978), *The Diary Of A Country Parson 1758–1802*. Edited by John Beresford. Oxford: Oxford University Press.

JOURNALS AND NEWSPAPERS

Ackermann's Repository of Arts, Vol. I, No. 3, 1809. London: R. Ackermann.
——June 1816.
Aris's Birmingham Gazette, 10 January 1791. Birmingham: Thomas Aris.
Bath Chronicle, 6 February 1798. Bath: Richard Cruttwell.
Bon Ton Magazine, Vol. II, No. 11, 1 March 1819. London: J. Johnston.
Hampshire Chronicle, 19 January 1810. Portsmouth: James Robbins.
St James's Chronicle, 'Extraordinary Female Affection', 17–20 July 1790. London: Henry Baldwin.
The Diary: or Woodfall's Register, Monday, 11 April 1791. London: William Woodfall.
The Gentleman's Magazine, December 1791. London: D. Henry.
——January 1806. London: J. Nichols and Son.
——May 1808. London: J. Nichols and Son.
——November 1810. London: J. Nichols and Son.
——April 1816. London: Nichols, Son, and Bentley.
——March 1825. London: Nichols, Son, and Bentley.
The Lady's Magazine, Vol. XLII, March 1811. London: G. Robinson.
——Vol. XLII, April 1811
——Vol. XLII, May 1811.
The Lady's Monthly Museum, Vol. 1, October 1798. London: Vernor and Hood.
—— Vol. 12, July 1820. London: Dean and Munday.
The Loiterer, Saturday, 15 August 1789. Oxford: P. Byrne.
The Morning Post, 18 April 1780. London: R. Bell.
The Public Advertiser, 13 August 1791. London.
The Rambler, Vol. II, No. 97, 1751. London: E. Earle.

Index